Obeying the Voice of God

Jack MacDonald's Journey

AS TOLD TO DONNIE MACDONALD

Obeying the Voice of God
Jack MacDonald's Journey
As told to Donnie MacDonald

ISBN: 978-0-9778545-1-6

Printed in the United States of America

BORREGO PUBLISHING
www.borregopublishing.com

Dedication

This book is dedicated to the Voice of the Holy Spirit, who still speaks to man today if they will only learn to listen.

Jesus said, "He who hath ears, let them hear what the spirit is saying."

Table of Contents

Acknowledgments

Thank you to my seven beautiful children; they all have made me proud to be their father.

To my whole family, thank you for all the fun times—(Lori Joy, Jack Jr., who we call *Jake*, Charity Lee, nicknamed *Chickadee*, Scottie Beth, nicknamed *Beaver*, Jericho, nicknamed *Coco*, David Joseph, nicknamed *Snapper*, Matthew Simeon, nicknamed *Little Bird*)—we had a blast. Larry Snapp, thank you for your computer tech support.

Caron Avakian, you came to our rescue and helped with the first manuscript reading.

Thank you, Diane Feia, for your moral support and your laboring with us through the editing process.

Preface

Thank you, Holy Spirit, for inspiring me to help my husband write this book.

In 2007, I attended an International Marriage Conference, where one of the guest speakers said that most Christian couples do not have a vision for their marriage. I told my husband that the Holy Spirit had impressed upon my heart that we should write a book. We appreciate the opportunity to share with you Jack's *Obeying the Voice of God*.

Donnie MacDonald
August 2008

CHAPTER 1

The O.K. Corral Showdown

It was in the middle of the winter in 1975 when word reached me a man from California was holding home meetings and teaching the Urantia book as a modern replacement to the Bible.

In Bible College, I had a whole semester studying false religions. Our text book was called *The Kingdom of the Cults*, by Dr. W. Martin. We had studied dozens of other forms of religion, but this Urantia movement was a new one to me. Some of the people from my church in Hungry Horse, Montana started going to his meetings, and they began to question the authority of the word of God. It made my blood boil. It seemed this man from California proclaimed himself to be a prophet and the Urantia book was supposed to become a New Age version of the Bible.

I felt as if one of Satan's disciples had come to the canyon area telling the people the Urantia book was the real word of God. I knew in my heart there was going to be a showdown. It turned out that's exactly what happened. We had a modern day O.K. Corral at John Bowles' gas station. By now, John was one of my deacons in the church. He and his wife, Liz, were growing in the Lord every day.

Now John's gas station was the local hangout. It was cold outside and there were over a dozen men standing around and visiting inside the station—half were from my church. While visiting with John, I noticed this large station wagon pull up to get gas. John said, "Pastor, do you know who that is?"

I answered, "No."

He replied, "That's the guy teaching the Urantia book."

I looked at John and said, "This is going to be interesting." After pumping gas, the guy came in to pay his bill. He had about five people with him; we could have had a regular Sunday school lesson with that crowd, and come to think of it, maybe we did.

One of the men that was with this fellow used to be a regular at our church, so he introduced me; I don't know who reached for their pistol (Bible) first, but the next thing I knew, we were involved in a spiritual firefight and were having a full-fledged debate over the authority of the Holy Scriptures.

I was stating the Bible was the only valid word of God, and this self-appointed prophet from California was trying to tell me the Urantia book was the New Age Bible for modern man. I said, "Any book that claims to be equal or better than the Bible is indeed a cult."

I happened to have a Bible in my coat pocket, so I pulled it out and he pulled out the Urantia book. It reminded me of the shootout at O.K. Corral in Tombstone, Arizona in the early 1880s. This guy was not only charismatic, but very intelligent and obviously well educated. I could see why many of the people were deceived by him.

Suddenly, an idea came to me and I recognized the prompting of the Holy Spirit. I said to him, "Let's settle this issue once and for all, right here and now. I will put my Bible down on this desk and you pray to your God to come down and burn this Bible right in front of our eyes. If it doesn't burn, you put the Urantia book down on the desk and I will pray to my God to come down and burn your book." John Bowles later told me his thoughts: "Jack, this is a gas station. This place will explode like a bomb if there is a fire in here." John was definitely a believer.

I looked the guy straight in the eye and said, "We will see just who the God of truth and miracles is. If your God burns my Bible, then we will all come to your meetings, but if my God burns your Urantia book, then you and your followers will turn your life over to Christ and follow him.

The super-intelligent man was without words; there was a look of fear in his eyes. The room was jammed with men, all listening and taking in every word. It was so quiet you could have heard a pin drop. No doubt he heard the conviction in my voice, and he saw the confidence in my eyes. There wasn't a shadow of a doubt in my mind that if the meeting had continued, God would have burned that Urantia book right in front of our eyes.

Finally, the leader said, "We can't do that," and I said, "Well, we can, do you want to see?" The man grabbed his

Urantia book and ran out the door; we never saw or heard from them again. I was told he left town the next day.

Word spread like wildfire about the showdown at John Bowles' garage—the kingdom of God versus the kingdom of the cults, with the word of God being victorious; it was a great piece of advertisement for the Hungry Horse Chapel. The Bad Rock Canyon area consisted of mostly loggers and their families. A very rowdy and rough bunch, they seemed to have liked the bold approach.

To give you an idea of just how rough these loggers were, let me share with you a couple of stories a friend of mine, Gene Sweeny, told me.

One time, Gene was in a bar and a logger was there drinking too much. He made a bet with another man for a bottle of beer that he could take a bite out of his beer glass and chew it up. Gene told me he saw the man do just that with his own eyes, and with blood running down his chin, grabbed his prize and then walked out. In my opinion, it was a little more stupid than it was tough.

Another story I was told about a logger in a bar who had too much to drink: This logger was very obnoxious. When he ordered another beer, the bartender refused and asked him to leave. He finally had to be physically escorted out the door, only to come back two minutes later demanding another beer. The second time they threw him out the door and locked it. When he couldn't get back in, he kicked the door. Then things got quiet for a few minutes. The men in the bar heard the sound of a chainsaw and soon the blade came through the door, and sawed it from the top to the bottom, just missing the hinges by inches. Again, the blade came through the door from the top to the bottom, just missing the deadbolt lock by inches. Soon, this four-foot wide door came crashing down and in walked this same logger, slamming his chainsaw down on the bar, demanding in a loud voice another beer! I could tell you logging stories all day long; some of them funny, some of them sad, some of them terrifying. It's a rough profession, not for the fainthearted.

I enjoyed the reputation that followed after the showdown at John's gas station involving the Urantia book. I remember walking into homes and meeting new families, introducing myself as pastor of the Hungry Horse Chapel, and tears starting to flow down the people's faces. It was nothing more than the convicting power of the Holy Spirit following me everywhere I went.

My sermons weren't anything to brag about, and I certainly wasn't any Tommy Barnett or Bob Ross, who are two of the finest expositors of the Scriptures I have ever heard, but we got the job done.

My messages were based on simple truths out of the Scriptures, but the presence of the Holy Spirit made them real and alive for the people. Simply put, God would make them hear what they needed to hear.

I would pray during the week and ask God to give me the message he wanted me to share at the next service. For example, while preparing for a Sunday morning service, I felt the Lord telling me to get a bowl of water, a mirror, some soap, and a razor, for the Sunday morning sermon—"I want you to shave in front of the congregation." I argued with God and asked Him what kind of sermon this was supposed to be. I finally told Him I would do it.

That Wednesday night, I announced that the following Sunday morning sermon would be one of the most unusual, shortest messages they had ever heard, but they would never forget it for the rest of their lives. I guess the word spread and we had a full house that Sunday morning.

Perhaps the showdown with the Urantia book was fresh in their minds and they thought to themselves, "What will this pastor do next?"

Our worship time usually lasted about an hour, but it seemed as if it were only fifteen minutes, it went by so fast. They sang in the spirit twenty minutes at a time, experiencing a strong presence of God.

Visitors came, sat in the back and began to weep uncontrollably; they came forward and asked if they could be saved. It was awesome to watch God move.

When I got up to preach, I read from the Bible, Luke 18:1: "Men ought to always pray and not faint." I closed the book, took off my jacket, removed my tie, folded my collar under, took a basin of water and sat it by the pulpit. I asked my son, Jake, to hold a mirror and I began to wet my face with the water. I applied some shaving cream and I began to shave.

As I shaved, I began to quote Psalm 1:1-3, Psalm 23:1-6, and Psalm 90:12, just to mention a few. "Teach me, oh Lord to number my days that I may apply my heart unto wisdom;" "Oh satisfy me early with your mercies, and I will rejoice and be glad all of my days;" "Let the beauty of the Lord, our God be upon me, and establish thou the works of my hands." For the next seven minutes, I shaved and talked to God.

One of the ladies later told me you could have heard a pin drop in the church. When I finished, I dried my face, fixed my collar, and took the mirror from my son. I turned and said, "Church, we are exhorted to pray without ceasing; when you shave or when you cook dinner, when you shower, while you drive your car. 'Men ought to always pray and not faint.'" I gave the altar call, as usual. Several came forward for salvation. It seemed like the whole church came to the altar and prayed.

Word spread around town that the pastor shaved for a Sunday morning sermon. It was great advertising. I could see now that the Holy Spirit knew what He was doing. It's a fun thing to be led by God's Spirit; very exciting and adventurous, not to mention, rewarding.

If you will allow me to hit the rewind button, I'd like to go back and share my very first experience of hearing and obeying the voice of God with you, along with the rest of my story.

✞

CHAPTER 2

The Early Days

I was born October 1, 1945 in Elmira, New York. My mother's maiden name was Eulaial Ellison. I have seen pictures of my mother when she was eighteen years old. She had long, chestnut-colored hair with an extremely nice figure. When my mother was eighteen years old, she met a young sailor stationed at the Brooklyn Navy Yard in the fall of 1944.

He was originally from Toronto, Canada, but he moved to the States so he could enlist in the navy. Whenever I would see my Aunt Dottie, I would ask her to tell me anything she could remember about my father, as she was the only relative who had met him. She told me he was about 5 feet 8 inches tall, on the skinny side, and very handsome. I remember her saying he looked like a little boy in a sailor suit. I have been told his name was Gordon MacDonald. Prior to shipping out to serve his country in WWII, he and my mother shared a romantic weekend. They were not married, but that did not stop the conception process. My mother became pregnant with me.

My Aunt Dottie told me my mother was about four months pregnant when she received a letter in the mail. No one knew what the letter said, as she was one of those extremely private people, but whatever the news, she cried for days. She never shared its contents.

My father had sent my mother several letters; some of the letters contained war ribbons. Apparently he was decorated on more than one occasion. The letters eventually stopped coming. My Aunt Dottie felt that he was killed, and that one of his best friends had sent the last letter. It was reported that the ship he was on was torpedoed off the coast of France and sank. I have tried many times to gather information about my father, but have not been successful.

In the 1940s, it was a big disgrace for a lady to be pregnant out of wedlock. My mother came from a wealthy family who completely disowned her and threw her out on her own. She had very few resources to support us. I do remember her taking me to an orphanage when I was about 3 years old. We arrived on Christmas Eve and there must have been a dozen kids opening presents. I cried because I didn't have any presents to open. The lady in charge of the orphanage asked one of the boys to share a dart gun with me; he objected, but the lady reassured him that he would get it back very soon. My mother slipped out the door while I was playing with the gun. I am not sure how long I was there, perhaps two or three years.

I have a few memories of that time in my life. One of them involves two teenage girls walking me around the farm property, each holding one of my hands. I found a pheasant feather and an older boy tried to take it away from me. When I cried the two older girls beat him up and got the feather back for me.

Another memory during that time is catching the school bus and going to kindergarten or first grade. I participated in a music class and played the cymbals. I remember looking out the school window and thinking I saw my grandmother's house; it made me very sad.

My mother's first cousin and best friend, who I called Aunt Dottie, has always been my main source of information pertaining to those early years. She told me that my mother had absolutely nothing and struggled just to have food to eat. This period of time was not only the post-depression era, but was also a time when the entire country had depleted itself in supporting WWII. I remember my Aunt Dottie telling me my mother would work at any job she could find, which weren't very many. She would save every penny she could with the hope of one day getting me out of the orphanage.

My next memory is of my mother and I living in this little house without any furniture and very little food. I recall my Uncle Albert, who was one of my mother's older brothers, came to visit. Uncle Albert was an outdoorsman with a muscular build. He was a skilled hunter, somewhat of a rugged man, and always wore logging boots with rawhide shoelaces. When he saw we had no food in the house, he went to his pickup truck and retrieved his twenty-two rifle. Many hunters feel a twenty-two rifle is too small to shoot a white-tailed deer, but in the hands of a skilled woodsman, it can get the job done. So at age five, he took me on my first hunting trip, trying to provide some meat for the little family.

We walked out behind the house in search of game, as we lived deep in the woods. I remember my uncle showing me a deer track in the mud; he told me it was a buck because it had wide-splayed toes and the dew claws were showing.

I got caught in the tall bushes and some vines with thorns on them and I cried for my Uncle Albert to wait for me. When we got back to the house, he told my mother we might have gotten a deer if I had not started crying. As strange as it sounds, even at that young age, I felt somewhat responsible for my mother not having food.

The farmer next door had chickens and I use to go gather eggs for him. I think I was around five or six years old. Each time I gathered eggs he gave me a nickel. In some small way, I felt like I was the man of the house and was helping to support my mother a nickel at a time. One day, the farmer gave me two eggs and said, "Here, give these to your mother." I put them in my front jeans pockets, and was so excited about bringing food home for the family that as I ran home, I stumbled and fell, breaking both of the eggs. I arrived home crying and told my mother what had happened. She took off my blue jeans, turned the pockets inside out and salvaged what she could of the two eggs. That was all we had to eat that day.

The next thing I knew, we were staying with Ellen Osborn, one of my mother's friends. She offered us a place to stay in her very large farmhouse until my mother could get a place of her own. At that time, Ellen had twelve kids; her husband had a good job at Klut Salt Factory. They raised chickens, a few cows, and grew wheat. One night I heard my mother ask Ellen if she could use their Model T truck to go to town; when she told me I couldn't go, I was upset. Perhaps I was afraid that I wouldn't see her again for a long time, as the episode of being left at the orphanage was still fresh in my mind.

It seemed like the next day that a man named Joe Morton came into our lives. I later learned that my mother had met him at the Garden Bar and Grill. Little did I know that he would be my stepfather for the next twenty years.

We moved into a house in the country that had no electricity or running water; we burned wood for heat. Because it had no utilities, it was less expensive to rent. I remember very little about the house except there was no furniture and it was very cold in the wintertime. It was located at the end of a mile-long dirt road with no other houses to be seen. While we lived there, I started kindergarten. My mother would walk me to catch the school bus because we didn't have a car. When the school bus would drop me off in the afternoon, it made me feel grown up to walk back to the house by myself. Soon I talked my mother into letting me walk the one mile to catch the school bus unescorted.

I remember going with Joe to set a half dozen traps to catch rabbits. There was a foot of snow on the ground and twice a day we would go and check the traps. There was a footpath beat in the snow and I learned where each trap was. Soon I was checking the traps by myself. I recall seeing a rabbit caught in a trap and I ran home very excited to tell my mother. Pancakes and rabbits were the only food we had, as both my mother and Joe were unemployed.

Apparently the tiny town of Logan offered no jobs; the closest town, Burdett, wasn't much bigger, and it was fifteen miles away. Without transportation (something that we take for granted today), employment was extremely difficult. The closest big town was Wilkins Glenn, probably forty miles away.

I do recall my Uncle Albert showing up unexpectedly with my Grandmother Morgan. She was a very close friend of my mother's; however, I don't think she was a real relative, but we called her grandma.

I understand Grandma Morgan opened her house to us when I was very young. My Aunt Dottie told me when my mother would try to spank me, I would run and hide under Grandma Morgan's bed and everybody thought it was so cute that they would forget about the spanking. From what bits and pieces I have been told, my mother was pressured into putting me in the orphanage by her own parents. Different things were mentioned that led me to believe my mother kidnapped me from the orphanage. Perhaps this would explain why she never signed up for welfare.

The only food we had in the house was pancakes. Uncle Albert got his twenty-two rifle and he and Joe went hunting. They came back with two raccoons. We had raccoon and pancakes for Thanksgiving dinner. The raccoons were greasy and as tough as shoe leather. I remember we sold the hides for $3 each. To us, that was a lot of money. They spent part of the money on kerosene to be used in our one oil-burning lamp. This was our only source of light because we had no electricity. My family was very poor and struggled with having the basic needs to survive.

My mother never went on welfare, but proved to be very resourceful. I recall going to this large city dump and seeing box after box of food set out on the ground. People who were on welfare were given cardboard boxes two feet long, two feet wide, and a foot deep, full to the top with a bag of flour, two bags of pancake mix, a sealed bag of macaroni, a sealed bag of rice, a brick of cheese twelve inches long, five inches high and five inches wide, sealed in a thick plastic wrapper, a can of peanut butter, a can of jelly, a bag of powdered milk, powdered eggs, a bag of sugar, a box of salt, a tin of butter, a can of spam, and the most treasured item was a can of cooked pork. Many people would get these boxes and take only the pork and the spam, and sometimes the peanut butter and jelly, then throw the rest away in the dump. I recall seeing several dozen of these boxes that my mother had acquired from this reject pile. Sometimes the cheese would have a spot of mold but she would cut the mold off and we'd eat the rest. No doubt, if it wasn't for these raids on the dump, we would have gone hungry.

I don't know why there would be dozens of boxes sitting there right along the edge of the dump. Perhaps they were outdated, but my first guess would be that every member of the family would go through the welfare line several times a day, mostly to get the canned ham. By the end of the week, they had so many boxes of leftovers that they took the extra food to the dump. Every once in a while, we'd find a can of this prized spam or a can of precooked pork that had the label torn off. My mother and Joe gathered up any unopened can that they could find in and around these boxes. Often it would be peanut butter or jelly, which we used on our pancakes. The most common items that we found unopened were bags of pancake mix, five pound bricks of cheese, large sealed bags of macaroni noodles, flour, and salt.

One day, when I was seven years old, my mother left for work at 4 a.m., and Joe had to make his own lunch for work that day. That evening, my mother found an empty can with a small amount of its contents left in the bottom. She asked Joe where the rest of it went. He told her he had used it to make sandwiches for work. The label was just barely clinging to the can, as she had torn it off the day before. She asked how the sandwiches had tasted. Joe said, "They were delicious." That's when she told him he had just eaten canned dog food.

During the first couple of years of grade school, I remember carrying my lunch in a bag that would contain pancake sandwiches with peanut butter, usually with no jelly or cheese.

Later on, when my mother finally got an oven, she learned to bake bread with these items she found in the dump. All the way through the eighth grade, my lunch always consisted of two peanut butter sandwiches or two cheese sandwiches, no mayo. Although milk was only 2¢ a bottle, I couldn't bring myself to ask my mother for the 10¢ for the week. I ate them dry, with nothing to drink.

All that changed in my freshman year, when I got a job with the school cafeteria, making 60¢ an hour, including all I could eat and all the milk I could drink. One time they had chicken salad sandwiches, and they were so good, I ate twenty-three of them in two hours. You guessed it—during football practice I got sick, but five minutes later, I was back doing calisthenics.

At the age of ten, I recall having a job with the neighbor, milking eleven cows, seven evenings a week, by myself. The owner would come and do the chores in the morning and then check on me to see how good of a job I was doing in the evening.

I must have passed inspection because I worked at this job for five months. Back in those days, I was a salaried man and earned $2 a week. I would have worked for $1 a week because I loved every aspect of farming. I would faithfully save every dime of my money to buy my own school clothes.

The family tradition was that every fall I would get two plaid shirts and two new pairs of blue jeans and that would last me one year going to school. Then the following year those two shirts and the two pairs of jeans would become my play clothes and I would get two more shirts and two more pairs of jeans for the following year's school clothes.

After about four months of work and putting my money away in a desk drawer at my house, I came home from school one day and noticed that all my money was gone. That night, my stepfather came home drunk and my mother asked him where he got the money for the beer. He said, "The boys at the bar just kept buying drinks." I never did get my $32.00 back.

When I was eleven years old, Uncle Albert gave me a single-shot twenty-two rifle. I felt like somebody had just handed me the world. Now I could help feed my family. I practiced and practiced and soon I was bringing home squirrels and rabbits every night, and by the time I was fifteen, I could hit the head of a sixteen-penny nail at fifty yards. I know this sounds like I'm bragging, but precision shooting had become my passionate hobby. I would pick up pop cans and pop bottles, mow lawns, work any job I could find, to get money to buy twenty-two shells. By the time I was twelve years old, I was harvesting white-tailed deer with a twenty-two rifle. Ninety-five percent of the meat that my family ate was what I brought home from hunting. It wasn't sport to me; it was a matter of survival. Many people today cannot comprehend living off the land, but this country boy can.

I am not sure why my mother never went on welfare; maybe it was pride, maybe there were other reasons, but she taught me to be self-sufficient and resourceful. To this day, I wouldn't know a food stamp if you showed it to me, and I have never received a welfare check.

Another thing I found myself doing to help support the family was running a trap line. A friend of the family had died and his widow gave me over fifty traps. I would get up at 4 a.m. and go check my three-mile long trap line, sometimes in waist-deep snow. Even though it was about a three-mile walk every morning, I only remember missing the 8 o'clock school bus one time, but then I hitchhiked and beat the bus to school. Some seasons, I would make $60 or $70 selling furs, plus the state would pay an additional $5 bounty on certain animals.

I also discovered that I was very good at picking concord grapes. I learned that instead of using grape shears, I could snap the grapes stems with my thumbs, enabling me to pick grapes with both hands; thus, I picked twice as fast as those who used shears. I would shuffle the basket between my feet. And when the grapes were extra heavy, I could make $10 an hour. That was good money for a teenage kid. I started picking grapes at age eleven in my landlord's vineyards. Because I could work my own hours, I would go down to the vineyard after school and pick grapes until dark. Because I was paid by the bushel, I would work very quickly and pick as many grapes as I could before it got dark.

I had never used grape shears before, so I thought I would give them a try. They are a lot like pruning shears, only sharper. I would hold the cluster of grapes with one hand and snip the stem with the shears, but in my haste to pick as many bushels of grapes as possible, I cut one of my fingers a half inch down from the end, almost completely off. I wrapped it up in a handkerchief and went home, washed it off, and poured some iodine on it.

A hundred yards up the hill from my house was the headquarters of a construction company, as they were reconstructing Route 14. I had already met a man named Shorty who had subcontracted putting out kerosene pots to mark the hazardous parts of the construction sites. Unable to pick grapes because of my cut finger, I went to talk to Shorty; he gave me the job of pumping kerosene out of a big drum while he filled up the individual pots. Eventually, I got a job refilling the pots, replacing the pots and retrieving them first thing in the morning. It was an extremely dirty job, as you got the soot all over your clothes and body, but I enjoyed the work. I felt like I was contributing to the family income. The money I earned would help buy my own school clothes so my mother would not have to. Shorty paid me $2 an hour. I thought I had found a gold mine.

The next job I held was in farming. Having made friends with my school bus driver, I learned that he had a dairy farm. After hounding him for a job, he finally asked me how old I was. At twelve, I was big for my age so I told him I was thirteen. That was the first summer I left home and went to live with the farmer. He provided me room and board at $15 a week. During the summer months I would get up at four a.m. to milk fifty cows; cultivate corn; mow, rake, and bale hay; stack and unstack the bales on a wagon; and then unload the bales in the hay mow. In my spare time, I would fix fences from four in the morning until nine or ten at night, seven days a week. I just loved it. In my young heart, I craved to be a man and I associated hard work with growing up, because I watched my mother, year after year, working extremely hard, waiting on tables and cooking at a restaurant. The next door neighbor would look after me because my mother would often work sixteen hours a day.

The farmer asked if he could pay me at the end of the summer. I said that would be okay. On my last day of work, he took me home late in the evening and as he pulled up to my house he handed me a handful of ones and said he was late for an appointment and that he needed to get going. After counting all the singles, I discovered why he had to get going—I was short $15. A whole week's pay, and I never saw him again.

I returned home for the school year. That following summer a neighboring farmer showed up in my yard and offered me the same type of work, the same hours, only $20 a week. I gladly accepted. I asked if I could be paid at the end of each week. That was the second time I left home. I would be gone from home three months this time.

At the age of 15, I left home in June for the third time and returned home the following April. I went to work on another dairy farm and after about six months the boss's wife, Barbara Crans, and I were talking and I said to her, "I really don't care if I live or die, it really doesn't matter." She said to me, "Someday you will meet somebody and that will all change."

Little did I suspect that her prophecy would come true. The following month, I went back to high school. My friend, Cransey, and I were walking down the hallway, and coming from the other direction was a thirteen-year-old girl. Her face glowed like a light bulb. I asked Cransey who that girl was, and he said, "Oh, that's Jeanetta Brimmer; you can forget her. She is a straight arrow. But that didn't stop me from feeling drawn to her.

That winter my parents had moved, and the following April I returned home since the farmer sold his dairy cows and didn't need my help anymore. After moving back home, I got on the school bus only to find at the very next stop, 100 yards away from my house, Jeanetta got on the school bus with her brother. I was wearing a cowboy hat and her brother, Steve, sat next to me and asked if I was a cowboy.

That was the beginning of a lifelong friendship. I got his phone number and asked if I could talk to Jeanetta. A month later, after many phone calls, Jeanetta's mother asked me down for a marshmallow roast, and that's when I met Jeanetta's father, Harry Brimmer. He was an old-time Pentecostal Holy Ghost, tongue talking, prayer warrior, man of God. He handed me the Gospel on a fiery spoon and almost scared me off. Then they invited me to go to church on Sunday. The only reason I went was to be with Jeanetta.

At the church, Pastor Winston Smock preached about Christ the redeemer, and for the very first time in my life, I heard the Gospel and understood that I needed to be saved. He gave the altar call and asked how many present would like to be born again. I said to myself, "That's me, but I am never going to raise my hand in front of all these people." The next thing I knew, I was raising my hand and standing on my feet. Then the pastor said, "If you really mean business and you really want to find God, come down and kneel at this altar." I said to myself, "There is no way I am going to walk down to that altar in front of all these people," but I did. Soon Jeanetta's father was kneeling by my side and leading me in the sinner's prayer. That was forty-six years ago and it is the most important decision I have ever made in my life.

I started going to church with them every Sunday morning, every Sunday night, and every Wednesday night; we never missed a service for the next four years, even though the church was eighteen miles away and we often had to drive in the snow and ice on treacherous mountain roads.

I can remember walking down the road to Jeanetta's house and hearing somebody praying in the barn loft. As I stopped and listened, I could hear Jeanetta's father speaking my name in prayer. I remember feeling so good that someone loved me enough to pray for me and to ask God for his will in my life.

During one Sunday evening service in mid-November, Brother Andrews gave a message in tongues. Brother Charles Hann gave the interpretation, saying, "Thus saith the Lord, pray earnestly for your country; it's about to experience great grief throughout the entire nation and there will be great turmoil in the government. Pray like you have never prayed before for the leaders of your country and for the Holy Spirit to be with our nation." Three days later, November 22, 1963, President Kennedy was assassinated and our nation experienced great grief and turmoil.

As a young believer, these gifts of the Spirit not only impressed and inspired me, but helped me grow in my faith, not to mention, they were somewhat exciting and adventurous to an 18-year-old boy.

Little did I know there was coming a day when God would use me in a similar way.

Harry and Blanch Brimmer took me under their wings and treated me like a son, even though I was not a blood relative. They drove me to youth camp and paid my registration fees in spite of the fact that they were not rich.

Harry was a factory worker and Blanch was a homemaker. They provided me transportation to church, 18 miles one way, three times a week, every single week for the next four years, until I was drafted into the Marine Corps.

After becoming a Christian, my whole life changed. At one time I had a mouth that would make a sailor blush, and I can remember stealing two football jerseys in my freshman year after football practice. That following summer, after being convicted by the Holy Spirit, I called up Coach John Ballard and said that it was very important that I talk to him. He invited me to his home. I took the two jerseys and handed them to Coach Ballard. He said, "I am glad to see these two jerseys come back." It was at that time that I shared with him how I was saved and how it had changed my life. Little did I know, that story would spread throughout the facility and I found great favor with many of the teachers.

During my sophomore year at Dundee Central High School in Dundee, New York, I was supporting a 1949 piece of steel made by Ford that I jokingly called my wife, because she required a lot of attention, tires, seat covers, and fuel (at 19¢ a gallon), and a constant need of new parts. My main source of income was working Saturdays, from daylight to dark, at a grape vineyard pulling brush for $1 an hour. Despite only being three hours into my shift one Saturday, I felt that I should leave work and go visit my friend and fellow wrestling team member, Lester Miller, and invite him to go to the Youth for Christ Rally with me in a town about thirty miles away. Now my old Ford only got nine miles to the gallon and I desperately needed to work for the gas money.

My flesh was arguing with my spirit about how much I really needed to work if I wanted to support my iron wife, but this inclination to invite Lester to go with me that night to the rally kept getting stronger and stronger. It was like a nagging thought that just wouldn't go away; in my heart I knew I needed to invite him to the rally. Finally I said to the foreman, "Mrs. Todd, I need to quit work early today." I told her why. She said to me, "Jack, I understand; I am a Christian too, and I respect what you are doing," so she gave me the rest of the day off.

Normally, I would get a load of kids on Saturday night and go to the Youth for Christ Rally. Usually there were six or seven of us squeezed into my '49 Ford. The large load of kids came in handy when we had to push the car in order to jump-start it in second gear.

One of the girls in our party was Carol Monagan, an extremely attractive brunette who picked red raspberries in the summertime and had a killer tan that was to die for. She definitely got my attention and we went steady for the next four years. She came from a very respected Polish family that had produced more than a few valedictorians and salutatorians. Carol's mother, Rose, was valedictorian of her class in spite of working at a full-time job to help support her mother, who had fourteen children. There is little doubt in anybody's mind that Carol would have been valedictorian of her class if it wasn't for me taking up so much of her time in and out of school. I remember standing outside her door at typing class and shooting rubber bands at her as she sat right next to the door. Needless to say, the poor kid almost flunked typing class.

I took the long road home, which brought me past Lester's house and there he was in the yard playing catch with a football. I stopped and told him that I had a strong urge to invite him to the Youth for Christ Rally that night and he agreed to go with me.

Lester had never been to a gospel meeting before. When the altar call was given at the Youth for Christ Rally, Lester turned to me and said, "I want to go up there and find God." I went with him and he asked Christ into his heart. That was my first experience being led by the Holy Spirit. I was seventeen years old and Lester was sixteen.

Sometimes I wonder if I was too fanatical in those early years; for example, we had a wrestling match scheduled for a Wednesday night with our arch rival wrestling team from Campbell. I knew it was going to be a close match but still I chose to tell the coach I couldn't wrestle that night because of the Wednesday night Bible study and prayer meeting.

My team lost that night by two points and my coach told me that if I had been there we would have won. He also told me he appreciated where I was coming from because he was a Sunday school superintendent at his own church.

My home church was what the kids would call a cooking Holy Ghoster congregation of people that meant business about praising and worshipping God. They would come a half hour early to pray before worship services and I can see now that the pre-service prayer meeting makes a big difference.

There was such a spirit of worship in that church, I remember Steve and I would often sit together behind

Brother and Sister Andrews; just sitting behind them sent tears involuntarily running down my face. They sang the old hymns of the church and the people worshipped God with their hands raised and their eyes closed. It gave me a great hunger to have what they had, even if it meant missing an important wrestling match. And now at age 62, I still have that same hunger to have more of God in my life, even if it means missing a little extra sleep in the middle of the night.

✝

CHAPTER 3

Going to Vietnam

In high school, I had worked several years for a man named Miles Houck, who took a liking to me. Being ready to retire and owning six or eight different farms, he made me an offer I couldn't refuse. If I would work one of the farms, which had over a hundred acres of vineyards, hayfields, a fifty thousand square foot barn, and a five thousand square foot farm house, all overlooking a five mile wide, thirty-eight mile long lake, I could buy this farm with nothing down and one annual payment a year when the grape crop came in. I absolutely loved farming and I thought my future was mapped out for me. I would do the work I loved for the rest of my life and be a landowner at the age of 19.

Then one day in August of 1965, I got a letter in the mail that said, "Greetings, from the President of the United States. This letter is to inform you that you are now being inducted into the Armed Forces of the United States of America." I couldn't understand how God could let this happen to me.

The war in Vietnam was getting stronger and stronger, and I had no desire to be a part of it. In Syracuse, New York, on November 10, 1965, I was drafted into the United States Marine Corps for two years. I discovered a few months later, however, that I had inadvertently extended my assignment to four years; it must have been in the midst of mass confusion while signing so many papers. What was I thinking? I had reached a bend in life's road that would change my life forever. From there, they sent me by bus to Parris Island, South Carolina. There I came in contact with the closest thing to hell that I have ever experienced in my whole life. It's called Marine Corps boot camp. After graduating from there, I was sent to Camp Lejeune, North Carolina for further training.

One of my disappointments of being drafted in the fall was the fact that I would miss deer season, which opened the middle of November. When I heard they were having an archery season beginning November 1, I went and bought a bow and arrows and began practicing. I had never hunted with a bow before and I knew nothing about it, but I was motivated by the fact that I had provided a deer every year for my family's freezer and I felt they depended on me. On the last day I had to hunt, I killed a white-tailed deer with a bow and arrow and without the use of a tree stand. I labeled it a miracle from God. But wait, there's more. Fifty yards from where that deer fell stood a hollow tree that the Holy Spirit directed me to five years later. You can read about that later in this book (Chapter 18).

My first duty station was Norfolk, Virginia, where I was attached to the military police division, and as it happened, my squad came up for a long weekend. So there I was, three days on my hands with nothing to do.

On an impulse, I decided to hitchhike home, which was 550 miles one way. Talk about impetuous; hitchhiking in a marine uniform was very productive. I got as far as Baltimore, Maryland and thought I should call my mother and tell her I was coming. She insisted on meeting me half way and giving me a ride. It was not my first choice, but we decided that if I hitchhiked two hundred miles and she drove two hundred miles, then we could meet in this small town in central Pennsylvania. She thought she would be there around eleven o'clock at night and I was to meet her at the north edge of town. I finally said okay and hung up the phone.

Sure enough, I arrived there about eleven o'clock that night, but she was nowhere to be found. I left Norfolk, Virginia in a short sleeve khaki shirt with matching hat and pants, certainly not warm enough for the mountains of Pennsylvania at eleven o'clock at night. I was very cold. As I was walking along the road, I passed a church. I felt the Holy Spirit say "go in and pray." I thought surel the door would be locked, but it wasn't, so I went in. It felt so good inside just to get warm.

I argued with God that I could easily miss my mother who was driving down to pick me up, but I was also trying to learn to be obedient to the Holy Spirit. I knelt at the altar and prayed for fifteen or twenty minutes, then I felt an urgency to go back out to the road. Not three minutes later, I saw headlights coming out of the North at a very high rate of speed, traveling so fast that I didn't recognize it as being my mother's car. The car passed me and was almost out of sight when it turned around and came back. It was none other than my hot rod mother, and my new fiancée, Carol.

My mother pulled up beside me and when I got in the

car, she said, "Sorry I'm late. I got lost and almost didn't see you when I drove by." I got to share with my unsaved mother that the Lord led me into that church, not only for a time of prayer, but to get warmed up. In my mind, that was one of those timed Holy Spirit miracles, but I never again had her meet me part of the way. The hitchhiking was too good and less stressful.

I had met Carol Monagan in my sophomore year of high school. I recall asking the Lord to give me the courage to ask her to go to the Saturday night Youth for Christ Rally, which was my custom. My game plan was to ask her to go to the basketball game on Friday and then to the rally on Saturday night. As it turned out, she was only free on Saturday night.

So that is how we started dating. We went steady for the next three years. When I was drafted into the Marine Corps, I was given a four-day pass and told not to leave town. The next morning I was walking by a jewelry store and I saw a diamond ring that caught my eye and I decided on the spot to hitchhike home, one hundred plus miles, gather up Carol, show her the ring, and become engaged. I recall asking her father if we could get engaged and to this day I can still remember his reply. "Well, you don't smoke, and you don't drink," and then there was about a sixty second pause. Then he said, "You don't drink and you don't smoke," and there was a two or three minute pause; then he again said, "Well, you don't drink and you don't smoke." After that, her parents gave us permission to get engaged. That was the first part of November 1965. I guess it could have been worse—Carol's father could have said only one good thing about me, so I guess two good qualities are better than one. A year and half later, we got married.

During the two years I was stationed at Norfolk Naval Air Station, I am sure I hitchhiked home fifty times. It even got so that I could predict how long it would take me. Carol would drop me off on the freeway at seven o'clock at night, and then I would be back at the base by seven o'clock the next morning after hitchhiking all night.

On one of these trips, I packed my dress blue uniform in a garment bag and took it home with me for Carol's senior prom. When I got ready to return to the base, my mother had purchased some reflective tape that glowed in car lights. On my garment bag, she put the letters USMC with tape. I argued with her that I needed to get going, I didn't have time for her to do that, but she won the argument. Little did I know that later it would be a blessing.

I was halfway through the Appalachian Mountains in Pennsylvania when it started pouring rain. It was a pitch-black dark night, and my dress green uniform turned very dark from the rain. I was not getting any rides. I told the Lord I was getting cold and I sure needed a ride. A car passed me going very fast and then slammed on its brakes. It turned out to be a fellow marine going all the way to Norfolk. He said he was half asleep, as it was two in the morning. He said he saw the reflected USMC on the garment bag, and that's what made him stop. I not only got warm but shared in the driving, and our conversation kept each other awake. I walked in the barracks at five minutes to seven, made muster (roll call), took a shower and went to work. Come Monday night I was ready for a good night's sleep.

In December of 1966, I received orders to go to Vietnam. I had a 30-day leave, so Carol and I decided to get married. Her mother pleaded with us to get married in the Catholic church and I finally agreed. She sent us to see the Monsignor, who kept postponing our meeting. Finally, I only had a week left on my leave. Carol's mother called him and forced an appointment for the next day. He informed us that he didn't like war weddings because he felt they never lasted. Carol's mother was furious with the monsignor for stalling us for three weeks and then refusing to to marry us, as I only had a thirty-day leave.

Before heading to Vietnam, I was stationed at Camp Pendleton, California to undergo intense guerilla warfare training. The area that I was training in was forty miles from nowhere, way out in the desert. I drew a weekend pass and hitchhiked down to see my new friend, Art Pratt, who I had met on the airplane while traveling from the East Coast to the West Coast en route to Camp Pendleton. Art had given me his phone number and address, and insisted that I come visit him before I left to go overseas.

I spent the next two days with he and his family, and then hitchhiked back to Camp Pendleton. About ten miles from the base, I caught a ride with two attractive ladies. One was a general's granddaughter in her mid-twenties, and the other was her college friend visiting from Ohio. She begged me to show them the base; she wanted to show it off to her friend. They did not have a Military ID card so I gladly used my ID card to get on the base. Of course, my tour of Camp Pendleton took us right by my barracks. I got out of the car and they asked if they could see the inside of the barracks. I explained that there were 80 men sleeping inside the barracks. They promised they would be very quiet if I would give them a tour. It was a foolish act on my part, but I have never claimed to be perfect, not even close. So I agreed to give then a very quick tour. I insisted that they not make a sound. We weren't 10 feet inside the building when one of the ladies bumped into a trash can and tipped it over. She squealed and said "Oh, I'll pick it up." Her female voice was all those guys needed to hear.

The lights came on, and the next thing I knew, we were surrounded by eighty young marines all wearing t-shirts and skivvies. Talk about being embarrassed! I kept trying to get them out of there, but the guys kept asking questions. So here's the scene: two extremely beautiful women inside a Marine Corps barracks in the middle of nowhere, with eighty marines surrounding them, asking questions, and only I knew that one of them was a general's granddaughter. Boy, was I sweating bullets! I kept saying, "It's two o'clock in the morning and these girls need to get back home, and you guys need your sleep. We have a big training day tomorrow!" But the girls said that they didn't need to get back home, and the guys said that they were not tired at all. I bet they weren't! I think these two ladies were enjoying the attention, but I was as nervous as a long-tailed cat in a room full of rocking chairs. I finally managed to push them out the door and get them loaded in their car. They wrote down directions on how to find the freeway again, thanked me repeatedly for the tour, and they both said that they would remember it for the rest of their lives. I bet they did. I also bet there were about 80 marines that won't forget it either! I have done some pretty dumb things in my lifetime and that was certainly one of them. But on the good side of the coin, for the next few days I was Mr. Popularity. The men voted me to be the Marine Corps Tour Guide of the Year.

It was probably a welcome break from some very intense training. We all knew what lay ahead of us, and many would not see US soil again for a long time, if at all.

I often thank the Lord for not letting the officer of the day walk in, because I would have been filling sandbags for the next two months.

In February of 1967, I called Carol and she informed me she was pregnant. I had $105 in my saving account and she didn't have much more, but it was enough to buy a plane ticket to fly her to California. Art Pratt, his wife and his son who lived in Escondido, California, played a huge part in helping Carol and I get married. On February 14, Valentine's Day, 1967, in front of three hundred marines dressed in combat utilities and four civilians, Art Pratt, his wife, Art Pratt Jr. and his girlfriend, we tied the knot. My company took up a collection for Carol and me as a wedding present, which amounted to over $200.

We stayed with the Pratts and for our honeymoon, Art Jr. suggested taking us to Tijuana, Mexico for the day to watch a bull fight and do some shopping. It was my very first time out of the country. I was twenty-two years old.

They were very supportive of our circumstances. Meeting the Pratts was a classic case of serendipity. This incident makes me think of the last verse of Psalm 23 where it says "surely goodness and mercy shall follow." The Hebrew word for follow means to pursue or to hunt down. I have experienced in my lifetime hundreds of thousands of times that goodness and mercy has hunted me down no matter where I went, because when I was sixteen years old, I made the Lord my Shepard. It's like I have two puppy dogs following me around named Goodness and Mercy. Many times later in this book, you will hear about serendipity. *Webster's Dictionary* defines it as a "seemingly chance meeting that is very meaningful." I choose to call it the blessing of the Lord in the form of a Divine Appointment.

My battalion at Camp Pendleton had 5,006 marines. The airlift that was to fly us from Camp Pendleton to Okinawa could only accommodate five thousand people. I was chosen as one of the six to stay behind.

Carol and I had an extra three weeks together to play in Southern California before I was to leave by ship for Vietnam. It was a blessing from the Lord. I remember taking her to the airport and watching her plane lift off. I felt as if my whole world had just ended. I was so sad, I wept. Saying goodbye to my brand new bride and getting on a ship to set sail to a war I wanted no part of was almost more than I could bear.

I told God I had no desire to kill anybody and I asked why this was happening to me. Little did I know that God had a plan. I joined a different battalion numbering over five thousand marines and we all boarded the USS Upshur, which was a troop carrier that would transport us to Okinawa for more intense training of guerrilla warfare.

I should mention here that part of our training was physical endurance. Every day we would go on a five mile run with heavy packs on our backs. We did the very same thing at Camp Pendleton, except we ran up a mountain. They were determined to get us that way even if it killed us, and sometimes it seemed like we were going to die.

The first day on the ship was a major shock to my system. The food was unpalatable—dried potatoes, powered eggs, powered milk, all dated 1943—it was 23 years old. Hardly any of the men ate it. We lived on peanut butter and jelly. I have always been a country boy and could eat almost anything and be thankful for it. I have had thousands of meals of rabbits and tree squirrels. I even remember having raccoon and pancakes for Thanksgiving dinner, but nothing was as bad as what they fed those poor marines crossing the Pacific on that ship; it was awful.

The second day at sea, I was walking around on the ship, which was as big as several football fields. It was many floors deep. I became lost in the maze of stairwells and passageways. In my attempt to find my way back, I opened a door and I came eye to eye with the civilian head cook who was in charge of the officer's mess. I said, "Excuse me sir, I made a wrong turn," and I tried to leave as quickly as possible. But the civilian chef said, "Wait." I thought to myself, "I am in trouble now," but he went on to say, "How would you like to work in the officers' mess? I will get you out of all your other duties and you won't have to eat that slop that they feed to the rest of the men. You will eat what the officers eat. Prime rib and pork chops and even trout under glass." I couldn't believe my ears. It was a blessing from the Lord.

He said, "Go get two or three of your buddies to help you and report back here in one hour; then get me the name of your platoon sergeant and I will take care of the rest." At that time, I was an E3, known as a lance corporal. I made sure that the other guys were E2 (PFCs) so I would outrank them, making me the boss. My momma didn't raise a dummy.

I knew if there were four instead of three there would be less work to do. As I recall my mother telling me, "Many hands make light work." As it turned out, we only worked a couple hours a day. The rest of the time, we ate T-bone steak and played cards, read books, and wrote letters. A seemingly chance meeting was a Blessing from the Lord. I honestly don't think I could have kept my health and eaten that twenty-three-year-old food for three weeks. I have never seen food so bad in all my life, before that voyage or since that voyage. I am sure it was World War II leftover rations and that my CO bragged that his men would eat anything, even nails for breakfast if they had to. At any rate, we were the human garbage cans that the navy used to dispose of food that should have been thrown out in the dump.

As we sailed by the big island of Hawaii, the captain announced over the PA system that we were looking at the town of South Point and that would be the last we would see of America for a very long time. Most of us knew that would be the last of America some would ever see before they died, what an awful feeling. Again my heart sank and I was extremely sad.

We had a rough trip. The ship would rise up on top of the waves and you could see all across the ocean. Then it would go down into a trough of water and all you could see on both sides of the ship were two walls of water and then back up you went. Almost everyone got seasick.The room where we slept was eight bunks high from the floor to the ceiling. I had the top one, which turned out to be a real sanitary Blessing from the Lord.

It took us three weeks to cross the Pacific; some of the guys were sick every single day. It was a very unpleasant trip but at least I had good food to eat, and even enjoyed trout under glass. Some of the officers would take two bites and throw the rest away. It would just make my blood boil—I could not tolerate waste.

✝

"The leaves that fall to the ground rot and turn into fertilizer, the millions of salmon that spawn and die turn into plankton that feed the whales, even the erosion of the banks of a muddy river make a fertile delta where crops are grown. Five loaves of bread and two fish fed five thousand people and the leftovers filled 12 baskets," Luke 9:13. I am convinced that God hates waste. If only America could get away from the sin of wasting food, I believe our economy would be much stronger.

✝

In March of 1967, we landed in Camp Schwab, Okinawa for more intense training. After about three weeks, my bunkmate fell in love with a prostitute and decided to go over the hill to be with her. I think it was the first woman he had ever been with. Two of us tried to talk him out of it. We even told him that desertion during wartime was punishable by death. We noticed about midnight he was gone. We were to catch the ship to leave for Vietnam at 0600 in the morning. My friend and I got some rope; we were going to find him, tie him up and bring him back. We had no idea which brothel he was in. The little town just outside the base had brothels side by side on both sides of the street, and there were dozens of them. He took one side and I took the other. We began to search every room of every brothel. It was a very interesting evening. I walked in not asking anyone for permission. I went from room to room looking for our friend. Not once did anyone try to stop me; all the doors were unlocked.

We never did find the young marine. My friend and I were no match for the strongest force in the natural world. I finished my side of the street at about three o'clock in the morning, and then I walked back to Camp Schwab feeling like I had failed my friend.

✝

CHAPTER 4

Assistant Chaplain

On my way back to the barracks, I passed the base chapel. Finding the door unlocked, I went in, went to the altar, knelt and prayed. About a half hour later, I heard the door open and footsteps coming behind me. With my fingers spread apart across my face, I begin to watch and pray. Soon a man was bending over looking at me; I didn't know what to do so I just keep praying. He bent over and touched my shoulder. I looked up and in the very dim light I could see it was a navy admiral. I stood at attention and he said to me, "What are you doing?"

"Sir, the lance corporal was praying, sir."

"Praying for what?" he asked.

I told him I was praying for my friend that went over the hill, and then I related the story of the brothel search and that I was praying just because I loved God. He asked me my name, and then he askedwhat unit I was in. He said "Do you know who I am?"

"No, sir."

He said, "I am the admiral in charge of all the navy chaplains in the South Pacific and I want you on my team. You will be hearing from me." I went back to my barracks, and didn't think anymore about it until two days later, when I was aboard the ship USS Enterprise, which served as our base for the many operations that we would perform in the jungles of South Vietnam.

The platoon sergeant looked me up, came to me and said, "The captain wants to see you pronto. I don't know what you have done, but I don't envy you right now."

I reported to the captain's office and there stood a senior chaplain, and he said to me, "Evidently you must know people in high places. You have been requested by name to be the assistant chaplain to the Second Battalion, Third Marine Division. Are you interested?"

I said, "Yes, sir."

He replied, "You should be; there are thousands of commissioned chaplains who would love to have this job. I will be sending you a memo of your duties." I thought to myself, "Could it be that this is God's way of delivering me out of taking another man's life?" The thought haunted me day and night. So it was, I became the field assistant chaplain, an E3, an absolute nobody in man's eyes.

My first sergeant, Kenneth Jones, always seemed to resent me after that; no doubt he assumed that I was some congressman's son or had a rich oil baron father who pulled strings with the navy admiral in an attempt to baby me. But come to think of it, maybe it was true. When I was born again at age sixteen, I gained a heavenly father who was the creator of the universe, which is far better than any congressman or rich oil baron. Being viewed as some spoiled rich kid might explain why the first sergeant refused to promote me to corporal, which was an E4, even though I had enough time in grade and was doing the job of an E5. My pro and con marks (proficiency and conduct) were 3.9 and 4.0 throughout my entire record book. (4.0 is the highest grade you can get.) Had I been in the army, I probably would have been an E6.

I am not sure, perhaps it was because I didn't smoke and drink with the rest of them, or maybe it was the touch of God on my life that this ungodly first sergeant resented. I don't think he ever liked me.

I was to preach in the jungle on Sundays when the main chaplain couldn't make it, which was 95 percent of the time, as the chaplain is often needed on the hospital ship to attend to the wounded and dying marines. I remember my very first Sunday. I checked in with First Sergeant Jones and told him it was Sunday and that I would like to hold a service for the men. He said, "Yeah, OK, fine," and pointed toward a bamboo grove down in a ravine. Then he said, "You can use that for your church building."

He promised to put the word out and I decided to help him on my own. The first two guys that I ran into were Rick Kucera and a guy named Dan. I told them we were having a church service at 11:00 in the bamboo grove down in the ravine. Rick suggested that I go check it out because it looked pretty thick.

So instead of continuing to spread the word about the church service, I went down to check out my bamboo church. Sure enough, it was thicker than thick but in the middle was a cleared-out opening about 8 feet by 8 feet, almost as if it was somebody's hideout. I knelt and prayed for the service. I remember pleading with God to give me the right message that would speak to the hearts of the men that would be the most receptive to the Gospel. I had my little New Testament, which I carried with me in my front pocket in a plastic sandwich bag to keep it dry.

I began to read from the Gospel of John and it wasn't long before I came to the story of how Nicodemus came to Jesus. That story seemed to jump out at me and lodge in my thinking, so by faith I took that as a leading of the Lord. I had my text now, and all I needed was the rest of my sermon. I was disgusted with myself for not preparing my sermon earlier, but I was pretty busy just trying to stay alive. I felt it hard to think about preparing a sermon while carrying a seventy-pound pack in the 115-degree sun. In my spare time, I found myself digging a foxhole every night that was six feet long, three feet wide, and four feet deep. Often the soil was as hard as cement and you had to chip it down one tablespoon at a time. So there I was the hotshot preacher with no sermon notes, called by the admiral himself to be God's man of wisdom and power. To be honest, I didn't feel like I was full of wisdom and power and I told God that. I prayed and said, "Lord, if you don't help me, this is going to be a big waste of time."

Before I knew it, it was five minutes to eleven and two guys showed up for church, Dan and Rick. I welcomed them to the bamboo chapel. I looked at my watch and it was one minute to eleven. I told the men we would get started with prayer. My opening prayer lasted about sixty seconds and I had no more said "Amen" when two shots of sniper fire rang out from the mountainside across from us. That sent us scrambling back to our foxholes, thinking we were in for a firefight. As we ran up the hill, I looked at my watch; it was exactly eleven o'clock. I thought to myself, "Could it be that the devil can tell time and this is a dirty trick to keep these men from attending church?"

✞

That was forty years ago, and since then, I have learned that, yes indeed, the devil can tell time and he has many tricks to keep people from going to God's House. One of the devil's most common tricks comes in the form of a disease, and over the years, I have given it a name called *sabatidious rigamitus* (missing church).

The characteristics of this disease are as follows: It usually strikes on Sunday morning at about 8:30, and by 9:15, you just don't feel like going to church. You are very tired, there is no fever involved, and it seems the best medicine involves watching TV. Pills don't seem to help, but potato chips and sodas will slowly make you feel better and if you lay on the couch for a couple of hours, you will usually feel better by noon.

The strange thing is that you feel fine for the rest of the day, even well enough to do some target practice, play tennis or do some chores around the house. The funny thing is, it strikes again about 5:30 Sunday night and by 6:15 the same old symptoms come back. The good news is that the same remedy works unless, of course, you run out of potato chips. Most of the time, you are in complete recovery by 9:00 in the evening. There is no doubt in my mind that in the devil's handbook, there is a chapter on "How to Get People to Miss Church," and surely part of this chapter goes into great detail of the many facets of *sabatidious rigamitus*.

I know what you are thinking, my dear reader. This Jack MacDonald guy has a dry sense of humor. But all jesting aside, let's get to the bottom line. Having Christian fellowship, where you worship God together as a body of believers is not only scriptural but is also important. "A place to bring your tithe into the storehouse" is described in Malachi 3:10. Acts 8 describes how to pray for one another and experience the revelation of the word of God through anointed preaching. Acts 2 talks about creating a haven where lost souls can become saved and also grounded in the word of God. This is absolutely essential for a Bible-based child of God. This is not only scriptural but is definitely God's plan for the believer according to the Bible. This process will mold, shape, and protect your spiritual man so that you will mature into a warrior for the kingdom of God. The apostle Paul tells us to not forsake the gathering of our selves together. This Scripture alone could and should act as a vaccination shot against *Sabatidious Rigamitus*.

✞

Meanwhile, back in the jungle, we waited in our foxhole for an hour. Apparently the sniper didn't want to give away his position because we didn't hear any more shots. I put the word out again, church at noon, and only Rick showed up this time.

Richard Kucera was from Lewistown, Montana. He was probably 6'2" and was as strong as any twenty-year-old you could find. He could outwalk and outpack anybody in the battalion, but he never could outwrestle me. He was a handsome fellow, probably 185 pounds of muscle that reminded me of spring steel. And his heart was hungry for God there in that little bamboo church. I told Rick about Jesus. I read him John 3 as best I could, and explained the spiritual rebirth to him.

We read in Romans that all have sinned and come short of the Glory of God and that the Gift of God is eternal life through Jesus Christ our Lord. I explained to Rick that he needed to confess his sins to the Lord and ask Christ to forgive him and invite him into his heart as his own personal Savior. When we finished praying, I asked Rick how he felt and with a big smile on his face, he said, "I feel like a dozen backpacks have been taken off my back." Rick Kucera was saved that day. He was the only one that I had led to the Lord in the entire six months that I was in the jungles of Vietnam.

I began to tutor Rick and teach him the scriptures—I taught him how to pray. I told him about water baptism. We were washing off in a cool river one day and as we stood there in waist-deep water, Rick asked me if I would baptize him. I told him I had never done that before, and that it was probably a job for the chaplain, so we decided to wait. It is a decision that I will regret for the rest of my life.

During my first month in Vietnam, we were transferred to Khe Sanh, which was a little more than a landing strip and a couple dozen bunkers. The North Vietnamese army, which consisted of a large percentage of Chinese soldiers, had captured hill 881 and hill 861 and they were dug in deep in the mountain.

The enemy was shelling Khe Sanh from their vantage points almost at will. My unit, which was the Second Battalion, Third Marine Division, started up hill 881. We were relieving the Second Battalion, Ninth Marine Division that was almost annihilated. On the march up the hill, the marines that we were relieving were coming down from the other direction. I recognized one of the men as Gunnery Sergeant Cox, who was one of my platoon sergeants at the

Marine Corps barracks in Norfolk, Virginia. Now this man looked to be in his mid-50s and he was worn out. I greeted him, shook his hand, and asked him, "How bad is it?" He told me it was the worst thing that he had ever seen in his life and that there was only a handful of them left.

It took us three weeks to take hill 881 and 861, and hundreds of our men died. Finally, we chased a regiment of NVA (North Vietnamese Army) off the mountain and they ran for Laos.

There were thousands of NVA wading in the river that separated South Vietnam from Laos, in chest-deep water. The river was almost a mile wide and four feet deep. We had them trapped, so we called for permission to fire, and someone sitting in a recliner chair on a ship nine miles off-shore, drinking a cold can of beer, denied us permission.

I don't know if we could have ended the war right then and there with one Hough gunship or not, but I am convinced we could have shortened it by years. We were trained to obey orders, so that is what we did, swallowing our pride and anger, after watching so many of our fellow marines die in our arms. Young men aged 20–24 years old were called the *flower of American youth*. These men would never have a chance to go to college, raise a family, or play with their grandchildren. I hope we never fight another war that we do not intend to win.

Those same NVA soldiers came back three weeks later, high on heroine; they bound themselves together with chains and charged our machine guns at Khe Sanh. Wave after wave, they came until they overran the base. It was one of the bloodiest battles in Vietnam, and all for what, I still don't know, but it haunts me that I was forced to be a part of it.

When the remainder of the battalion that was still alive and able to walk left Khe Sanh, we got orders to walk out. All the troop-carrying helicopters, which are called 46s, were grounded. They were having a lot of problems with the rear engine conking out. The 46 is a big helicopter that can carry fourteen combat-ready marines. It has two big blades on top, one at each end, with a seven foot-wide hydraulic-controlled tailgate on the back that was usually left in a down position. This ramp served as a walkway for the men to board the helicopter.

I remember flying to Khe Sanh in one of these 46s. We were maybe a mile or two up in the air when the rear engine quit and the tail end of the helicopter dropped. It started falling toward the earth, tailgate first. I was sitting on the very end seat closest to the tailgate. I was thrown out of my seat onto the floor, and rolled down the tailgate. I had seventy pounds in my backpack and just before I rolled off the tailgate, I grabbed onto something. I didn't know what it was at the time, but I hung on. There we were, falling through the sky, tail first, with me hanging onto the tailgate. I thought to myself, "So this is how I am going to die." However, before we crashed in the jungle, the pilot got the engine going again and brought the tail back up where it was supposed to be. Somehow, I managed to crawl back up to my seat. I looked at my captain sitting there and his face was as white as snow. I could only imagine what my face looked like. Once again, God had spared my life. I will say that Vietnam was one big adventure, or maybe I should say thousands of little hair-raising scary adventures. Thank God for a praying home church. Thank you, Pastor Smock and Harry and Blanch Brimmer, for bringing me to Jesus.

✞

CHAPTER 5

Public Relations

They couldn't fly us back to the ship from Khe Sanh so they decided to force-march us over to the ocean, pick us up by boat, and take us to the ship. It was a 67-mile march and 120 degrees in the sun. We heard that a marine general bet a navy admiral that we could do it in one day. So away we went, a seasoned second lieutenant with a map and compass in his hand walking straight east to the ocean. It was the second time in my whole life that I had ever experienced my second wind kicking in.

We were shot at by snipers most of the way. We marched all night and all day and all of the following day, when we finally got to the ocean. We soon figured out that they were just Viet Cong and not snipers, as they were very poor shots. We got so that we wouldn't even dive for cover; we just kept on marching. We would even joke with each other about how the next bullet has your name on it—that's how tired we were.

On our way, we passed through a village and little kids began to beg us for food. It was impossible to say no. We gave away most of our food to the starving kids. We stopped at a village to rest in the shade. A small boy came over. He was about nine years old. He said, "Hey marine, you got chop, chop (food)?" I had two crackers in the bottom of my little tin can; I gave him the two crackers and the tin can. About five minutes later, he came back and he said, "Marine, come," and motioned for me to follow him. I was a little suspicious of a trap, but there were eight more guys in my fire team, so I had them cover me as I followed him. On the way, I walked by the captain and told him what had happened. He said, "Go ahead, maybe it will do something for public relations".

The boy kept pointing toward this mud hut and saying, "Popason." I followed him in and there sat an older man and woman, neither one over five feet tall and each weighing less than one hundred pounds. There must have been a half dozen kids huddled in the house. The room was fifteen feet by fifteen feet, and in the middle was a large altar with a big statue of Buddha. The lady of the house offered me tea. She poured one for me, the man and herself. I waited and let them drink first for fear of being poisoned. Then I sipped the tea that had leaves floating around in the glass.

The man of the house kept bowing to me saying something that I didn't understand. I pointed to the Buddha and then I pointed toward my heart and I said, "Marine Christian, Jesus is God." We tried to communicate for about a half hour when I heard the call "saddle up," which means we are leaving. I stood, bowed to the man, shook his hand, and pulled my little New Testament out of my pocket and gave it to him. I then bowed to the lady and shook her hand, and then I put my hand on the little boy's head and said, "Jesus loves you," and left. As I was leaving, the little boy ran up to me and waved, smiling from ear to ear. I had almost forgotten the joy of seeing glee on a young kid's face. It brought tears to my eyes. He made my day. My experience, in a remote way, reminds me of a true story as told by an esteemed Bible teacher named Marilyn Hickey.

✝

The story started seven hundred years ago in the deep jungles of Africa. There was a group of natives known as the Wah tribe. A prophecy had been handed down from generation to generation that a white horse would lead them to a man with a white face who would give them a Holy book that would tell them how to find God. (They had never seen a white man before.)

A little over eighty years ago, the spiritual leader of that Wah tribe said, "Now is the time to follow the white horse that will lead us to the man with the white face to get our Holy book." So they got a white horse and chose one of the tribesmen to follow the horse wherever he went. They turned the horse loose and much to the man's surprise, the horse walked in one direction for a very long time. Then one day, the horse came to a village and the Wah tribesman asked, "Is there a man with a white face here?"

They told him that there was, and pointed to a hole where an American missionary was digging a well. The American missionary climbed out of the hole and was told the story of finding the Holy book. The missionary gave him a Bible and would have gone back to the village with him, but he was having a revival, and he couldn't leave. The native took the Bible back to the Wah's village and the entire village was saved.

I would truly love to believe that the little New Testament caused the entire village to be saved, which would indeed be a miracle. However, the book was written in English and they only spoke Vietnamese. It was a good feeling anyway, just knowing that I had planted the word of God in the village. Perhaps in heaven someday, that little Vietnamese boy will seek me out and say, "Hey marine, I learned English from your New Testament and that's how I got saved." Stranger things have happened.

The captain told me later that it was the mayor that had invited me in for tea—he was the chief of the village. Maybe we did do some good public relations work. The mayor slept on a bamboo mat on a dirt floor—no furniture, just some cups, some bowls, a pot with some water in it, and a small fire. That was all those people had to their name—no TV, no refrigerator, no Chevy in front of the house.

We got to the ocean right at dark; we were so hot and exhausted that we took off our backpacks, laid down our rifles and waded out in the ocean, boots and all, and took a swim.

For a while, it looked like a beach in Miami, Florida with hundreds of marines ready to pass out from heat exhaustion. They were all just lying in that ocean water, but soon reality set in that we were definitely in enemy country. We went back to the tree line and dug in for the night. Unbeknownst to me, two guys in my squad had run into some Vietnamese girls and these two guys began to follow the girls when they said, "Hey marine, want boom-boom, come." (I shouldn't have to tell you what boom-boom is.)

Needless to say, they were led into a trap, and ambushed by a dozen riflemen. They came running back to our position. One guy had been shot in the leg, and his arm had been almost shot off—the other guy didn't have a scratch on him. The corpsman had no more than given him first aid when we were attacked. It seemed like bullets were flying everywhere in the pitch-black darkness. Something hit me in the shoulder and I realized that it was a grenade. I couldn't see where it went, so I stuck with the standard procedure drill and yelled, "Grenades incoming." I began to run away in the opposite direction from where I thought the grenade was, when it went off. The blast was like a pickup truck hitting me in the back going 50 miles an hour. My helmet went flying and I tumbled end over end into a huge cactus patch the size of half of a football field. I had no shoes on, no flack jacket, no shirt, just a pair of pants.

After rolling some distance in the cactus patch, I acquired hundreds of cactus quills. The blast of the grenade left my head bleeding and a back and neck ache that wouldn't quit. We fought the enemy most of the night; they eventually left when it started getting light. We were finally picked up by boat and taken back to the ship.

Johnny Rivers, the corpsman, put me in for a Purple Heart, as I was wounded in action, but the powers that be denied it. He came back and told me, and I said, "Oh well, no big deal." But my friend, Smitty, picked up my helmet and handed it to Johnny and said, "Go show them this." The canvas cover on the helmet was ripped to shreds and there was blood all over it. Smitty said, "Ask them if they will reconsider," and that was how I got my first Purple Heart. If it wasn't for Smitty picking that helmet up,

I probably wouldn't have gotten it. The worst part of the whole ordeal were the cactus quills all over my entire body—in my ears, eyes, nose, mouth—and everywhere you could think of. I had never been more miserable in my life. The night this happened, the enemy had overrun our position and it was so dark you could not tell who was who; fortunately, they couldn't tell us from their own men, so they finally backed off.

Back on the ship, I got a hot shower, a good night's sleep, and then spent the next day with a pair of tweezers, picking out cactus quills. I believe that was called *Operation Star Light*. Three days later, we made another landing. I have forgotten what they called this operation; it could have been called *Whiskey One*.

The 46 helicopters were still grounded, so they loaded us up on beach landing boats, which were probably the same boats they used on D-Day in World War II. With fixed bayonets, we came charging out of this boat, and to my disbelief, there stood a newspaper reporter with his camera rolling. I charged right at him and just before I ran into him, I veered off to the right, went another ten feet, then stopped and turned around. Facing the camera, I waved and said, "Hi mom." And then into the jungle we went. We didn't get very far as we ran into a heavy fire fight with the enemy. My squad was called up front to reinforce the other squad that had been hit.

We always carried ten magazines for our M16 rifles, which each held twenty rounds of bullets. I quickly shot all two hundred rounds. I unbuttoned my shirt and shoved these twenty empty magazines down my shirt and went to the command post to replenish my ammo. There were bullets flying everywhere. I was running bent over, with one hand holding my stomach so my empty magazines wouldn't fall out.

As I ran, I looked up and there was that same reporter filming me as I ran back to the command post holding my stomach. It probably looked like I was wounded and, wouldn't you know, my mother saw that piece of film. I did write her a letter that day to tell her I was OK, but she worried for a week before she got the letter. It was a terrible strain on her. The last time I'd talked to her on the phone was at Camp Pendleton, and she'd said, "I just know I am never going to see you again," and she cried uncontrollably. I pleaded with her several minutes to stop crying, as it really bothered me. She just became more and more hysterical. I think she had some kind of breakdown. I just couldn't take it so I hung up the phone. It was the last time I ever heard my mother's voice—she died before I got home.

My family has a history of men dying in war. My great-grandfather was a union officer in the Civil War, and was killed freeing the slaves. Another great-grandfather was killed in World War I, and my father was killed in World War II. I guess my mother had reason to fear.

✝

God had been dealing with me about going into the ministry. But a big part of me didn't want to listen. I loved farming and I had a great opportunity waiting for me back home. Little did I know that God has ways of getting your attention.

I fell in love with that farm, hundreds of acres of grapes and hay fields, one of the biggest dairy barns that I had ever seen, rolling hills with lush grass all fenced and ready for cattle, overlooking beautiful Seneca Lake.

I thought I had my life all mapped out for me, but life has a lot of little twists in the road, and some of those twists are sharp bends. Being a Christian is not so much how well you walk down the straight and narrow, but how well you negotiate the curves in the road. It would be one of the hardest lessons I ever had to experience.

✞

Sometime later, my platoon was walking across this dried up rice patty, when we found a little island of trees about the size of a school bus. We took a break in the shade in the trees, and as I looked across this open field into the timber three hundred yards away, I saw what looked like walking trees. I knew immediately that they were NVA. I also noticed the Fox Company off to my right, walking right toward them in the open.

We always had to ask permission to fire, so I had my radioman call the command post and tell them what we saw and request permission to fire; permission was denied. I turned to the radioman and said, "Those men are going to be slaughtered because we obeyed our orders." I had no more than finished the sentence when I heard what sounded like a hundred machine guns firing automatic fire.

The men in the Fox Company were falling like hay in front of a mowing machine. In a matter of seconds we were in a full-fledged firefight, and we just happened to be at the vantage point. We could easily see the enemy slaughtering our fellow marines. The dreaded time had come—what would I do when I came face-to-face with the issue of taking another man's life? I didn't even think about it, I just did what came naturally—I tried to save my fellow Americans' lives.

Back home in the States, precision long-distance shooting was my hobby, only I shot targets the size of a pop can at three hundred yards. These enemy soldiers were much bigger than that. One by one, we began to pick them off; it was somewhat like a turkey shoot. Little did I know that soon the tide would turn. I had gone through about sixty rounds of ammunition when all of a sudden, the guy next to me fell over dead. I turned to my left and said, "There's a sniper over there somewhere." The tree line must have been five hundred yards away, and I figured he was over there, but I didn't know where.

The next thing I knew, I was struck in the head by a round from an AK-47. The reason I knew what type of gun it was is that the bullet glanced off my head and hit my radioman in the shoulder. He saved the bullet and gave it to me later.

There was a furrow under my right eye a half-inch wide and a half-inch deep, and it continued across my face and went above my right ear. I was stunned; I had blood in both eyes and couldn't see. I heard someone yell for the corpsman. The next thing I knew, Johnny Rivers was kneeling over me saying, "No, not Jack." He washed my eyes out with water and put some gauze around my eyes and on my wound.

The next thing I knew, two guys each grabbed one arm and carried me back to the rear where it was safe. I could see from underneath the gauze with my left eye that all around us bullets were biting the sand; it looked like raindrops on a pond. I remember thinking to myself, "So this is how I'm going to die." There is no way we could run through these bullets and live to tell about it. We made it back all right. I had cheated death again; "The Lord is a shield to me."

As I laid there waiting for a 46 to pick us up, the enemy attacked our command post in another hail of bullets. Richard Kucera ran over by himself and dragged me back to the chopper, which by now had begun to take off; we jumped on the tailgate, which is three feet off the ground. Rick pulled me toward the front of the chopper and laid me down on the floor. I later found out he had returned to the tailgate and jumped about fifteen feet back to the ground. I don't know why he didn't break both legs.

The chopper began to pick up speed and gain altitude. I kept hearing this popping noise, and after a couple dozen pops, some fiberglass sprayed me in the face. I realized that those pops were bullets coming through the helicopter. Again, I thought to myself, "I am going to die." At any minute, I expected a bullet to come through the floor and take my life, but after a couple of minutes, the pops were less and less and I thought to myself, "Maybe we are going to make it." *The Lord is a Shield to me and a lifter to my head.*

✞

CHAPTER 6

Miracle on the USS Repose

They flew me back to the USS Enterprise and the doctors there said that my wounds were too extensive and they didn't have the equipment to operate on me. They took me off that helicopter and put me on a different one. No one was sure how the chopper stayed up in the air being riddled with so many bullet holes. In my opinion, an angel must have put his hands under the chopper and carried it back to the ship.

I would like to take a moment to thank those extremely brave marine chopper pilots who would fly into a hot zone to rescue their fellow warriors, knowing that they could be shot down at any moment. The good news is they made an extra $65 a month in combat pay, the very same amount that the guys back at the ship made, nine miles out in the ocean.

They flew me over to the USS Repose, which is a full-fledged hospital ship. I was so weak from the loss of blood, all I could do was lay there. I remember one of the sailors that was carrying the stretcher en route to the operating room had a heavy southern drawl; he said, "I's knows he's dead. I's can tell he's dead just by looking at him, I's have never seen so much blood, they can't make me touch no dead man." I thought I should say boo or something, but I could tell they were carrying me down a gangplank on the side of the ship. I could hear the waves beating on the side of the boat. If I make a sound, this guy is going to throw me in the ocean.

Soon I was being operated on. There was no ether or anesthetic—cold turkey gets the job done—the pain was unreal. I heard the doctor saying, "I think he'll live, but I don't think we can save the eye"; then they wheeled me down to a recovery room. I was exhausted; in spite of the pain, I fell asleep. Both eyes were covered with gauze and I couldn't see a thing.

The next day, somebody who was cutting the gauze off my face woke me up. Then a female voice said, "Can you open your eyes?" The first thing I saw was an extremely beautiful blond nurse with a snow-white uniform on. I looked past her to a snow-white ceiling, snow-white walls, snow-white sheets and then there was me, as filthy dirty as I have ever been in my life. Dried dirt and blood covered my sweaty body. The first words out of my mouth were, "You're a woman!"

"Well, I was the last time I looked," she said.

I replied, "I didn't mean it that way, I haven't seen a lady in four months, and I thought for a minute that you were an angel all dressed in white and I was in one of heaven's white rooms." I really thought that I had died and gone to heaven.

For some reason, this lady seemed to like me. Over the next two weeks, we became good friends. She even smuggled me out of my room and used her "stone fox" influence to get me the use of the ship's radio. They radioed somebody in California who had a ham radio, who in turn radioed someone who had a ham radio in Pennsylvania, who in turn called my wife on a landline. It was one of the nicest gifts anyone has ever given to me. I talked to my brand new wife for ten minutes. She assured me there were a hundred prayer warriors from my home church praying for me to be healed.

The Bible says, "The effectual fervent prayer of a righteous man availeth much." Now my home church consisted of over a hundred born-again, Bible-believing, tongue-talking, righteous believers, and they were all praying for me, 12,000 miles away.

✟

We see thousands of miracles written in the Scriptures as a direct result of prayer. I will give you one or two. God's people were in a war and they were on the verge of winning, but it was getting dark. If darkness came, the enemy would have a chance to regroup and fight the next day. A man of God prayed that the sun would stand still and it did and God's people won. Another time, a man of God prayed that the sun would go backward; now you have to agree with me that is an absolute miracle. The Scripture says that it went back ten degrees.

Now you may be reading and thinking to yourself that this is a little hard to accept, but let me offer this as proof.

NASA was planning a moon shot and they needed to know the exact position of the sun ten days in advance. To do this, they had their computer go back in time as far as it could reach, which turned out to be thousands of years, and then track the sun's path.

Their hope was to discover the sun's exact path in its entire history to the best of the computer's ability, and then figure out the sun's exact path in the future, but they ran into a snag—the scientists discovered that they were missing twenty-four hours and twenty minutes. They could not figure out how anyone could lose twenty-four hours and twenty minutes of history. It had all of NASA at an impasse for days. Finally, one scientist said, "I remember when I was a kid in Sunday school and learning about the sun standing still and I also remember when it went ten degrees backward." Read II Kings 20:8–11 and Isaiah 38:2–9, especially verse 8.

When they typed in the exact data from the Bible, the computer produced an astonishing statement, which is this: The twenty-four hours and twenty minutes that is missing in the history of time is now accounted for with the information supplied from the scriptures. Now do you believe in miracles?

Meanwhile, back at my wife's house, she had received several telegrams from the US Department of Defense. The first one was delivered by two marines in their dress blue uniforms. The same guys were visiting my wife's parent's house for the second time in two months. It was part of their duties to hand deliver all telegrams concerning men who were wounded in action (WIA) or men killed in action (KIA). My mother-in-law began to cry.

The first thing they said was, "He's not dead, he is alive." They delivered their telegram and left, and an hour later the state police showed up with another telegram stating that I might lose my eye, but God healed me and to this day you can hardly see the scar. The doctors on the ship called it a miracle, and I took the opportunity to tell the blond nurse about Jesus and the healing power of the Holy Spirit. Fourteen days later, they discharged me from the USS Repose, completely healed.

Eight sailors dressed in steel helmets, flack jackets, each carrying a half-dozen hand grenades and M14 rifles with fixed bayonets gave me a boat ride to shore. They even had camouflage paint on their faces. I was placed in the bow of the boat and was told that as soon as the boat touched the shore, I was to jump out. I thought surely they will throw me a rope, tie up the boat, and then escort me back to my unit.

When I jumped on shore, they put the boat in reverse and started to leave. I said in a loud voice, "Where are you going?" And they said, "We did our job," and they left me there. All I had was a pair of boots, a pair of pants, a shirt, no hat of any kind, no weapon of any kind, and no food or water in 118 degree heat in a Viet Cong-infested jungle.

If you have a praying grandmother or a praying church, you have a great heritage; never take it for granted. My home church prayed for me when they heard I was shot and God even gave Blanch Brimmer a personal revelation for me in the form of a scripture, which she put in a letter and mailed to me. Psalm 91:7: "A thousand may fall at thy side and 10,000 at thy right hand but it shall not come neigh thee."

So there I stood at the edge of the jungle, not having a clue what direction to go to find my unit. I was aware that I was a prime candidate to be captured. It sort of reminded me like deer hunting back in the states. I would take a step and look and listen, scrutinize the jungle floor for trip wires or any other disturbance that shouldn't be there. I knew that if I ran into the Viet Cong, or worse yet, the NVA, I ran a very high risk of being killed or captured. For two days, I inched my way through the jungle. Every sound I heard, I had to assume it meant trouble. Twice I heard Vietnamese voices and I stayed hidden in the brush for six hours. No water, no food—I admit it, I was upset with those sailors.

Finally, I came to a road and I thought that if I hid in the brush and waited, a GI convoy would come by. I remember waiting there for a long time. And then finally, here comes my taxi, in the form of a track vehicle painted marine green, with a .50 caliber machine gun mounted on the roof and USMC painted on the side. I flagged them down and told them what had happened. They gave me some water and a sandwich. Wherever these guys were based out of, they had made some sandwiches for lunch. I thought to myself that it must be nice.

Away we went on down the road at a very high rate of speed. I don't know if that was to keep from getting ambushed or if the guy driving was just having fun. I remember seeing a half dozen bodies lying in the road and the guy steered the vehicle over to where they were so we could run over them with the track vehicle. That's when he said, "I heard that there was an ambush up here last night; it looks like Charlie got the worst of it." It didn't sit well with me running over those bodies like that, but I didn't say anything.

We traveled for some time and then we finally arrived at the village of Danang. I remembered that my friend, Paul McConnell, was stationed in Danang at an air base. Paul was my neighbor during my childhood years. Although he was fifteen years older, we were good friends. I hadn't seen him since I was fifteen years old. He had made a career out of the air force. Once on the air base, I asked around and sure enough, everybody knew Paul McConnell. They directed me to his Quonset hut and I sat down on a locker with his name on it.

Pretty soon here he came. He gave me this blank look, and said, "How are you doing?"

"Paul, don't you recognize me?"

His eyes got big as saucers and in a very loud voice he yelled, "Jackie!" We hugged and cried—a face from back home—what a morale booster. He asked me what I was doing there and I told him. The next thing I knew he was taking me to an officers' club to feed me.

Paul was an E8, the next highest rank you can get as an enlisted man. If he wanted to take a lance corporal to lunch at an officers' club, nobody could stop him. We had T-bone steak; I had not eaten a decent meal in three days. Paul gave me a shower and a place to sleep; I think I slept for 36 hours. He wanted me to stay, but I felt like I needed to get back to my squad; little did I know they were all dead except me. That sniper was very good at what he did.

When I finally got back to Hotel Company, I heard that my good friend, Johnny Rivers, had been killed. He was shot right after he finished tending to my wounds. I later wrote him up for a Silver Star. I felt he was killed saving my life, but the office boys; nine miles out in the ocean on the ship, said they had given out too many Silver Stars that month. They didn't have any left. Johnny got nothing; he was one of the finest Christian Americans I have ever known in my life, the best of the best that ever came out of the state of Georgia. I have tried many times to find his relatives, but to no avail.

Five minutes after I had heard of his death, I went to see the first sergeant; I told him that I quit. He replied, "What do you mean?"

"I have had it with this pointless war where good men like Johnnie Rivers die for nothing. I am resigning from the Marine Corps."

He said, "You can't do that."

"Watch me," I said.

"That would be called desertion during wartime, and you could be stood against the wall, shot, and it would all be legal," he replied.

I looked him right in the eye and said, "You don't have the guts."

I could see the captain in the background, cringing; even he didn't backtalk First Sergeant Jones. Sergeant Jones is about five feet eleven inches tall and 250 pounds, with very little body fat. His arms were as big around as my head and his face had a half dozen long scars. He looked like he ate nails for breakfast. Everybody, including the captain, gave Sergeant Jones a wide girth.

I turned and walked away. We stayed at that camp for ten days; I guess by then I had a chance to cool off, and then the order came to saddle up. I found myself picking up my backpack, shouldering my rifle, and going back to work. Later on, I ran into Sergeant Jones again and he said to me, "You're not a bad marine for a WIA (wounded in action)." It appeared I had gained his respect.

The episode with the sniper's bullet had won me my second Purple Heart. I knew it would be an uphill climb to get my third one. It seemed liked my battalion didn't like handing out Purple Hearts to begin with, as congress had passed a law; if any one man receives three Purple Hearts, he is immediately sent out of the combat zone.

By now, I was very skilled and experienced at my job and the government had spent tens of thousands of dollars training me to be an American fighting man to serve in the armed forces that guard our country. I was prepared to give my life in its defense, and they wanted all the return on their investment they could get.

I suspected that I would almost have to die to get my third Purple Heart. As it turned out, I was right. Speaking of almost dying, we were deep in the jungle and had gone three days without water. We were ordered not to drink out of the streams as they were intentionally polluted, but after three days, I found myself chewing on banana tree bark, just to get the moisture out of it. It was very bitter. I even ventured out on an eight-foot-wide trail in search of a stream. I noticed that the trail was especially beaten down with jungle boot footprints. I even noticed some fresh blood in the mud. After a half mile, I turned around to go back to our position. That's when I noticed my own boot print in the muddy trail. For some reason, I assumed our company had just gone down that trail on a patrol and somebody had cut themselves on the razor-sharp elephant grass, but now, on my way back up the hill, I noticed that all the tracks were the same except mine. My vibram sole boots made a different print than NVA boots. I was mad at myself for not noticing this before, but three days without water and you lose some of your mental capabilities. I could tell by the fresh blood that the tracks were less than an hour old. That's when I realized I was in trouble. I put my M16 on fully automatic after I fixed my bayonet on the end of my rifle. I put a full magazine in my shirt pocket so I could reload my rifle very quickly. As quietly as I have ever walked, I started up the trail, expecting to meet the enemy head on as I rounded every bend. To make matters worse, the jungle was so thick, a man could be standing one foot off the trail waiting to run you through with a bayonet and you would never see him until he moved. I rehearsed in my mind what I was going to do if I met just one man. I also rehearsed in my mind what I was going to do if I met twenty of them. I decided that being captured was not an option, no matter what the odds. I would stand and fight. I really thought that I had a chance of being killed. It was very much like deer hunting in the deep woods back home, walking along, not making a sound, stopping every few feet to listen, looking for tracks that jumped off the trail, smelling the air for any smell at all that was different. I finally made it back to my squad and breathed a sigh of relief.

When you get thirsty enough, you will do unusual things that you ordinarily would not do to quench your thirst. No doubt you know what I am about to say next. If you really want to be filled with God, thirsting after righteousness is a key ingredient. We stayed alive by chewing on moist banana tree bark and drinking out of mud puddles that still had frog scum on top of them.

I ended up contracting malaria. When we finally got back to the ship to regroup, I had a temperature of between 104 and 105 degrees for five days. The doctor told me there was nothing they could do; they were just too overwhelmed and busy with treating men who had been wounded. I lay on my bunk for three days in a pool of sweat; no one came to visit me. It seemed like they had left me there to die; but, I knew that Brother Andrews, the Brimmer family, Charles Hand and his wife, the Rook family, and many others were praying earnestly for me back in my home church. I cheated death one more time and again God's healing hand touched my body.

✞

CHAPTER 7

Angel in the Pit

Meanwhile, back in the jungle, we faced grave danger every hour of the day and every minute of the night. We had to wear a flack jacket that was a half-inch thick and supposedly bulletproof. It had to be zipped and buttoned up at all times. We also wore a steel helmet that must have weighed 5 lbs. In our backpacks, we carried two or three mortar rounds that weighed twenty-two pounds each, two full canteens of water, a razor-sharp K-Bar knife, and two hand grenades. In addition to this, we carried an M16 rifle that weighed six pounds, and ten magazines containing twenty rounds each for the M16 rifle. To round out our pack we carried a poncho to sleep on and cover up with when it rained, and enough food to last us three days. I can remember it being 118 degrees and they ordered us to run while carrying all this equipment. *Yeah, right.*

On one occasion, we were ordered to turn our flack jackets in as we were to be issued a new and improved version. As a fire team leader, I was responsible for picking up the new jackets for my men. When asked how many were on my team, I told them nine men. I did not bother counting the flack jackets, but when I handed them out, there were only eight. By the time I went to get the last one, the chopper had already left, so I told the lieutenant that we were one flack jacket short. He told me we would get it later. Later on that day, I crossed paths with First Sergeant Jones. He asked, "Where is your flack jacket, MacDonald?"

I told him what had happened. He said, "You and your platoon sergeant, report to me at 1800 hours and bring your entrenching tool (foxhole shovel)." You guessed it—I was ordered to dig a hole six feet long, six feet wide, and six feet deep. I was told if it wasn't done by sunup, I would dig a second hole the second night. My platoon sergeant was to guard me to make sure it got done. Talk about pure ignorance. There we were in a war zone, playing Parris Island drill instructor games.

The ground was pure bedrock; it was as hard a dig as I have ever seen. First, I would adjust my entrenching tool to be a pick and chip at the rock until I got several shovels full of loose rock, change my tool back into shovel mode and shovel the loose rock out; by two o'clock in the morning, I was worn out and only half done.

I could see that I was not going to finish digging the hole by sunup, which was four hours away. My platoon sergeant leaned back against some brush and went to sleep, and then I had a brainstorm. I thought that if I got Rick Kucera to help me, I might get it finished by morning and avoid digging the second hole the following night. As quietly as I could, I crawled out of the hole and tip toed past the snoring sergeant. It wasn't a pitch-black dark night, but almost. How I ever found where Rick was sleeping was a miracle, and not being shot at by one of the sentries was another miracle. I woke Rick and told him of the situation. He grabbed his shovel and said, "Let's go."

Rick Kucera reminded me of a human backhoe. He put his tool in pick position and he hit that rock so hard, I thought it would break the handle. He never stopped swinging for four hours. He chipped the rock up and I shoveled it out.

It was just getting light when the platoon sergeant woke up. Rick sat down in the corner of the hole and I stood in front of him. The platoon sergeant must have talked to me three minutes before he noticed Rick. When he asked me who the other guy in the hole was, I said, "What other guy?"

"That guy behind you."

I said, "You must be seeing double."

"No, I am not."

Then I said, "You must be seeing an angel in the hole with me," and for a whole minute, I think I had him convinced.

Finally he said, "Well, I am going to the head and that angel better be gone when I get back." He left, and I thanked Rick for the help. I was just finishing the last two inches by myself when the first sergeant showed up.

I had my shirt off, I was dripping with sweat, my pants were drenched, and I was filthy dirty. The first sergeant never guessed that I had help. He took one look at the hole, threw his cigarettes in the bottom of it, and said, "Fill it up." That's when I suggested that we use it for a garbage pit; he snapped back at me—"I said fill it up!" It took me another two hours to fill it back up.

I had my breakfast and then the first sergeant set me up on sentry duty. I was totally spent—I had nothing left. I lay back on some sandbags. I cried out to the Lord but soon fell fast asleep. I never woke up until that evening. If I would have been caught sleeping on sentry duty, I would have been court-martialed. That would have been the good news—if the enemy would have snuck up to my position, they would not only have killed me, but the whole company would have been compromised. Now do you understand when I say that the first sergeant didn't like me? I still stand by my judgment; it was an act of ignorance and machismo. If Charlie had decided to hit us that day, I was so tired, I do not think I could have lifted a grenade.

An officer we called Lieutenant B, as his last name was too long to pronounce, was about thirty-five years old, and had worked his way up through the enlisted ranks. He was accepted at OCS at Quantico and had become an officer. He sought me out the following night, and told me he laid there and listened to me dig all night. He said, "I don't know how you did it. I felt sorry for you and I didn't agree with your punishment but we all know who runs this show." Two days later, a mortar landed right next to this lieutenant and blew his leg completely off above the knee. I never did find out if he lived long enough to get back to the hospital ship; it was fifty-fifty chance at best.

✞

CHAPTER 8

God Spared My Life

One morning I was point man, a position I often found myself in. I am not sure why, but as a country boy, I could read the jungle far better than my city raised brothers. My first guess is they all knew I was a Christian and by now they believed I had divine protection. Being point man wasn't my first choice but I drew the duty often because many of the men begged, pleaded or refused to do it. In the next few paragraphs you will understand why. As I was leading my company across a dried-up rice paddy, everything was quiet. Then all of a sudden, a thousand bullets started striking the dry sand around me. It looked like raindrops hitting on a pond. Fortunately for me, I was able to dive into an irrigation ditch that was about two feet wide and two feet deep. I laid there on my stomach for what seemed like three hours. My backpack stuck up about a foot above my back and several times I could feel bullets striking it. *Mother earth was protecting my vital organs; I cheated death.*

I managed to reach back and slip off my backpack. I gave it a throw as not to give off my position, and I rolled over on my back. I could see the tracer rounds going over my head; some of the rounds were just inches from my nose.

Finally, the first sergeant yelled, "Hotel Company, fix your bayonets and on my command, charge!" *Yeah, right.* But that is what we did. It must have been a terrifying sight to see hundreds of marines jump to their feet all at once and charge, because the enemy that had ambushed us turned and ran, giving us a chance to get to some shaded cover. We were never even sure who they were.

It was 120 degrees that day. We were all about to die from heat exhaustion. They called in an air strike and after about an hour of dropping bombs on their location, we thought they were annihilated. *Wrong!* We learned many times the hard way that these people were extremely resourceful and very resilient. They regrouped and pinned us down again, but at least for now, we were lying in some shade and not in the hot sun.

All of a sudden, I heard a loud bellowing off to my right and looked up just in time to see a 2,000 lb. water buffalo bull with horns that were four feet wide and as big around as my legs. It was badly wounded from shrapnel from the bomb. He was running straight at me, I guessed at about thirty miles an hour. All I had in my hand was an M16 rifle shooting a .223 bullet. This was something you would use on a ten-pound woodchuck or a twenty-pound coyote, not an animal this large. Facing an angry buffalo, charging straight at me, I knew that in order to stop him,

I had to shoot him in the head or the back. I really did not want to do this, because it would give away my position and I would draw enemy sniper fire. What should I do?

There was a bush about 40 yards away and I decided that if he came any closer than that bush I would have to try to drop him or be trampled to death. I took careful aim at his head and put my rife on fully automatic and waited. He came straight at me, but just as he got to the bush, he turned to the left and ran away from me. Was there an angel playing matador that day? That would be my first guess. If that bull had reached me, I am sure he would have gored me to death. They have a very bad temper, just like their first cousin, the Cape buffalo, which is one of the most feared animals in the world. *God protected my life a second time that day.*

The first sergeant yelled again, "Hotel Company, prepare to charge on my command. Ready charge." We all jumped to our feet and charged the enemy. Bullets were flying everywhere; we were shooting from the hip as we ran, and it looked like a John Wayne movie. The only difference was, when the men were shot, they didn't get back up, dust themselves off and go home for dinner. This was for real.

As I was charging toward the enemy, there was a sapling in front of me about six feet tall. As I approached it, I veered off to the left, almost brushing it with my shoulder when I noticed that the sapling suddenly snapped off about eye level. A bullet had struck it in the middle and cut it off, and if I had not sidestepped to go around it, I would have been shot in the head. *God spared my life a third time that day.*

As we continued running across the dried-up rice paddy, I became extremely exhausted. My boots felt like they weighed a hundred pounds each. The hot sun had taken its toll, not to mention all that weight we were carrying; I got to within thirty feet of a hedgerow that was in front of us and I knew we would all take cover there, at least until we caught our breath.

I was so exhausted and I thought to myself, "I will just leap forward and then crawl the last thirty feet to the hedgerow." I could not run another step. But just as I took a leap, I caught myself changing my mind, since I only had another ten steps to go. Just then, a bullet struck the ground in front of me at the exact same place where I would have landed. If I had followed through with my plan to crawl the last thirty feet, the bullet would have struck me right in the middle of the back. *God saved my life the fourth time that day.*

About twenty of us reached the hedgerow and began to return fire. Ralph Yellow Thunder, a full-blood Sioux Indian, was on my left, just two feet away from me. He asked me if I had any water. I reached for my canteen and handed it to him. Just then, a tracer bullet streaked between us at eye level. I gave him a very hard shove away from me and I went the other way. He said, "Why did you do that?" He never even saw the tracer bullet.

A tracer bullet comes out of a machine gun and usually is about every seventh round. I do not know what happened to the other rounds before or after, but I do know that the white glowing tracer bullet missed my nose by eight inches. *God spared my life for the fifth time that day.*

What really upset me, though, was there were so many bullets being shot in our direction that the bullets were mowing down the trees that we were using for shade and the trees were falling down on top of us. I could tolerate the rest of it, but shooting down our shade trees was the last straw. I thought of an old cartoon of Popeye saying, "I am really mad now, and I can't stands no more!"

✞

I remember Bob Coughman, a friend of mine back in high school. He was a mild tempered farm kid who was truly a gentleman, not easily riled. We were on the wrestling team together—he wrestled the 180-weight class. Bob was a six foot tall, purebred farm boy. He was a peace loving and quiet kind of guy if there ever was one. He was as strong as three men. He could pick up a rock the size of a coffee table, carry it ten feet, and then put it on a stone boat. That is something country boys do for $1 an hour, all day long.

There were five or six of us at a dance once. I was about sixteen years old, and about a half dozen guys from a rival town showed up half drunk. The biggest one of the bunch started mouthing off to Bob, calling him every name he could think of. Then he started shoving Bob. All this time Bob was keeping his cool pretty well. One of the guys shoved him and ripped two buttons off Bob's shirt. Bob looked down and said, "You ripped my shirt and I just bought it with some hard-earned money."

Bob began swinging his arms in a fashion that I would have to describe as two windmills and his two fists started to come down on this guy like sledgehammers. I think Bob must have hit him twenty times before the guy finally yelled, "I am not going to fight any more! I give up. I think you broke my arm!" It seemed like when that guy ripped Bob's shirt, Bob "couldn't stands no more." You think of the dumbest things at the worst times.

✞

Meanwhile, back at the hedgerow, the firefight raged on. The firefight had been going on for six hours now. We did not know how many enemy soldiers were back in the tree line. We guessed that we were up against a whole battalion. There had to be hundreds of them in order to produce that many bullets in the air all at once. Everywhere you looked, there were bullets snapping off twigs or kicking up dirt. You did not have time to be afraid. You had to concentrate on doing your job well because that was the only way you were going to get out of this mess alive. To say that there was danger in the air would be an understatement.

There was a marine out in the middle of the rice paddy screaming for help, but a sniper killed everyone that went to try to help him. They were using him as bait. The first sergeant had my fire team put down a base of fire in an attempt to rescue the marine. The guy on my right, named Jim, was from Wilkes-Barre, Pennsylvania. He was one of the nicest guys you will ever meet.

Dropping out of college, he came to Vietnam to fight for his country. He was one of those guys that had everything going for him, extremely handsome, charismatic, very intelligent, and a Christian. We had become good friends and he would often show me a picture of his fiancée back in the States. We developed a very strong bond, having been on many patrols together; he was almost like my brother. The next thing I knew, the dirt spit up in front of me throwing sand in my eyes. I went to get some water to rinse my eyes out, and while I was doing that, a bullet went through Jim's helmet and creased the top of his skull. You could actually see his brain through the jagged bone splinters. He lay in my arms asking me how bad it was. I said, "You lucky dog, you got yourself a ticket to go home."

Jim said, "Thank God." I was sure I lied to him because soon his brain swelled. He kept saying he had a raging headache. I tried to joke with him, telling him he had a right to have a headache. Jim died in my arms. *God spared my life the sixth time in one day.*

Finally, the enemy had had enough. They turned and ran, and the CO sent our company to chase them down. We soon became lost in the jungle and the captain called up the second lieutenant, who was our own schooled-trained navigator. He pulled out his map and his very sophisticated compass and for the rest of the day led us through the jungle.

I am a country boy, very used to being in the deep woods and I knew all about the moss growing on the north side of the trees; I could even tell what time it was by looking at the sun. I told the guy in front of me that we were walking in a big circle. Sure enough, we came right back to our old trail that we had cut through the jungle with a machete. That is when we coined the saying, "The most dangerous man in the Marine Corps is a second lieutenant with a map and compass in his hand."

It was getting dark and we were very lost in the jungle. The enemy was everywhere, so we climbed up on this knoll and started digging in for the night. We formed a circle about 100 yards across with our command post in the middle, and started digging; the ground was as hard as cement.

At this point, let me give you a piece of interesting information. Those who survived Marine Corps boot camp, which was not everybody, entered into the second most elite club in the world. The French Foreign Legion takes first place and you have to join for life and sign a vow of celibacy. Our club gladly takes a back seat to those brave and insane men.

In Vietnam, the brotherhood took on a whole new life; there was no minority or majority, the man watching your back was your equal and you loved him like he was your own brother. This world would be a better place to live if we could experience more of that type of unity.

We all shared the foxhole—it was so hard digging that we only got it about twelve inches deep, three feet wide, and six feet long when way off in the distance, at least a mile away, we heard a bang. It sounded like a cannon going off. We heard this whistling sound, just like you hear on the Fourth of July. It was a mortar round coming closer and closer and louder and louder. It fell short of our defense perimeter, but then we heard a second bang and it came closer, and a third and a fourth, until they were landing right on top of our perimeter.

These NVA were expert mortar men. They marched 179 mortar rounds in ten minutes around our perimeter several times and in the middle of our command post, killing our gunny sergeant. I remember him saying, I do not care if I lose a leg, a hand, or an arm, or even both eyes, but what I really care about and fear most is getting killed. The thing that he feared most literally came to him.

These mortar rounds were so well placed, they would hit one foxhole, then they would turn the dial five clicks and the next mortar would hit the next foxhole. They knew just how far apart our defenses would be. I heard a mortar coming and it sounded like it was going to hit us, but it hit the guys next to us. I began to pray aloud at the top of my voice and worship God. It didn't occur to me to ask for protection. I just shouted, "Hallelujah, praise you, Jesus!" and I began to pray in tongues as loud as I could. I said, "Have your way in my life, Lord," and then I found myself saying, "Lord, if you will get me out of this alive, I will go into the ministry and I will give up the idea of farming."

I fell back on my faith in the Holy Spirit, who was always with me, no matter where I went, and no matter what happened. He is just a prayer away; what a friend, always there in time of need. I tell you, being a child of God is a good deal. I can only imagine how extremely terrifying it was for the men who knew nothing about the supernatural, but at that time, I appreciated greatly my connection with God. Perhaps that is what this book is all about—God connecting with us on a daily basis through the study of the Scriptures.

I heard a round coming closer and closer, but instead of landing in our foxhole, it was a *short round*. It fell in front of us about 10 yards. Chief was the first to jump into our little foxhole; Snowden and I jumped in together on top of Chief. Mind you, this hole was only three feet wide and twelve inches deep. If anybody was safe, Chief was, but a hot piece of shrapnel stuck in his back like a knife, and I burned my hands pulling it out. Chief was screaming in pain. *God spared my life a seventh time that day.* To make matters worse, we didn't even get paid overtime.

They would have killed us all if it was not for one man, Richard Kucera, who got up in the pitch-black dark with mortar rounds exploding all around him. He felt around and found the two sections of the 81 mm mortar base plate that has to be twisted precisely together. Then he found the mortar tube, and assembled the mortar tube into the base plate.

A guy named Dan held the tube up in the air by hand while Rick felt around for a mortar round and unpackaged it. He guessed how many increments to take off (small sacks of powder the size of a carrot). Remember, he did this in the pitch-black dark with mortars exploding all around him.

He guessed where to hold the tube and while Dan held it steady, Rick dropped it down the tube and away it went. Evidently, it landed close enough to the enemy that they stopped shooting. It was the longest and most horrifying ten minutes of my life that I have ever experienced. I felt helpless.

Most of the company were either killed or wounded. The order came to "dig your holes and get ready for an attack." Cement ground or no cement ground, our foxhole was three feet deep and six feet long in no time. I wrote up Richard Kucera for a Silver Star. I felt like he and Dan had saved us from *annihilation*, but the office boys back on the ship, nine miles out on the ocean, said, "We have given out too many Silver Stars this month. We don't have anymore." *Yeah, right!*

Several of the guys came up to me later and said to me, "Hey, Mac" (they used to call me that), you might want to know that you taught us how to pray last night. Whatever that was you were saying seemed to work and it was a big help. When we heard you praying, we were praying with you. We just wanted you to know you were not praying alone."

This brings me to a question that keeps coming back to me: Why Johnny Rivers, why Richard Kucera, why Jim

Thomas, why did they have to die, but not me. Sometimes I feel guilty because I was not killed and they were. That's how strong the bond was between us.

That night deep in the jungles of Vietnam, I experienced a little glimpse of hell. It was a terrifying experience that I remember as if it were yesterday. Even though it was forty years ago, it took that experience for me to surrender to God's call to the ministry, a call I had been struggling with for many years. In a sense, it was a very memorable night in my Christian experience.

Many men died that night and I could have easily been one of them. However, I am convinced there was an angel there protecting me. Here is the picture: a very small foxhole with a marine PFC that we called Chief laying in the bottom of the hole, with me and another marine named Snoden laying on top of him. However, it was Chief who was hit with a piece of red hot shrapnel. Do not ask me how it happened; there must have been only a square inch of his back showing.

We stayed awake all night waiting for an attack, and when it didn't come, we were sure it would come first thing in the morning. But for some reason they left us alone. Could it be that Rick Kucera's estimate at the range, and also his guess at the amount of charge that he left on the mortar round, hit their commanding officer? Or was it a ring of fire the angels brought down to protect us?

In my opinion, Richard Kucera singlehandedly saved Hotel Company of the Second Battalion Third Marine Division from total annihilation on that summer night in 1967. This marine deserved at least a Silver Star.

Most of the company was dead or wounded, but for the grace of God it could have been me. *I had cheated death seven times in the last 24 hours*. No doubt Psalm 91:4 could have been a good Scripture for that day; it says, "He shall cover you with his feathers and under his wings shall 'thou' trust. His truth shall be thy shield and buckler."

The entire company, what was left of it, was exhausted from putting in a twenty-four hour day. We would have been easy pickings for them, but God protected us.

✞

I heard about a mission in Mexico back in the 1800s that was being attacked by bandits who intended to rape, rob, and kill the missioners. They spent half of the night riding around the mission and then finally left. A year later, one of the bandits was saved and told the story of a wall of fire burning all around the mission and he said their horses would not go through it. The missioners said they saw no fire, they didn't even smell smoke, and they thought it must have been the Holy Spirit messing with those bandits.

There is a little lighthouse on the big island of Hawaii; it used to be utilized as a church meeting place. It is east of Kalapana beach on the south end of the island. A volcano erupted and the lava flowed down toward the ocean. When it came to the lighthouse the lava went around it. To this day, you can see a ten foot border of grass all around the lighthouse, with a three foot deep wall of lava forming a natural fence. In my opinion, God protected that little lighthouse. If you ever get to the Big Island, it is worth going to see.

I could go on and on about how God protected me in Vietnam, but I don't want to risk sounding too redundant. I will say I now know that part of the reason I was sent to Vietnam, my seemingly "chance meeting" with the admiral, and being appointed the assistant chaplain—all of these incidents seemed to be a nudge from God, drawing me into the ministry, and giving me the experience of orchestrating Sunday services. As humble as they may have been, it gave me a glimpse of things to come. I soon learned more often than not, you have to make things happen.

"Making things happen" are good words for today. It is a necessary facet of the marketplace if one is to survive in business. I never could comprehend a healthy grown man saying, "I can't find a job," when all you have to do is to discover a need and fill it. Maybe the need is your next door neighbor not having food on the table. Go down to a major grocery store at 8:30 at night and ask the manager to donate all his leftover soup; seventy percent of the time he will, rather than throw it away, and twenty percent of the time, you can buy it all and a lot more for $1. I promise, if you go around doing good, God will give you a job.

In the Old Testament, there was a man named Nehemiah who would qualify as a high-powered leader. He humbly and graciously made things happen. Leo Godzich is the founder of an organization called NAME (National Association for Marriage Enhancement), which is located at Hwy. 101 and Cave Creek Road in Phoenix, Arizona. This organization offers free marriage counseling and has a well over ninety percent success rate. God bless you, Leo and your staff, we support you and pray for you. No doubt you are ministering to a modern day mission field that's been somewhat neglected for some time.

If you ever want to see someone make things happen, I suggest trying to follow Leo around for one day. In his office, you will find an army of workers who are inspired by Leo's example. If our federal government could be one-half as efficient and cost effective as his office, we would no longer have a national debt. If it can be done on a small scale, it should be able to be done on a large scale. If there are any super powers who happen to be reading this book and find yourselves at a crossroads not knowing what to do, I suggest giving Leo's office a call at 602-971-7127. I promise you, you will talk to a straight shooter who will not talk in circles, and I will assure you, when you hang up the phone, you will have direction and not wonder what he just said, which is a lot more than I can say for many speeches I have heard in my lifetime. Visit Leo's office and see for yourself. Who knows? This could be the voice of God for you.

✞

CHAPTER 9

Third Purple Heart

Meanwhile, back in the jungle, the monsoon season had begun. There were two inches of water on the ground everywhere, so a platoon of large track vehicles picked us up. Eleven of us were riding on a track vehicle, when all of a sudden there was an explosion. I was later told that the Viet Cong had booby trapped a 500-pound bomb that turned out to be what we call a dud (meaning a bomb that didn't explode). The way they do this is dig up a dud, bury it in an anticipated trail, and install a grenade underneath it. The dud will then be triggered when a heavy vehicle runs over it.

It blew the track vehicle I was riding in completely off the ground. I was thrown in the air and when I came down, I landed in the engine. I thought I had broken both thumbs, and my elbow and my shoulders felt like I had been hit with a sledgehammer. My back hurt and I couldn't move my legs, but I was still alive. I cheated death again.

The shells inside the tank began to explode as the fuel tank caught on fire. I had to use my hands to push myself so I could roll off the track vehicle. It was a soft landing in a foot of mud. After dragging myself for about fifty yards, I was very exhausted. I wondered if I was the only one that made it out of there alive. By now it was dark and the rain was coming down harder than I have ever seen it rain before. I leaned up against a bush, pulled my helmet over my face, and then spent the night laying in six inches of water, shivering from the cold. I did not mind missing supper; I was just glad to be alive. There were four or five tanks that had run over mines and were on fire all around me. Their live rounds were cooking off. It was a night to remember; in fact, it was one of the most miserable nights of my life.

We were ordered not to move because we were in the middle of a minefield, so we lay there until morning. Finally, a track vehicle came in with a huge v-plow on it. It plowed up three feet of earth and made a safe path through the minefield as the blade plowed up the land mines. Talk about a scary job.

The corpsman took me back to the command post that morning. The feeling had returned to my legs. I was bruised and battered with a half dozen deep cuts on my body and I was starved to death.

They were debating whether to give me a Purple Heart when at that precise time, a telegram came for me. My wife had had a baby girl, eight pounds, two ounces. Up to this point, the command post was trying to weasel their way out of giving me my third Purple Heart. The delivery of the telegram seemed to change the mind of my first sergeant.

Could it be that he had some daughters of his own? If so, I wouldn't want to be one of their boyfriends. Anyway, I got my third Purple Heart on September 16, 1967, the same day my first daughter, Lori Joy, was born. I knew I had qualified for five Purple Hearts, but these three would do just fine. The office boys told me that I could sign a waiver, and I wouldn't have to leave the jungle—I wouldn't lose my extra $65 a month hazardous duty pay. I just looked at them as if they had lost their minds and said, "I'm out of here!"

They gave me my orders to go back to Okinawa to finish out my thirteen-month overseas tour, but before I arrived, my sea bag was lost or stolen. When I inquired about my pay records and record book, the record department for the battalion informed me they were in a helicopter that was shot down over the ocean and were never recovered.

All I had was a copy of my orders folded up in my pocket. I arrived at Camp Schwab the next day, no clothes except what I had on, no record book, zero money, but I was alive and that is all I cared about. I prayed to God and told him I really did not want to spend another seven months away from my family, and that is when a corporal paged me and told me to report to the American Red Cross.

An older man sat me down and told me there had been a tragedy back home. "I am afraid I have the worst possible news for you," he said. My mind raced ninety miles an hour. My only thought was, "Is my wife all right?" The man put his hand on my shoulder and said, "I am afraid it is your mother; she has passed away." I cried. I thought to myself, "Jack, you have held death and looked at death for six months and now you are crying. What is wrong with you?" I remembered telling myself this was my mother and it was all right to cry.

They loaded me on a huge deuce and a half truck and sent me down this narrow mountain road. The civilian driving was probably 40 years old, less than five feet tall, scared to death of that big deuce and a half truck. The corporal kept yelling at him, "hicyko, hicyko," which means "faster, faster" in Okinawa. He would speed up to twenty miles an hour and then slow back down to ten miles an hour. We had to hurry to catch a cargo plane back to the States. I did not care if it was an ultralight, as long as it was taking me home.

We finally arrived at the airstrip and I boarded a C130 bound for Dover, Delaware via Anchorage, Alaska. All I had to sit on was a wooden bench, no armrest, no padding, and a row of caskets down the middle of the airplane. I was not the only one going home.

I landed in Anchorage, Alaska fifteen or twenty hours later on October 5; it was twenty-seven degrees above zero and all I had on was a short sleeve shirt. I was cold but I did not care; I was back in America. It could have been fifty below zero and I still would not have cared. I almost kissed the ground, but I knew the best was yet to come. The C130 was refueling and leaving immediately for Dover, Delaware. There were vending machines where you could get sandwiches, but my pay records had gone down in the ocean and I did not have one dime to my name. I was not about to leave that terminal to go to the mess hall to get food, even though I had not eaten for a day and a night.

The flight to Delaware was another ten or twelve hours. I was good and hungry by the time we got there, but the joy of being home made two days without food seem like nothing. I got off the plane late that evening in Dover, Delaware. I had made a collect call to my wife from Anchorage. I told her approximately what time I would be landing in Dover, and then asked if she could make the three hundred mile drive to pick me up. After I arrived, I sat there in the terminal on the base for about an hour when I looked up and saw my Uncle Jack walk through the door. When I saw him, I yelled "Yes!" as loud as I could. Everybody in the terminal was looking at me. I did not care. I was reunited with my family; nothing else in the whole world mattered to me. We shook hands and hugged each other and I said, "It's good to be home." Next, my wife walked in the door. I hugged her and then she opened up this little bassinette. There lay the most beautiful baby I had ever seen—my three-week-old daughter, Lori Joy.

My bones no longer ached from the long plane ride, sitting on the wooden bench. I did not think about my empty stomach. Indeed, I felt like a very rich man; as they say in West Virginia, "Yes indeed, I'm a fortunate man."

It was a very emotional time. I felt as if I had died and gone to hell, and then rose again. We got out of there and started to drive home. I had no luggage—only the clothes on my back and not one dime to my name. Unknown to me at the time was the fact I would not be paid for six straight months. What lies ahead are a series of miracles and a testimony of what you and God can do with very little money.

We drove all night and got home the next morning. My mother's funeral was that afternoon. I did have my dress blue uniform stored at my house, so I wore it to the funeral. I wondered why there was no headstone. In addition, there was no hole dug in the ground. We stood around a vacant piece of grass and were told that this would be the gravesite for my mother. Not having been to very many funerals in my life, I did not know any better. Could it be that my mother's body had to be disposed of quickly, before an autopsy was done?

My stepfather told me he had ordered a headstone and it would be installed in the near future. A few years later, I visited my mother's grave and noticed there was still no headstone. When I inquired with the cemetery superintendent, he said there was no record of her being buried there or anywhere else in the cemetery.

My stepfather was a longtime alcoholic and I have seen him cheat, steal and lie in the past for beer. I could only imagine what he did with my mother's body. All I know is that she did not get a proper burial, and to make matters worse, I later learned that she did not have a heart attack. She died in the dentist chair while being given sleeping gas, and the same dentist was being charged by a different family with manslaughter for the misuse of sleeping gas. The case was tied up in court, but he was still practicing dentistry. Nonetheless, within an hour of my mother's death, my stepfather was called in and was somehow manipulated into signing a hold harmless waiver stating that the dentist was not liable in any way for the events surrounding my mother's death.

I am convinced she was given too much sleeping gas and it stopped her heart. Moreover, I am convinced my alcoholic stepfather was capable of accepting money for my mother's cadaver. I had seen him, in the past, go to great extremes for beer. I do understand there are different scientific institutes and medical experimentation institutes that will pay good money for such cadavers.

To make matters worse, if that is possible, I had an eleven-year-old adopted brother. However, he was not legally adopted. My stepfather had met this pregnant woman in a bar, who stated she already had five kids and did not want another one. She told my mother and Joe that if they wanted this child, they could have it.

The woman delivered Robert to us when he was three weeks old. She also insisted that we take his older sister, Sonya, who was two, but she failed to mention that Sonya was mentally challenged. My mother tried for one year to raise them both, but it was too much for her, working two jobs and being the main breadwinner. Don't ask me how she did this week after week. I have never known a harder worker than my mother. My mother ended up giving Sonya back. The woman didn't want her back, and got so angry with my mother that she came and got both of the children. It broke my mother's heart; however that same woman came back a year later and gave Robert back to my mother to raise.

We later learned that this same woman got pregnant again and tried to give my mother a second child, but it died at birth. The doctor said the baby died from a combination of alcohol, nicotine, and drugs. To this day, it baffles my mind when I see a pregnant woman smoking. With all the information available on how deadly nicotine is to your system, I truly believe it is a slow form of suicide, not to mention the complications it can do to an unborn child. It has to be the height of selfishness to smoke while you are pregnant.

✞

CHAPTER 10

Posttraumatic Stress Disorder

After my mother's funeral, I remember walking into my father-in-law's backyard. It was in the fall and spruce hen hunting season had just opened. Suddenly, two hundred yards down the hill in the creek bottom, somebody flushed out a bird and fired a single shotgun blast at it. The next thing I knew, I dove head first under the lilac bush and crawled in the dirt trying to conceal myself. Can you imagine how foolish I felt? My dress blue uniform looked like it had just come out of the dump, my hands were black, and my face was dirty. It was my first flashback of Vietnam, perhaps a mild form of posttraumatic stress disorder.

I thought to myself, surely this reaction will dissipate as I ease back into a normal life. I was very wrong. Fourteen years later, working as a carpenter, I was bending over nailing a stud wall together. Back in those days, we did all the nailing with a 22 oz. framing hammer with a 19-inch handle. Unbeknownst to me, a carpenter's helper walked up behind me with a dozen 8′ 2x4s in his arms. Instead of setting them down, he just dropped them from a chest-level height. When they landed on the plywood deck, they sounded like a mortar round going off eight feet behind me. For a whole ten seconds, I was back in the jungle being ambushed all over again. My thoughts went into survival mode; I jumped to my feet, whirled around in midair, and just missed his nose by inches with my hammer. I yelled at him and said, "Don't ever do that again." The poor kid's face was as white as snow. If the superintendent had seen it, I would have lost my job.

For twenty years after that, I would plan a camping trip on the Fourth of July, as I hated firecrackers with a passion. Worse yet were the rockets that sounded exactly like a mortar round coming in on top of you.

War is a terrible thing; it can scar you for life. To this day, I do not make a lot of men friends. The VA counselor told me it is because my mind is afraid I might watch them die in my arms, and I have absorbed that type of pain to such an extent that my mind refuses to accept any more. Subconsciously, I go to great lengths to avoid that scenario.

The first fifteen years I was back from Vietnam, I often experienced two different dreams. The most common one involved riding down a steep mountain road that had no guardrail and a thousand foot cliff off to my right. My entire family is riding in the back seat of the van and I'm sitting in the passenger's seat. We are traveling a little too fast for my comfort, as the road is very steep and full of sharp curves. Suddenly, the man driving the van disappears and the van is about to go over the thousand foot cliff. Each time, I leap from the passenger seat to the floor, and try to push the brake pedals with my hands to stop the van. At that very second, I would spring straight up out of the bed, and would land on my feet, sometimes on the bed, sometimes on the carpet, yelling at the top of my lungs the word "no." My entire body would be dripping with sweat. Sometimes I would start to weep. It would take several minutes for my heart to stop pounding.

The other dream that came less often would be one where I'm lying in bed with my wife and a scoop shovel, three feet wide, three feet long and eight inches deep, heaped full of hot glowing coals, was slowly being elevated to dump the cinders on me and my wife while we were lying in bed. At that point I would leap to my feet, usually landing on top of the bed, and often trampling my poor wife. I would put both hands together as if I was trying to catch the coals from burning my wife and at that point I would yell in a loud voice the word "no." Again, I would be drenched with sweat and sometimes I would cry uncontrollably. The surgeon general calls it PTSD (Posttraumatic Stress Disorder); even to this day, 40 years later, if someone walks up behind me and I do not hear them, I have a very negative reaction.

One time in Water Valley, Mississippi I was at a Christmas party, and this lady, who was about five feet, ten inches tall and weighed 170 pounds, walked up behind me and, before I knew what was happening, threw her arms around my neck. The next thing I knew I had grabbed the woman's wrist and flipped her in a complete cartwheel. Fortunately, she landed on the couch. I firmly grabbed her shoulders, and I yelled at her, "Don't do that." Then I hugged her and apologized, and said, "You startled me." I helped her up and asked her if she was OK.

I was so embarrassed. I went to find a cold drink and tried to hide in a corner. I noticed the owner of the home, Nathan, talking to the woman quietly, and about five minutes later, she came over to me and said, "I am very sorry. I now realize that I could have been killed." I do not know what Nathan told her but he knew about my background. I bet it will be a while before she ever does that again.

✞

CHAPTER 11

Unlikely Candidate

At this time I would like to bare my heart to let you know that I am human. Here is the picture of a born-again, spirit-filled Christian trying to serve God, sometimes successfully and sometimes not so successfully, with the background of Marine Corps boot camp. The Marine Corps goes to great length to produce an American fighting man who has vowed to protect his country and live the American way, even at the cost of giving his own life.

In Vietnam, a portion of your mind goes into survival mode and often you find yourself in situations where you have one-half of one-half of a second to size up a situation and act accordingly. It seems like this acquired instinct burns into your mind and it is always there, even thirty years after you have left the jungle. When someone walks up behind you and grabs you around the neck, your mind automatically goes into survival mode. Had I taken longer than one-half of one-half of a second to size up that situation at the Christmas party, I would have never sent that woman flying over my head. Nevertheless, it seems once your mind is programmed to react, it is hard to push the erase button.

Mixing together thousands of haunting memories of real live war with a very large portion of God's grace, and trying to understand how the Holy Spirit can visit a heart like mine in a very real and exciting way is impossible for the human intellect to understand. I do not know why God has chosen me to be a spokesperson for the Gospel. But I know that He has.

As I read the Scriptures, I find other unlikely candidates in history whom God chose to use. For example, we know Abraham lied to a king, telling him Sarah was his sister. In addition, Moses killed an Egyptian in a rage of anger and smashed the tablets of stone the finger of God had written upon. Of course, we all know David, who tried to hide his adultery by having his mistress's husband killed? And then there's Peter, who was such a coward that a servant girl got him to curse and swear and deny that he knew Christ three different times. Let us not forget the apostle Paul, who held the men's coats while they stoned Steven to death. If you will look in our day and age, it does not take long to find a multitude that have failed God, and really blown it in their spiritual walk. Yet the grace of God is so huge and abundant, we can only conclude that love covers a multitude of sins, and if we will repent and confess our sins to the Father, He is faithful and just to forgive us of our sins and cleanse us from all unrighteousness. Here is the part that is so hard for us to understand. We are all sinners in need of a loving God to grant us redemption.

In addition, the Bible goes on to teach us that when God forgives, it is just as if we have never sinned. If only we could grasp that truth, God's family would be better off. Surely, this process about being able to grasp the truth about forgiveness would help us to be candidates to be used by the Holy Spirit. Maybe the key is the word "candidate"; are you a candidate to be used by God? Are you willing at the prompting of the Holy Spirit to stand up in a large group of people and give a message in tongues or an interpretation? Let me ask you this question—when is the last time you witnessed to anybody, or heard real live prophesies given to even a small group of believers? A poll was taken largely in the Assembly of God churches and the finding was that 48 percent of the born-again believers who were polled spoke in tongues.

At this point I could go to great lengths and take up a lot of room in this book and speak about the baptism of the Holy Spirit, but you can read it for yourself in Acts 1:8, 2:4, 19:1-10 and in First Corinthians 12:1-10, especially First Corinthians 12:1, where Paul said, "now concerning spiritual gifts brethren [this leaves no doubt who he was talking to], I would not have you ignorant."

There are hundreds of verses in the Bible that talk about the voice of the Holy Spirit. If you are hungering for more of God in your life, you will find them. Remember this—one of the secrets of being filled with the Holy Spirit is to hunger and thirst after righteousness. The Scriptures say, "The kingdom of God suffers violence and the violent take it by force." What this means is if you really want something in the spiritual realm you will pray and fast and wait on God in a very aggressive way, and if Satan opposes you, and trust me, he will, you will take up your sword, which is the word of God, and fight like a warrior who is fighting for his life.

You may think that statement sounds a little strange, so let me explain. There are some things in the Scriptures we have to see with our spiritual eyes and hear with our spiritual ears. That verse in Matthew 11:12 that speaks of taking the kingdom of God by force can be seen in the life of Daniel.

Daniel prayed three times a day for three weeks straight over a certain matter, and finally an angel arrived. The angel apologized to Daniel for being late, but he had a good excuse. He said," The prince of the air did hinder me." So we see that Satan will fight to delay or stop the answers to our prayers, so now that we are aware of this spiritual warfare, we can gear up to do what we have to do to win our spiritual victories.

We learned about the full armor of God in Sunday school, Ephesians 6:13-17, and the verses right after that are also important. For example, it says, "When you have done all to stand, stand." The reason that I emphasize standing is because in Ephesians 6:12 it says, "We wrestle not against flesh and blood, but against principalities, against powers, against the rulers of the darkness of this world, and against spiritual wickedness in high places."

Having a heavy collegiate wrestling background, I can tell you this for sure—you cannot step out onto the mat with an indecisive attitude and expect to win. When you shoot for a takedown, you have already visualized it several times in your mind and you have already decided nothing was going to stop you from taking that man off his feet.

If he is as quick as a cat, and most wrestlers are, then you have to be determined to be quicker. If he is very strong, you have to believe that you are stronger. If he is a smart wrestler, you must tell yourself you are smarter, and that's what makes collegiate wrestling so interesting.

Sometimes these two men go at it so hard and so fast it looks violent; that is because they are both determined to win. If you really want to hit the ball for God, be warned; you will experience some wrestling against rulers of darkness. The only way you are going to win is with a disciplined prayer life, which will require you to feed the spiritual man, not submit to the natural man and the lust of his flesh.

Fasting is a powerful exercise for the spiritual man, and it causes the person doing the fasting to deal with this very issue. The bottom line is that gain only comes by much prayer and fasting. A man who runs a lot will build up his physical endurance, and if we will pray and fast often, we will surely build up our spiritual man.

Be prepared to do it by force and sometimes violently. Realize it is not just the carnal man that you wrestle with, but often demonic powers. Be encouraged, and as you read the Holy Book, feel free to peek to see how it ends, because when it is all said and done, we win.

I have spent thousands of hours guarding a gate and even a foxhole, and at least half of that time on my feet. I am here to tell you—you get tired, your legs hurt and your back aches, and you become physically exhausted. When we decide to take a stand for the Gospel, we enter into a spiritual battlefield that is similar to the battlefields here on earth. It will require endurance, knowledge, training, and ability from the Holy Spirit. Another element that is very important—a will to win and a very strong sense of want-to-ism. If we are going to have God's government in our lives, we have to take it by force. Satan will do everything in his power to hinder us, and that is what it means when it says the violent take it by force.

Daniel was a spiritually violent man; have you ever prayed for one thing three times a day, every day, for three weeks straight? Daniel did. Allen Redpath does an excellent job of writing about this concept in his book, *The Making of a Man of God*. Of all the books I have read in my life, I would list this as number two in my must-read category. The Bible, of course, is number one, but books like *Pilgrims Progress* by John Bunyan and *The Making of a Man of God* are excellent reading material for those who are serious about their walk with God.

There is a devil out there that will do everything in his power to silence the church, especially the gifts of the Holy Spirit. If you care to read about the great revivals in the past where the Holy Spirit manifested itself, read about Topeka, Kansas, Azusa Street in California, and Brownsville, Florida. You will see a golden thread that runs through them all. That thread is the gift of the Holy Spirit. Has God changed or have we changed? Has God's priority changed, or has ours?

It seems as if many of our mainline churches from the past have turned into machines. Those machines have built empires, but somewhere along the way, the Holy Spirit has taken a back seat to social standing, in an effort to be more accepted by the intelligentsia, which *Webster's Dictionary* says are intellectuals considered as the social or political elite.

✝

CHAPTER 12

Hometown Celebrity

I did enjoy being somewhat of a celebrity in my hometown when I returned from Vietnam. The local newspaper printed a number of articles about me and my near-death experiences. My classmates sought me out just to chitchat, asking me if I needed anything. Even the mail carrier stopped and welcomed me home.

My history teacher, Mr. Ballard, who had also been my football coach, the same guy I took the stolen football jerseys back to, contacted me and asked if I would address his history class to tell them firsthand about Vietnam. I accepted the invitation and as I sat there waiting to be introduced, Mr. Ballard produced a sea ration postcard I had written to him from the jungle.

A sea ration postcard comes from a little box—8 inches tall and 6 inches deep—that holds field rations of ham and eggs, beans and franks, beef stew, or spaghetti and meatballs. One side of the postcard is blank, handy for writing messages back home, while the other side was the label stating the date manufactured, which was quite often 1943. Those were our choices, three times a day, seven days a week. Now these meals may sound delicious, but they were not. We ate for fuel, not for fun. The modern day field rations are called MRIs, and they are a thousand times better.

We would fold the postcard in half and tape it together with some tape acquired from the corpsman. The word "free" was written in the right-hand corner because it didn't require any postage.

I had written to Mr. Ballard on August 20, which was the traditional day our football practice began. I told him I had traded my football spikes for jungle boots, my shoulder pads for a flack jacket, and my football helmet for a steel helmet. I remembered how the heat felt during those few weeks of practice, but it was nothing like the hot sun I was experiencing in Vietnam. I thanked him for pushing us so hard during those practices. It truly helped me endure the extreme conditions of life in the jungle.

Mr. Ballard told the class this postcard was one of his prized possessions. I did talk to him about forty years later and he mentioned that he still had it—spoken like a true brother pack rat. Some of you brothers out there know what I am talking about, only we prefer to call it our collectables, treasures, or, as I sometime refer to it, inventory, but never trash.

I stood there in front of a huge history class; many extra faculty members attended the meeting, as well as another history class. There was standing room only. People wanted to know exactly what was going on in Vietnam. I talked to them for a whole hour, and the last twenty minutes I spent telling them about God's mercy and grace toward me, and the miraculous healing and divine protection I experienced over there.

I ended by saying, "Let every head be bowed and every eye be closed so that we may end this session in prayer." I ask, "Is there anyone who is not sure if they are going to heaven? Raise your hands—I would like to pray for you. If you sincerely would like Christ to come into your life, pray this prayer after me because salvation is available to you." At that time I led them in the sinner's prayer.

Over a dozen hands were raised. We had ourselves a regular Gospel meeting, compliments of the school district. Mr. Ballard later told me he probably could have gotten into trouble for that. However, when you have been teaching school for 20 years, you can get away with a few extra things. He said if he had it to do over again, he would not have me change a single thing.

✞

CHAPTER 13

Treasure Island, California

My 30-day leave went by so fast that I could hardly believe it. I was due to report to Treasure Island, California on November 5, 1967. When I arrived at Treasure Island, I found myself in a huge barracks full of transit marines.

We had nothing to do but wait. I was waiting for orders to Okinawa to finish my overseas tour. Most of these men were fresh out Vietnam. All they could think about was picking a fight—they all seemed very angry. No doubt, they had a lot of anger stored up inside them from all the atrocities they saw overseas.

One black man got in my face and tried to pick a fight with me. I looked him square in the eye and said, "You don't want to fight me, you want to thank me." Then he asked me why he should thank me for anything. I said,

"I am from the North; my great-grandfather was an officer in the Union army, and he gave his life setting your grandfather free from slavery. I even have the sword he fought with." (Little did I know that sword was soon to disappear out of my stepfather's house where I had it stored.) The black marine's eyes softened. He raised his eyebrows, looked away, and all he said was, "Yea, that's cool." It is amazing how powerful our words can be.

Consequently, I spent very little time in the barracks. I began to wander around the base, meeting new people. One day I wandered into this small building where there was a marine standing behind the counter. There was a chalkboard on the wall behind him. At the top of the chalkboard was written the name Richard Kucera, Lewistown, Montana and there was a date after his name. When I inquired what the chalkboard was, I was told it was one of many stations the fallen soldiers came through on their way home to a military burial.

I was so sick to my stomach that I had to sit down. The man asked if I knew Richard Kucera. I said, "Yes, he saved my life in Vietnam." He said, "It's too bad you couldn't have gotten here earlier; we would have made you a part of the military escort. His parents would have liked that. They just left on a plane two hours ago."

At the time, I could not understand how I had missed such an important opportunity. In a way, I was grateful the Lord led me to that chalkboard. Those names are only up there half of a day. Once processed, the name is replaced by another name. Somehow, I felt like it was serendipity.

I went back to the barracks feeling very depressed, when they announced we were all getting a 3-day pass for the weekend. I felt sorry for some of the local guys that might run into these Vietnam warriors after they had been drinking, because back in the barracks, all they wanted to do was fight and argue—it would be an interesting Monday.

I grabbed my pass and walked out the door. I had no idea where I was going. The only clothes I had was one pair of pants, one short sleeve shirt, and a hat. It was very cold and damp in the San Francisco Bay area in the middle of November. I had not walked two blocks when, just as it was beginning to feel too cold for me, a car stopped and asked me if I needed a ride. I accepted; as it turned out, it was a staff sergeant in charge of supply. He was an Assembly of God Christian who asked me if I could use a home-cooked meal. I said, "Does the ocean have water in it? That would be very nice, thank you." We became good friends.

He had a guest room I stayed in, and he took me to church on Sunday. On the way back to the base on Monday morning, he said, "We can't have you running around in a short sleeve shirt; everybody else is wearing their dress greens." I told him I did not have any money, not even a dime, and that they had lost my pay records. He told me I was in luck, because he was in charge of handing out all of the uniforms. I was to come by his office that afternoon. Sure enough, by evening I had socks, pants, new skivvies, a belt with a buckle, shirt, tie, tie clasp, jacket with marine emblems, a soft cover (hat), and even a Purple Heart ribbon with two stars on it. At least I would not freeze to death in California. He invited me to go on a men's retreat the following weekend—Thursday, Friday and Saturday. I told him I did not think I could get Thursday or Friday off. He told me to leave it to him and he would handle it.

The next thing I knew I was handed a 96-hour pass, almost unheard of in the Marine Corps. I do not know where the registration money came from for the retreat (R100), but someone paid it.

It was a regular Holy Ghost weekend with prayer meetings in the morning, classes until noon, Christian fellowship, and worship services in the evening with great preaching.

When the people heard I had just gotten back from Vietnam, it seemed like everybody wanted a firsthand account. I told them I hoped we would never fight another war we did not intend to win. During these three days of prayer, Bible studies, worship services, and sharing each other's testimonies, with over 500 men raising their hands and praising God, the Holy Spirit spoke to me and told me to have my wife fly to San Francisco.

At first I argued with the Lord, saying, "I could be shipped out of here any day now, and I have no money for a plane ticket or anything else." However, I knew it was the still, small voice of the Holy Spirit. I shared this with my friend, the staff sergeant. He said, "I am willing to pick her up at the airport and she can stay at my house; my wife needs the Christian fellowship during the day while I am gone. You can ride back and forth with me."

Therefore, I made the call and told my wife the plan, and she said, "Where are we going to get the money?"

I told her, "I own two cars and a dozen guns. Sell whatever you can, and bring as much money as possible, because I don't know how long you will be here."

She had to make the airline reservation two weeks in advance or the price was almost double. Her parents loaned her the money for the ticket, and she held a garage sale, where she sold half of my life's treasures.

That following Wednesday night, as I sat in church—there were less than 100 people there—the pastor opened up in prayer, led the song service, had some testimonies shared, and then I witnessed one of the most incredible things of my entire Christen experience.

Pastor North introduced his sixteen-year-old daughter, who would sing a special song for the congregation. This very young looking girl sat down behind the piano and began to play. She was not an accomplished piano player. She played mostly cords, but I have never in my life, heard a more anointed song than the one she sang. "When I survey the wondrous cross on which the Prince of Glory died, my riches gain I count, but loss and poor contempt on all my pride, were the whole realm of nature mine that were a present far too small, love so amazing so divine demands my heart, my soul, my all." As I sat there listening to her sing, tears rolled down my face as I have never experienced before. Something happened in my spirit, a very good thing, and to this day, I can't explain it.

I could tell this girl had spent time with the Holy Spirit in prayer. It seemed like an anointing flowed through her and dramatically touched my life. I think I received some kind of a healing. I have never seen a sixteen-year-old so anointed; she was dripping with the Holy Spirit. Nor have I ever seen such power in a single song. Brother and Sister North, I salute you for indeed raising your child for Jesus. That does not just happen overnight, but is a result of many faithful family altars on Saturday morning.

✞

Perhaps some of you have never heard of a family altar. Let me explain: As a teenager, I remember Harry Brimmer gathering his five children and wife in the living room. They would read a portion out of the Bible, sing a church worship song, give prayer requests, and everybody there would take turns lifting these requests up in prayer. Maybe it would only last twenty or thirty minutes but I truly believe it pleased God.

Brother and Sister North were a living example of Jesus to their children. You could tell when this girl prayed, she touched God. That was forty years ago; I remember it like it was yesterday. It is a lot of fun walking with God. Thank you, Sister North, you are grown and married now. I cannot tell you what a blessing you were to me in that humble church at a Wednesday night prayer meeting.

Fifteen years later, I met another Brother North on the big island of Hawaii. He was the pastor of a very small church. I got to know him rather well and he even asked me to preach for him. It did not dawn on me at the time that this may have been the same Pastor North I had met in San Francisco.

✞

CHAPTER 14

Going to Placerville

Back at the barracks, they announced that everybody had four days off for Thanksgiving. My Uncle Jack had sent word that his daughter, my cousin, Sandy, and her husband, Dale, who I was very close to, would be visiting his parents in Placerville, California. If I could make it there, we could have Thanksgiving together. I soon learned that hitchhiking in a Marine Corps uniform was extremely efficient; a trucker picked me up—he was going all the way to Placerville. Thank you, Jesus.

We were on a freeway, and had just passed through Sacramento, when we passed a building along the side of the road. It was all lit up and I thought I saw a cross on top. The Lord spoke to me and said, "Get out here and go back to that church." I argued with God, "I have a ride all the way to Placerville," but like an obedient son, I did as he asked.

I told the trucker to stop; "I have to get out here."

He said, "I thought you were going to Placerville."

I said, "I am, but I feel led by the Holy Spirit to get out and go to that church back there."

"All right," he said. "I understand." By the time I got out of the truck and thanked him for the ride, I had a half-mile walk back to the church. I needed the exercise so I ran, and wouldn't you know, it was an Assembly of God church just starting the Thanksgiving prayer meeting. I had forgotten it was Wednesday night, and the next day was Thanksgiving.

As I walked into the church, I was handed a candle and joined about one hundred people standing in a circle. They were all lighting their candles one at a time and sharing what they were thankful for. I shared how God had spared my life and how I was thankful for being miraculously healed in Vietnam.

After the service, a couple came up to me and said, "Our son is in Vietnam and we have been praying tonight for his safety." I told them about my home church, and my adopted Christian parents successfully praying for me. The mother began to cry and said, "You will never know what this means to me. I now have a new assurance that my son is going to be alright."

God knew this woman's name and what her worried heart needed. It was as if I had a divine appointment at that church to comfort these people. In addition, they were going to drive to Placerville that evening to be with their family and they were happy to give me a ride wherever I needed to go.

I knew my cousin's father-in-law was the pastor of a Nazarene church and I knew his name and phone number, but the cool thing was these people knew where he lived.

We pulled up next to his house but it was dark, and as I was saying goodbye to these folks, a car pulled into the driveway. It was the pastor and his wife. They were just returning from their Wednesday night church service. The pastor said, "I've been expecting you; come on in."

I said, "First I would like to introduce you to my new friends who gave me a ride." I soon learned that I had brothers and sisters, lands and homes, hundred-fold, that I have yet to meet.

✞

This experience reminds me of the rich, young ruler when Jesus told him to leave all that he had, to "come, and follow me," which, by the way, was the very same call He gave to Matthew. The rich, young ruler walked away sorrowfully, because he had great riches. He walked away from an offer that might have made him the thirteenth disciple. Peter, taking all this in, came to the Lord and said, "We have forsaken all and followed you."

The point I want to make is addressed in Mark 10:29-30. The answer Christ gave Peter says, "No man that hath left house, or brethren, or sisters, or father, or mother, or wife, or children, or lands, for my name's sake, and the Gospels, but he shall receive a hundred-fold in this time, houses, and brethren, and sisters, and mothers, and children, and lands, with persecutions; and in the world to come eternal life."

✞

So there I was, three thousand miles away from home, meeting a woman about my mother's age, who was terribly worried about her son who was fighting in Vietnam.

For two hours, I became like a son to her, bringing her comfort and reassurance. But the story doesn't stop there—they not only invited me to their home for Thanksgiving dinner, which I graciously had to decline, but they gave me a ride right to the door of my destination, which no doubt was a better deal for me than the ride in the semi truck.

When we are saved, we enter into the family of God. And this family spans the entire world. It's a great blessing to know we can move from Houston, Texas to Phoenix, Arizona and there will be a whole new family there waiting for us, and they will be just as close, or closer, than our natural family. I tell you, this life in the supernatural is a good deal.

It was cold and rainy that night; if I had stayed with the trucker, I would have arrived there two hours early and had a very uncomfortable time sitting on the front step.

The Nazarene pastor fed me supper and shortly after that, my cousin, Sandy, and her new husband arrived. Sandy and I had grown up together and were very close. It was a great joy to spend Thanksgiving with her. Those four days flew by very quickly. Sandy's father-in-law found me a ride back to San Francisco.

It was good to be alive. Amen.

✞

CHAPTER 15

The Barracks

Once back at the base, it was more of the same—the barracks was full of warriors—most of them were Vietnam vets, fresh out of combat, with overwhelming, pent-up emotional issues. All they wanted to do was fight. I think we all had anger problems—by now, we knew that we were being used to make others rich, and in the process, a lot of good people died. Living in that barracks was like being thrown into a boxing ring with one hand tied behind your back, not to mention most of us were dealing with delayed grief of the memory of our friends dying in our arms.

I did receive some good news. My wife's garage sale had raised over $500. She paid her parents back, and she and my brand new daughter, Lori Joy, got on the airplane. My new friend, the supply sergeant, picked her up and took her to his home. After a couple of days, I found a room to rent at the Presidio, which was a military base near Treasure Island. It cost me $2 a night, and came with a refrigerator, stove, microwave, clean bed with maid service, even a TV and a private shower. What a deal. We stayed there for six weeks while the military tried to figure out what to do with me. *Jehovah Jira (the Lord is my provider).*

During those six weeks, we learned how to get a transfer on the trolley cars, and we could ride all day all over San Francisco for 25¢ each. Eating on base was ridiculously reasonable. One price that I remember was 10¢ for a delicious bowl of soup; a steak dinner was $2. All that was required of me was that I check in every morning at eight o'clock to see if my orders had come in yet. The rest of the time was my own, playing in San Francisco with my brand new daughter and my brand new bride. The blessing of the Lord makes us rich, and little is much when God is in it.

It was important for me to remember that during the six weeks I was at Treasure Island, I could be transferred back to Okinawa at any time. I knew they had lost my record book along with my pay records, but I had no idea how it would affect the military process. I did have a copy of my orders, which included a 30-day emergency leave; after the leave, it stated I was to report to Treasure Island and be transferred back to Okinawa. It was a by-faith venture, flying my wife and daughter out to California. For all I knew, I would be sent overseas before she landed. The funny thing about this story is that I had heard from God and *He* knows the future. So there we were, playing in the San Francisco Bay area for three weeks, when unexpectedly, they decided they needed me in Quantico, Virginia.

I finally got my orders on December 22. My little family and I flew back to Rochester, New York, where my wife's parents picked us up. They had given me seven days travel time, coupled with the holidays, and we were able to spend Christmas at home.

On January 2, 1968, I hitchhiked down to Quantico, Virginia, leaving what little money we had with my wife and daughter, who stayed with her parents.

The barracks at Quantico was much like Treasure Island, overrun with returned warriors from Vietnam. The transition back to a normal life was not an easy one. They kept talking about debriefing us, but it never happened. I do not think they knew how. While they decided what to do with me at Quantico, I worked the detail that involved placing sea bags in their designated companies.

There I was, in this warehouse with thousands of sea bags and fifty other marines, sorting them out, and the first sea bag I picked up to be processed had the name Ralph Yellow Thunder on it. What a small world. Now I knew that at least one member of my squad made it back. I took "Chief's" sea bag, set it aside, and wrote him a note on the back of a large tag. I told him where I was and suggested that we stay in touch. I never did hear from him, as Quantico was a huge base.

The next day, I was assigned to Camp Barrett, a place all the guys said to avoid like the plague, as it's way out in the middle of nowhere, and they train second lieutenants, FBI agents, and conduct Officers Candidate School.

I remember at the time complaining to the Lord that I really did not want to go to a place commonly called "Grin and Bare it," instead of Camp Barrett. Now I can see I would not have been happy staying at main side, participating in all the parades and inspections every week. I appreciated my steps being led by the Lord. Camp Barrett was much more relaxed, a little like McHale's Navy. There, the war veterans were given a lot of respect, and the officers and the candidates listened to you as if their lives depended on it.

My new platoon sergeant's name was Al; he seemed to like me. He gave me time off to look for a house to rent for my family. After a lot of searching, I found a little one-bedroom trailer I felt I could afford. My wife had all our money, so I didn't have any money to put down to hold it.

I told the sergeant, "All I need is to get my family moved down here before this rental trailer is taken by someone else." My mouth fell open when he handed me a 96-hour pass.

I hitchhiked home, loaded up the family in my Plymouth Fury and drove back to Quantico, only to find someone else had taken the one-bedroom trailer. Again, I felt disappointed and complained to God. Later that day, we found a two-bedroom mobile home for less money. Retired Sergeant Major Saville, who was fresh out of the USMC, was running the mobile home park.

We got along well, and he seemed to like me; six months later Sergeant Major Saville used his influence to persuade the owner of the mobile home to sell it to me for a ridiculously low price.

Our little family settled into our new home and I took up my duties, training men how to stay alive in the jungle. It was kind of a fun job—it made me feel important. It was a lot better than marching on a parade deck with a thousand other men, trying to impress some dignitary. Those poor guys spent hours and hours in the hot sun, and believe me, Virginia has some hot sun with humidity.

As an added benefit, just behind my barracks, which was a Quonset hut, was a small lake. I soon discovered it was full of large catfish. You guessed it—my family and I ate catfish several times a week.

After about a month at my duty station, I felt like I needed to check on my twelve-year-old adopted brother and my alcoholic stepfather. Sergeant Al gave me another 96-hour pass. We pulled into my in-laws' home about midnight and spent the night there. The next day, my brother-in-law, Herbie Monagan and I drove over to my mother's house. I walked right in as I had done a thousand times before, and I noticed a different table and chairs in the kitchen and a strange woman standing at the sink. I stood there with a bewildered look on my face and this woman freaked out and yelled, "George," and a second and third time, each time getting louder and louder. Soon a middle-aged man appeared from the other room and the woman ran over to hide behind him. The first thing the man said to me was, "You must be Joe's boy. I have been expecting you. We bought the place from Joe and he doesn't live here anymore."

In my stepfather's home, I'd had all my worldly belongings stored. My beloved '49 Ford with dual carburetors that was polished so well you could see your face in the reflection of the hood was gone. I had also stored over fifty steel traps, three hunting rifles, an excellent white-tailed deer mount, a full collection of archery equipment, a knife collection, and a rare coin collection. All my civilian clothes, a barbell set, and my prized varsity letter with the three stripes on it—one for football, wrestling, and track—numerous pictures from Vietnam, everything was gone. Even my great-great-grandfather's Civil War sword that was handed down four or five generations was gone. The sword was taken out of the bloody hand of my slain great-great-grandfather as he died trying to free the slaves. It was priceless, yet easily converted into a six-pack of beer.

All these things just disappeared when my stepfather sold the house my mother had worked so hard to buy. My stepfather sold it to one of his drinking friends, who told me he just took over the payments. Nobody knew anything about how my belongings disappeared or where they went. Perhaps they were converted into beer, or maybe an angel came and took them to heaven.

✞

CHAPTER 16

Bible College

In April of 1969, the Marine Corps decided they were being overrun by returning Vietnam vets; out of the blue, they offered me $20,000 and a promotion to E5 if I would sign up for another six years. This meant I would have to sign a waiver making me eligible to go back to Vietnam.

I sat there and looked at the recruiter like he had lost his mind. I even thought about bursting out laughing, but instead, I simply declined the offer. A week later, I was informed I had an option of an early out. Instead of being discharged on November 10, I could be discharged on May 1. All I said was, "Where do I sign?" At 8 a.m. on May 1, 1969, I received an honorable discharge.

I was aware that I was eligible to draw unemployment insurance up to nine months after my discharge, but the idea didn't sit well with me.

Please read carefully, my dear reader, as I have something important to share with you. I hope and pray you don't receive this as boasting or proud or haughty, but only as a testimony to the grace of God, and to show you that God provides. I tell you this: I am now 62 years old, with seven children, and so many grandchildren I have lost count, and I have yet to cash an unemployment check, and I wouldn't know a food stamp if you showed it to me. My hardworking wife was a housewife 99 percent of the time with the exception of doing some babysitting.

I can't say I am against unemployment insurance and food stamps, but for me, they never seemed to fit into my economics. My mother was a very hardworking woman, and she definitely instilled that in me.

I had spent the last two evenings looking for a secular job. I was lucky enough to find one, and one hour after my discharge, I went to work as a carpenter. It paid $3 an hour, with a promise of a $1 raise in the very near future. Two weeks later, when I asked my boss about the raise, he said the company was getting short on funds, so I told him I had to look for another job.

Up to this point, my family and I had attended the Triangle Assembly of God church faithfully, three times a week, for well over eighteen months, and the people there really liked us. One guy in particular, Brother Clay, who had been in the Ironworkers Union for over thirty years, knew I was saving money to go to Bible College, so he arranged for me to get a worker's permit in the Carpenters' Union in Washington, DC. I went to work the next day building a giant grocery store for $6.85 an hour, and before the end of the summer, I worked my way up to $12 an hour.

The day before I was supposed to leave for Bible College, I asked the superintendent if I could get fired so I could pick up my check that day. He tried to talk me out of it, saying he was shorthanded. But when I told him what I was doing, he said "OK, but we will do it my way." At three o'clock that afternoon, there were a dozen of us up on huge scaffolding forming up a wall in the very hot sun, and we were all dragging a little bit because of the heat. That is, until the superintendent came along and said in a loud voice, "You, in the red hat, go pick up your check. You're fired!" Of course, I had the red hat. The rest of the men looked at each other and started working like beavers. I did feel a little used, but I picked up my check and went home.

We sold our mobile home the day before we left for two and half times what we had paid for it. Now we had a nest egg to start college. We arrived in Green Lane, Pennsylvania two days before classes started and managed to purchase a 14 × 70 foot trailer that we lived in for the next three years.

School didn't come easy for me, as I am not what you call a quick study. I had to work very hard for Bs and Cs. Well, six weeks into my first semester, there was a mighty move of the Holy Spirit. Instead of going to classes, we stayed in the chapel for ten days. I called it the School of the Holy Spirit.

I was sitting in Bible school, listening to Brother Hobart Grazer's lesson. The lesson was about God miraculously providing food for the children of Israel. First, he spoke about the manna from Heaven; after that he told how huge flocks of quail flew three feet off the ground and the children of Israel killed the quail with clubs.

At the exact moment he spoke about the children of Israel killing the quail, I heard a loud thud about one foot from my head. I was sitting next to a large picture window.

As I looked to see what made the noise, there lay a sparrow on a six-inch-wide ledge made out of brick; it was even slanted to shed water. The poor little sparrow had some drops of blood coming out of its mouth. That bird had flown into the glass window at eye level from where I was sitting, at the very precise time that Brother Grazer was talking about God providing the quail for his people.

The bird broke its neck and without twitching, stayed on that slanted window ledge. The Lord spoke to me and said, "Jack, this is how easy I can provide for you." From that time on, I had no doubt God would meet our needs, and He always did.

✞

CHAPTER 17

Treasure Hunting

During my sophomore year of Bible College, my wife and I wanted to go home for Christmas, but the trip involved about $50 for gas. The GI Bill paid us $243 a month and after we paid our tuition, books, electric, and tithe, what was leftover paid for food. We had very little leftover to pay for gasoline. We decided to pray about it. The Lord spoke to me and said, "Jack, do you remember three months ago when you were deer hunting in the mountains and on the steep mountainside buried under a foot of leaves was an old dump? Go back there and gather some of those bottles and sell those bottles for gas money." I thought to myself, what a strange thing, couldn't God simply have someone write me a letter and send me $50?

The thought has often crossed my mind that the Holy Spirit asks me to do things to see if I will obey his promptings. I decided to go back, and I miraculously found the same place deep in the woods. As I began to kick the leaves away, I found different colored bottles. Most of the bottles had a cork, not a screwtop; I suspected that they were very old.

I knew a little bit about bottles—I could tell the older bottles from the newer bottles. I also found some with dates on them of 1843 and 1848. Then it dawned on me—this was an old Civil War dump, about the size of a football field. I had brought a large burlap sack with me and I filled it full of these bottles. I took them to a collector, and I sold them for enough money for gas one way. I didn't know how I was going to get back, but I was confident that God would supply our needs.

The Holy Spirit had given me, personally, a couple of Scriptures. One of those Scriptures was, "With God, all things are possible." I knew that God would supply the money that we needed for the return trip.

We drove home for Christmas, and sure enough, I got a couple of Pentecostal handshakes from the people in my home church, but we still lacked about $7. No doubt, some of my precious readers have never even heard of a Pentecostal handshake, so let me explain. It's simply someone in the body of Christ feeling led to give someone else some money. And the transfer is made by folding up a bill, concealing it in your right hand, and shaking hands with the person you want to bless, simply by saying, "God bless you."

It really is a lot of fun to watch the eyes of that person when they feel the bill touching their hand. Pray and ask God to direct you to a needy brother or sister and ask God what denomination bill you should give them. If you are not sure, simply start out with a $1 bill. The shocked and surprised look in their eyes will be the same.

I went to pray and the Lord spoke to me and said, "Jack, remember that patch of woods up behind Marvin

Wright's farm?" I told the Lord I did. Then he said, "Do you remember the hollow tree at the edge of the woods where you drive in? There is a raccoon in that hollow tree and that will be money for the gas that you need for your return trip."

If there are any animal lovers reading this, you will have to forgive me, but I need to share this true story just as it happened. I called up my friend, Steve Brimmer, and asked him if he would like to go with me to get a raccoon. He asked me how I knew there was a raccoon in that tree. I told him it was a word of knowledge.

Steve and I went there, climbed the tree, and ran a long, skinny stick down the hollow tree. Sure enough, here comes the raccoon. Things got exciting for a minute; it was the biggest, black raccoon I had ever seen. I will spare you the details; suffice to say, I sold that raccoon pelt for $7. We had enough money to go back to Bible College.

Another time, I got home from class about two o'clock in the afternoon. I tried doing some homework, but I had this overwhelming desire to go pheasant hunting. I was a little disgusted with myself, as I had a lot of homework to do, but finally, I put down my book and grabbed my Winchester shotgun. I drove across the street where there was a big open field; half of it had been mowed for hay, but the middle half was still knee-high grass. As I was getting out of the car, I heard a cock pheasant crow. I quickly loaded my shotgun and began to zigzag the field where the tall grass was. Much to my surprise, nothing flew out. I thought they had probably run off without me seeing them. As I was getting ready to go back to the car, the Holy Spirit told me to stop, turn around, and look. At the far end of the field, the mowing machine had missed a little spot of grass about ten feet by ten feet. I felt compelled to go look there, even though it was way down at the other end of the field—it was a walk of faith.

I had only taken one step into that little patch of grass, when out flew two cock pheasants. I only had three shells—my first shot missed, but the second shot dropped the first bird. I pumped my last shell into the chamber of my twenty-gauge shotgun and took careful aim on the second pheasant, which was by now forty yards away. I shot, and one BB hit him in the head; we had pheasant for dinner that night. *Praise God!*

Once we tried to eat pigeon for dinner; it tasted so bad, I got up from the dinner table, grabbed my fishing pole, and walked down to a lake, which was about two hundred yards through the woods by my house. On my first cast, I caught an eight to nine pound bass. I cast a dozen times after that and caught nothing.

I carried it back up to the house and when my next door neighbor, Roger Smith, saw the fish, he told me that was the biggest bass he had ever seen, and asked if I was going to have it mounted. I laid the fish on a chopping block by my house and picked up a hatchet. After chopping his head and his tail off, I told him I was going to mount it right in my frying pan, and he laughed. We had bass for supper that night. I have never shot another pigeon since.

Sometimes God provides for us in mysterious ways, and possibly we don't even realize it is our provision. For example, we were coming home from Wednesday night church when the car in front of me hit a deer. The only damage to the deer was a broken neck, killing it instantly. The lady that hit it had a big hole in her radiator and was losing her antifreeze fast. I told her she only had two to four minutes to get home before she ran out of antifreeze and then her car would overheat.

She asked me if I would take care of the deer because she didn't want it. I took the family home, got a piece of plastic, and put it in the car. My neighbor, Roger Smith, and I went back and got the deer. I was happy to give him half of it.

One year, in the middle of deer season, I was doing homework and a fellow student knocked on my door and asked me if I had a rifle. He had seen a deer a couple of hundred yards back in the woods. That year, the Lord provided us with another deer to share with that couple. Although the only rifle I had was a .22 Magnum (not exactly a deer cartridge), but we got that deer with one shot. Little is much when God is in it.

I know some of you may think, why would God send you to shoot a deer? Little did I know I would raise seven children, and 99 percent of our meat would come from hunting and fishing. We would eat wild meat or fish every single night of the year, and we fed hundreds of guests. The scenario repeated itself for twenty-nine straight years. That was one way God provided. Perhaps He provides for different people in different ways.

In Hungry Horse, Montana, my first pastorate, God provided us with one black bear, four hundred salmon, eight deer, eight antelope, and one elk, which fed my family, and guests that we fed regularly, for one year. I remember catching thirty salmon with thirty casts and I got so I could clean thirty fish, head off, tail off, skin off, in thirty minutes.

✝

CHAPTER 18

Hearing God's Voice

Looking back, I learned a lot from one professor, Walter H. Butler in particular. He taught me to know God and hear his voice. Later on in my junior year, I felt a strong prompting of the Holy Spirit to take the Old Testament course over again, only this time with Walter Butler as the teacher. I knew I would not receive the GI Bill for that month, and I knew I would be three credits short for graduation. But I hungered to be a follower of God's voice no matter what the cost.

During this semester, Brother Butler taught about the prayer life of the prophet Daniel in the Bible and how he prayed three times a day. With this lesson, he challenged the students to try doing just that. He told us to pray at nine, noon and at three. So I began to pray three times a day and about two weeks later, I had an incredible experience.

I arrived home shortly after noon one day and went straight to my bedroom and knelt by the bed and prayed. After twenty or thirty minutes, I got off my knees and stretched out on the bed. A couple minutes later, a voice spoke to my mind. This was not an audible voice, but two words came into my thinking that I somehow knew was from the Lord and they lodged in my heart.

The two words that I heard God say were "Hungry Horse." Somehow in my spirit, I felt this was a town in Montana, Wyoming, or Colorado. I also knew that I was supposed to go there. Except for sharing this with my wife, I kept this to myself for several days.

I wondered if this was the Holy Spirit leading me to the following summer's ministry. One day, my friend, Frank Stanley, was visiting my home and I shared with him what had happened in my prayer closet. He urged me to call Montana information and ask if they had a town called Hungry Horse.

Up until that time I had no idea there was such a town. The operator on the phone told me they did have a town named Hungry Horse and asked me who I would like to reach there. Somewhat surprised and not knowing what to say next, I requested the number for the Assembly of God Church. She said, "Hungry Horse doesn't have an Assembly of God Church, but I do see an Assembly of God Bible camp." That was all this young preacher needed to hear. I just knew God wanted me to be the Bible camp evangelist; God's man of the hour, full of power, teaching a family Bible camp. Yes indeed, that was me. *WRONG*!

Walter Butler taught at Northeast Bible Institute for a very long time; in fact, he taught Brother Winston Smock, who was my first pastor. This was back in the 50s and he was a spiritual inspiration to many young pastors, including me. He seemed to specialize in teaching his students how to wait on God and be led by the Holy Spirit. He told of the Lord calling him to minister overseas during his summer breaks. He told the Lord he was willing to go but he had no money. God said to him, "Let me worry about that!" That winter, through the mail, money began to trickle in, and by summertime, he had enough money to make his trip.

In my sophomore year, this inspired me to do the same. I wrote to half a dozen different pastors, telling them I would be available to hold special meetings that summer. One pastor responded way up in northern Vermont.

I, too, began to receive letters with unexpected money from unexpected sources. So as soon as school was out, we loaded up and drove to Vermont. It was a small church; nonetheless, I was excited to be in the ministry. We arrived on a Saturday night and stayed in the pastor's guest room.

That Sunday morning, I noticed him making several phone calls. He called each and every member of his church, reminded them of the Sunday Service, and asked them if they needed any extra help, or a ride to church. This was his approach to church attendance. I thought to myself, "These must be absolute babes in Christ." The pastor later told me if he didn't call them, they probably wouldn't make it to church.

That first service came and I was very much surprised to see middle-aged people who had been saved for a long time, but never grew to the point where they would be faithful to God's house without a call from the pastor.

I have to admit, the service was very dry and almost lifeless. When I preached, it was as if my words bounced back at me. It was more of the same on Sunday night, but after the service, the pastor informed me the service on Monday night would be different because the sectional presbyter was attending the meeting.

I don't think I will ever forget the song service for as long as I live. The presbyter led the singing. He was a very energetic man, vigorously swinging his arms to the beat of the music, but you could barely hear the people singing. As he led the singing, all I could think of was someone with a tire pump trying to pump up a tire that had a very large hole in it.

I got up to preach and again my words bounced off the walls. I felt like I was getting nowhere. No one responded to the altar call, nor would they come to the altar and pray. That week I faced great discouragement. I had such great hopes of being God's man of power with great wisdom for the hour; it didn't happen.

I preached all week and not a single soul raised their hand for salvation. I prayed harder and harder, but to no avail. At the end of my week of being a visiting evangelist, they took up a love offering. If I remember right, the amount of money raised in the offering was $18. I was soon to learn, little is much when God is in it.

The day before I left, the pastor had a flat tire on his car and I went out that afternoon to help him change it. We were having trouble with the bumper jack; we couldn't seem to get it to work. As we fiddled with it, a teenage boy walked by, and I asked him if he knew anything about bumper jacks. He seemed willing to try to help, and as we worked on the tire, I introduced myself and I told him where I was from and what I was doing in Vermont.

To make a long story short, I shared with him about Jesus and he genuinely seemed interested. I prayed with him there on the sidewalk and I invited him to come to church on Sunday. I was leaving the next day and never did find out if he made it to church.

As I said goodbye to the pastor, he said, "Brother Jack, after watching you with that boy, changing the tire, I feel I have learned a great lesson in how to reach people for Jesus. Thank you very much." Maybe something was accomplished after all.

✞

CHAPTER 19

Dreams

I have only had a few dreams in my life I am sure were from God.

One of the dreams came while I was in Bible school in my sophomore year, and it went like this: I was sitting on the platform of the church during the song service, waiting to get up and preach, when a man walked in dressed like a lumberjack with hobnail boots, known as corks. Every time he took a step, he would snag this beautiful red carpet in the church and you could actually see every place he stepped as the carpet was being pulled up. In the dream, the Lord asked me, "Jack, what would you do in this situation?" and I answered, "Lord, I would get all the board members together and we would pick this guy up and carry him out to the parking lot." Then the Lord spoke to me and said, "Are you more concerned about your red carpet or about that man's heart?"

The following weekend, after this dream, my wife and I went to Brockport, New York for a wedding. The next day was Sunday, and as was our custom, we went to church. The pastor introduced himself to me and when he found out I was in Bible College, he asked me to preach that night. I accepted. There I was on the platform that evening, sitting behind the pulpit during the song service, waiting to preach, when in walked two men, both kind of scruffy. One of them was smoking a cigarette and he sat down in the back pew. One of the ushers walked up and tapped him on the shoulder and apparently told him there was no smoking in church. The man nodded his head and took the cigarette, dropped it on the floor, and crushed it out.

I couldn't believe my eyes as I realized the church floor was covered with a beautiful red carpet. These two men were obviously drunk as they soon got into an argument with each other and got up and left. Little did I know this was God preparing me for an incident that would happen some years later in Hungry Horse, Montana.

The incident I am referring to happened like this. I was playing my guitar and leading the song service when a man walked in and sat in the back. I knew this man's name was Don Downing, one of the toughest, meanest alcoholics this logging town had ever seen. Don had a reputation for out-drinking, out-fighting, and out-cursing any logger in the county.

As usual, the worship service lasted about an hour; we sang in the spirit, and had manifestations of God's gifts. I got up to preach and I found myself explaining the simple plan of salvation. As usual, we had a heavy presence of the Holy Spirit. When I gave the altar call, Don Downing raised his hand, came forward, and knelt at the altar. He came to the altar drunk, but when he got up, he was sober.

To make a long story short, Don was delivered from alcohol, never to touch another drop for the rest of his life. He told us later he had been planning to commit suicide that night and as he was driving by the church his car stalled right in front of the parking lot and it wouldn't start. He came into the building looking for help and found more than he bargained for. Don reeked with the smell of beer; perhaps some of it was spilled on his clothes. As we prayed with him, the smell was so bad our eyes watered, but I have since learned God only looks at the heart.

Don became a great witness, leading his entire family to Jesus, and to this day, thirty years later, his grandson faithfully attends the Hungry Horse Chapel. Was the dream just for Don or was it just for me? I am not sure, but I do believe in dreams from God.

In another dream, I found myself walking down a dirt road, carrying my guitar, when I came to this small town. The first building was a general store with bales of hay and feedbags stacked everywhere, with several rocking chairs and a bench on the porch.

There were at least a dozen men on the porch and they were all wearing bibbed overalls with neatly trimmed beards. Every one of them was sleeping, apparently taking a nap. In the dream, I strummed the G chord on my guitar and they all woke up. I asked them if they knew Jesus and they said, "You bet we do," and they all began to sing together, "Are you washed in the blood of the Lamb."

They were very lively for the first verse, but the second verse was much slower, and by the third verse, they were all sleeping again. I turned and left town the way I had come. A half mile down the road I could see a man sitting at a stop sign in a Cadillac convertible reading his road map. I walked down to where he was and asked him if he was lost. He told me he certainly was, and then I said, "May I give you some directions?" As we talked, he asked me which way I was going. I told him, "I am going the same way you are," and he invited me to ride with him. I put my guitar in the back seat and we drove off. As we drove, I told him about Jesus.

Perhaps God was trying to prepare me for the church in Vermont. Somehow, I felt like the sleeping men with the well-trimmed beards represent many of our mainline churches that indeed know the words to the song, "Are you washed in the blood of the lamb," but have fallen asleep on the job and are in desperate need of a new awakening and a fresh revelation of God's plan for their lives.

The man in the Cadillac represents the lost sinner just sitting at a stop sign, lost and not knowing which way to turn. Any one of those men with the well-trimmed beards could have ministered to the man in the Cadillac had they not fallen asleep. I really believe there is such a thing as Christian immunization shots, where we receive a small portion of the real thing, namely the Gospel. It makes us immune to the full revelation of Jesus Christ.

I don't know how many times I have heard people say, "You believe the way you believe and I will believe the way I believe." It's as if they have had a spiritual immunization shot where they have received a small dose of religion and it's made them immune to growing to a higher level in their spiritual walk. That's what this book is all about, encouraging you to grow to a higher spiritual level by not only hearing the voice of God, but also obeying the voice of God.

This brings to my mind an incident that happened while my wife and I were out garage saleing on Saturday morning. As we were driving, we saw a sign for a rummage sale. Out of curiosity we turned in and stopped. It was a large campus of a well known mainline church. As we walked around, there must have been a dozen pockets of little treasures here and there for sale. The trails led us to the main sanctuary where we found a dozen or so high-priced paintings. There sat two ladies at a table next to the very last pew. One was a blond and one was a redhead, both in their late fifties. What happened next was a first in the life of Jack MacDonald. It was almost like the prompting of the Holy Spirit that I get when giving an interpretation of a message in tongues (which you can read about in 1 Corinthians 12). I looked at the blond lady and found myself saying, "Did you know, you cannot worship God in spirit and in truth unless you have a personal revelation of who Jesus Christ is?"

The blond lady's eyes got very big. She became very defensive, saying, "Who are you to tell me I can't worship God without a revelation of who Jesus Christ is? What do you think we are doing here at this fund raiser for the church?" At that time, the red-haired lady started to side with her friend, but changed her mind and sat back and quietly listened. Apparently these ladies thought they were working their way to heaven by selling their very expensive paintings. As we talked, the blond lady became very belligerent and said, "By what authority do you talk to me like this?"

I said to her, "Jesus said in the New Testament, 'no man can come unto the father but by me.' So I guess to answer your question, it is by the authority of the word of God."

She immediately said to me, "Well, when you can talk to me in Hebrew, then I will listen to what you have to say about the word of God." Again I felt the prompting of the Holy Spirit, much like when you give a message in tongues. I looked her in the eye and I began to speak in my prayer language. I spoke to her for several minutes in my unknown tongue. Immediately the blond lady's countenances changed. It was almost like throwing a bucket of water on a lit candle. She sat down and just looked at the floor. I excused myself and said, "Have a blessed day."

All that day I pondered the incident. I even said to myself, "I have never witnessed that way before." That next morning, the Holy Spirit woke me up at three a.m. As I sat there waiting on the Lord, I found myself asking God about the incident that happened in that church the previous day. As clear as day the Holy Spirit spoke to me and said, "Jack, that message wasn't just for the blond lady. It was mostly for the redhead who thought she could get to heaven by good works. She needed to hear that there was such a thing as having a personal revelation of who Jesus Christ is." This lady's heart was hungry for more of God than what she had.

It is one thing to be saved and even filled with the Holy Spirit, but it is another thing to present your body as a living sacrifice, holy and acceptable unto God, which is our reasonable service (Romans 12:1).

I believe God is looking for men and women who would dare to say, "I am a candidate to be used for the Glory of God. I am available even at a minute's notice to allow the Holy Spirit to direct my steps, my words, and even my actions." Someone once said availability is more important than our own personal ability. The way I see it, the vast majority of God's promises are conditional.

If we will trust in the Lord with all our heart, then He will direct our paths and I am here to tell you, God is still in the business of directing our paths.

I should warn you right now, though. It might just turn out to be a very exciting adventure and it's possible some of these exciting adventures are not for the faint-hearted. But if you will stand in the gap with prayer and fasting and be available to the leading of the Holy Spirit, I promise you a very fulfilling life with unspeakable joy and full of glory.

✞

CHAPTER 20

Evangelistic Meetings

During my week of meetings in Vermont, a neighboring pastor attended who lived in Harden, Vermont. He asked me if I would come to his church the following week. I looked at my schedule, and immediately told him I was available and asked him when he would like me to start. We decided I should come over that day and start services the following day.

This second church I went to preach in for a week was a huge ten thousand square foot building. It was an old, closed-down Baptist Church in desperate need of repair.

The congregation met in the foyer, as it was easier to heat; they didn't need that one thousand-seat auditorium. The pastor had purchased the building for $1 and had been holding services there for about six mouths. It was a very different crowd. These people stood and worshipped God, and sang in the spirit for an hour at a time. Preaching to them was a joy; it just seemed to flow, and they were hungry for the things of God. Several were saved and filled with the Holy Spirit and many were healed.

I recall one lady that came forward; she was gasping for air, and said she had suffered with asthma all her life. Right after she said that, she passed out. We laid hands on her and prayed for her immediately. Within two minutes, she was standing back up, saying she could breathe without any difficulty. The next day she called the pastor and proclaimed she was still healed. She had had an uninterrupted night's sleep, which she had not experienced in two years, and she had not had to use any asthma medication since we prayed for her.

The last night of my meetings, there was a visiting pastor from Lancaster, New Hampshire. She asked me if I could come and fill in for thirty days while she and her husband went on vacation. When I said yes, she thanked me and mentioned they had not had a vacation in fifteen years. By the time I arrived at their church, they'd already left on their trip. We were greeted by a lady named Ruth, who was one of the pastor's former Bible school students. Although she felt called to Africa as a missionary, she moved to Lancaster to assist with the ministry there.

The church welcomed us with open arms. I felt very much at home there. It impressed me that the people would come to church early to pray. No doubt that is why they had a very sweet spirit and a powerful worship service. Preaching to them was easy. Again, we saw several saved and filled with the Holy Spirit.

I was only there a week when a knock came on the office door, and one of the board member's daughters asked to speak with me. She sat down and began to cry. The Lord spoke to my heart and told me that she was upset because she thought she may be pregnant.

I wrestled with that piece of information for a few minutes; it was delicate, to say the least, but finally I said to her, "Kim, are you upset because you think you are pregnant?" She stopped crying and looked at me. "How could you have possibly known? I just discovered it today and I have only discussed it with my boyfriend." I simply told her the Holy Spirit whispered it in my ear.

What happened next was a series of miracles. I first ask her who the father was. She named another board member's son, who was also the youth group president. I told her I would need to speak with her parents, but I wouldn't do it without her permission. We prayed together and decided to have another meeting the next day; she would let me know what she wanted to do.

To make a long story short, she brought her parents and we all cried and prayed, and the young man brought his parents and they cried and prayed. The absence of anger and condemnation was very refreshing. The two families met together to discuss what their next step should be. The love that flowed between these two families was a testimony to a healthy church. It turned out the young girl was not pregnant, but it drove both families into deeper prayer.

There was such an anointing on that church; the services often lasted longer than planned. One Wednesday night, I preached on the book of Ruth and the message flowed like oil out of a bottle. I asked several times, "Shall we stop here or shall we go on?" They voted to go on. I covered the entire book of Ruth that night in three hours;

it was the longest sermon I have ever preached. To me, that was a miracle; a hundred plus people sitting in hard pews, who seemed to be very interested in a Bible school sophomore preaching a much too long sermon.

Unbeknownst to me, Ruth, the assistant pastor, called the pastor every week and gave her a report on how things were going. On my last few days there, the pastor called me to say she was very excited about the glowing reports she was getting from our services. She asked if I would be interested in a permanent position as senior pastor, as she had decided to resign for health reasons.

I told her I would pray about it; I would not accept the position unless I heard from God. I was very flattered that one of the largest churches in the New England district considered a Bible school sophomore student for a position of senior pastor.

By now, it was the first part of September and I returned to Green Lane, Pennsylvania. Every few days, the chairman of the board called me and prayed with me. Finally, I heard from the Lord as clear as anything I have ever heard the Holy Spirit say to me. These words came to my heart, "You can go there and pastor that church, Jack, if you really want to, but I have something I think you will like better."

That night, the pastor called me and said they were feeling guilty about pulling me out of school early. They wanted to wait a year to see what developed. I said I thought that was a good idea. I returned to classes that fall. My junior year at Bible College was very eventful; I will share just a few things that happened.

✞

CHAPTER 21

Valley Forge

About two weeks into the first semester of my junior year, the Lord spoke to me and said, "Go to the Valley Forge Hospital." I had never been there, but I knew it was nearby. After class, I was walking up the road toward my home and I told my friend, Bob Nobel, what I was feeling. Bob Nobel was a puppeteer, and had a puppet ministry. In Corinthians 1:28, it lists eight different ministries. One of those ministries is teaching, and puppets have become a great tool in teaching children the word of God. He said he was available that afternoon, so off we went.

Now understand, I didn't have a lot of gas money and I was probably a little on the conservative side, but I was sure that I had heard from God. As Bob and I drove the fifty miles to the hospital, we talked about how we would get on the base. We decided the Lord would just have to make a way for us. We finally got to the front gate, drove up to the guard shack, and nobody was there. We just drove in as if we owned the place. We found the base chapel, which doubled as a recreation room. We went to the nurse's station, called the chaplain, and asked permission to use the chapel for a Gospel service. The chaplain informed me that he had 21 assistants and if anybody was going to have a Gospel service there, it would be one of them.

I thanked the chaplain for his time and hung up the phone. As we were walking down the hall talking about the situation, the head nurse and her assistant just happened to be walking behind us, and overheard our conservation. She asked me if I was looking for a place to have a Gospel service. We said, "Yes, we are, but the chaplain denied us permission to use the rec room."

She said, "Half of that rec room belongs to us, and we have the say as to how it is used. We will not only give you permission, but will have the chairs set up and your service announced."

At that time, it was six o'clock and the patients were just finishing dinner. She announced over the loud speaker that a Gospel service would be held in the rec room at seven o'clock if anyone would like to attend. Bob and I had one hour to prepare. We found a quiet place and began to seek God. I remember specifically praying, "We claim Valley Forge for the work of the Gospel. We claim the entire base for the kingdom of God." Little did I know what a huge campus it was. There were dozens of large buildings, mostly hospital rooms, used for the wounded Vietnam veterans. It included a very large gymnasium that would make an excellent place to have a meeting with a large group of people. There were also dozens of administrative buildings, a base exchange building, and a huge supply building.

Seven o'clock came around and we met in the rec room. Thirteen men showed up; we opened with a prayer, then had some singing and read from the Scriptures. I prayed for God's rich blessings to fall on this historic place of Valley Forge. Bob put on a fifteen-minute puppet show, which showed the Gospel in a child-like fashion.

I then preached a very simple sermon about Christ the redeemer, concluding with John 3:3; it was the same message I had preached with Richard Kucera back in the jungle. I asked if every head could be bowed and every eye closed.Then I asked the question of how many here knew, without a shadow of doubt, that if they died tonight, they would go to heaven. I explained the plan of salvation and asked how many would raise their hand and ask Christ to come into their heart as their Savior. Thirteen hands were raised. Then I said, "I would like to pray with you. If you really mean business with God, I would like you to stand and come to the front." Thirteen men stood and came for salvation—the entire congregation was saved. *Hallelujah, God is good.*

The nurses had made available to us a box of Bibles to be handed out to the men. We handed out thirteen Bibles that night and instructed them to read the New Testament, beginning with the book of John. We told them that before they read, they should pray and ask God to help them understand what they were reading.

We thanked the nurses for the use of their rec room and said we needed to get back to the college. As we drove out of the base, we noticed that there were now two guards standing at the front gate. Driving through the base toward the front gate, we held our hands up and claimed that campus for Jesus, and all the way home, we prayed for those men that got saved. That is a nice story, but it doesn't end here.

That winter, the Valley Forge Military Hospital was shut down and totally abandoned. Northeast Bible Institute, a poor and struggling college, purchased the entire Valley Forge Campus, lock, stock and barrel, from the United States Government, for $1. The following year, Northeast Bible Institute became Valley Forge Christian College. *I just love to see God's Work. Amen.*

Had I accepted the pastorate in New Hampshire, I probably would not have had that experience, or the milestone in the January semester, when the Holy Spirit spoke to me and said, "Hungry Horse." I wouldn't trade anything for my three years at Northeast Bible Institute.

During the summer, they held Bible camp within one hundred yards of my house. There I was able to experience the excellent preaching of many precious men of God. I always felt that the highlight of Bible camp was the prayer room after the service. It always seemed to have an extra heavy presence of God.

I recall one night when Hardy Steinberg had preached an excellent message on mounting up with wings of eagles. After the service, the prayer room was filled with people; many only stayed twenty or thirty minutes. It was about eleven-thirty at night when all of a sudden, I heard someone screaming. I looked over and there was a young girl lying on her back, flailing her arms and striking the wooden floor with her knuckles. She rotated her hips in a sexual, suggestive manner while making these awful screams.

I noticed that there were a dozen elderly people sitting around her watching and praying. I felt led to pray for her. I walked over and put my hand on her shoulder and I prayed, "Dear Jesus, help this young girl." At that time, she turned her face toward me and growled in such a voice it actually frightened me. I had just spent four years in the Marine Corps, was fresh out of Vietnam, and I didn't scare easily. I thought I had seen everything that Hell had to offer.

I quickly pulled my hand away because I really thought she was going to bite me. She reminded me of a mad dog, only with a voice I have never heard before or since. I stood up to leave when an older gray-haired man stopped me and spoke quietly in my ear. "You shouldn't touch people when they are receiving something from God," he whispered.

I couldn't believe my ears. The Scripture is clear about the laying on of hands for spiritual purposes. I looked over at the girl and she was still rotating her hips in a sexual manner and banging her knuckles on the floor while making awful screams. In my opinion, that girl was not receiving something from God and the gray-haired man was mistaken. I haven't had a lot of experience with demons, but I suspected this young girl was under demonic influences.

✟

I recall an incident in Hungry Horse, Montana when a nineteen-year-old girl came to my door and asked for money to help her get to Germany. She said she had only been married a few months, and her new husband was in the Army, and had been transferred to Germany. She wanted very badly to follow him.

We told her we had no money, but we would be glad to pray with her about the situation. My wife and one of the men of the church, named John Attard, laid hands on her and began to pray. She threw herself to the floor and began to strangle herself. It was all John and I could do to get her hands away from her neck. She was incredibly strong. Neither John or I were weaklings, but we had our hands full keeping her arms pinned to the floor.

A strange voice came from her mouth that said, "She loves you, Jack." My wife spoke back, "She does not love Jack, she loves her husband." Again, she tried to strangle herself. John knelt on one arm, and I knelt on the other arm, and my wife sat on her ankles. She could pick John and me right up off the floor as if we were two loaves of bread. She began to curse and swear. She said, "I hate you and I am going to kill you." At that time, we began to plead the blood of Jesus over this girl. We began to rebuke the devil and bind him in Jesus name—we commanded that he loose this woman and set her free.

She calmed down and began to cry. The following evening, she called and asked if she could be prayed for again. John, who lived in the basement of the church, came over at my invitation to help pray for this girl. We had pretty much a repeat of the first night. This strange voice came from her and said, "She loves you, Jack," and again my wife said, "No she doesn't, she loves her husband." After about an hour, she began to cry as she returned to normal. The following day, she called us again, wanting to come over a THIRD time. I told her, "OK, but this time, we are going to have some of the elders come too." I invited about a dozen of our prayer warriors and I made one of the biggest mistakes I've ever made in my ministry.

There was a very sweet girl name Barbara Walters, who was about nineteen years old, and engaged to a man named Paul, who was attending Southeast Bible College. They planned to get married and pastor a church. I thought perhaps this may be an opportunity for Barbara to see spiritual warfare firsthand.

Sure enough, the third night was very much like the other two, only this time, we had God's Marine Corps with us. We rebuked the devil and commanded that he leave this woman alone, to bother her no more, and commanded those demons to go to the place prepared for them in the pit of hell.

I didn't realize at the time that Barbara was in the corner, terrified. She couldn't wait to get out of there. I did get a phone call the next day from her mother suggesting that had not been a good idea.

There are a number of mistakes I can think of that I have made in the ministry, and inviting Barbara that night was surely one of them. I am not much of a demon chaser (perhaps I should be), but what little experience I have had in that arena was not something that I enjoy.

I guess we each have our separate gifts; some of us are hands that build God's house, some are feet that carry Bible tracts from door to door, some of us are mouths that preach and teach the Gospel, some have the ministry of hearing, and some have visions, but we are all in this together, joining forces to build the kingdom of God.

If only all God's people could grasp this concept and realize we are not all the same, but that we are all still part of the same body, I think the work of God would go a lot smoother and be a lot more efficient.

An example of this would be a lady name Lynn Gilder, who was in a hospital room visiting her dying aunt. The lady in the bed next to her had to be tied to the bed with restraints, as she was thrashing around in the bed violently, screaming uncontrollably and crying.

Lynn Gilder felt led to pray for the crying woman, so she walked over and laid her hands on her. Not knowing what to pray for, Lynn decided to use her prayer language. After praying in tongues for five minutes, the older lady calmed down, smiled at Lynn, and began to talk to her in a language that Lynn did not understand.

About that time, the woman's daughter came in to visit, and began speaking to her mother in a foreign language. After a lengthy conversation, the daughter shared this incredible story with Lynn.

The daughter said, "Our whole family is Polish and only the children speak English." It seems that Lynn had prayed for her mother in perfect Polish and told her that Jesus loved her and she loved her and everybody in this hospital was here to help her and meant to do her no harm.

Maybe you are reading this thinking to yourself that you don't have anything to give to God. This story illustrates that you don't have to have great ability, but you need to have availability, and God will use you.

I can't help but think about the little two-year-old girl playing in her backyard, wandering out into a vast wheat field in central Montana. The mother frantically looked for her, calling her husband, her friends, and her neighbors. They walked the wheat field all night long to no avail. The next day somebody suggested that they all join hands and systematically cover the entire wheat field.

Several hours later, the child was found. She had died of exposure, as it had rained in the night. I will never forget the words of that mother as she stood on that farmhouse porch with her dead child in her arms. She said, "I want to thank all of my friends and neighbors for helping look for my baby. I only wish to God we would have joined hands sooner."

What a lesson for the church; people are lost and dying in the vast wheat fields of life all around us. Many times God's people are unable to put their differences aside, join hands, and work together; too often, jealously and pride become stumbling stones.

The book of Romans is a letter Paul wrote while in prison, and in Romans 1:7, he addresses this letter: "To all that be in Rome, beloved of God called to be Saints." Paul knew there were many groups in Rome who were believers, and he absolutely assumed these different groups were in a channel of communicating with each other.

Historians tell us in Corinth alone, there were 25,000 believers, but Paul always addressed his letters to the Church of Corinth. Paul assumed all the Christians in Rome would be in fellowship with each other and pass his letters around. The idea of a lot of groups all calling themselves Christians, but being totally alienated from each other, is not the New Testament way.

I can't help but think about a small body of believers in Phoenix, Arizona—many of them are of Jewish descent. Rabbi Harlan Picker addresses the congregation in Hebrew and English.

Beth Yachat is a place where Jews and Gentiles worship. It is known as a Messianic Synagogue. While I am sure it is not perfect (and come to think of it, what church is?), there is such a sweet spirit of worship there—you can sense a love flow among the brethren. I feel these people are sincerely seeking God. They may dress a little different than we do, and their service may last longer than most, and perhaps they do things differently than I am use to, but they are a part of the body of Christ. I would encourage you to check it out for yourself.

The Assembly of God is a very strong Pentecostal organization. It is known for its good teaching and widespread evangelistic outreach. It is the only organization I know of where 100 percent of your offering to missions, for example, actually goes to missions.

You will find many brothers and sisters in the Assembly of God movement, but I need to make a statement I believe is very true, so listen carefully. The Assembly, sometimes called the A/G, does not have a corner on God—no church has a corner on God.

My wife and I are members of the most powerful Assembly of God Church in America—Phoenix First Assembly. But Rabbi Heron and Joyce Picker at Beth Yachat, are seeing people healed and even filled with the Holy Spirit, evidenced by the speaking in tongues.

Back in the 70s, I attended a number of Catholic prayer meetings and witnessed them receiving the baptism of the Holy Spirit, evidenced by the speaking in tongues. The Holy Spirit is not limited to any church or domination.

I also participated in several Catholic Cercis [men's retreats], which involved hundreds of men from all over the state gathering in one place for three days for the purpose of experiencing more of God. There was such a spirit of love there; sinners would come, cry uncontrollably, and get saved and filled with the Holy Spirit.

✝

CHAPTER 22

Heading for Hungry Horse

I wound up writing the district superintendent, Brother R.L. Brant, who I later found to be a mighty man of God and a great mentor. I told him of of my experience in my prayer closet and hearing God speak to me the words "Hungry Horse." He wrote back, "It's interesting that you write about Hungry Horse because there is a rather large church building and a parsonage there, but it has been closed down for nine years. It seems the Hungry Horse church and the neighboring church in Columbia Falls merged together so they could afford a pastor."

Brother Brant went on to say, "A few months before I received your letter, a man from the Columbia Falls church was trying to open a Sunday school in the old Hungry Horse church building. It has been sitting empty for the last nine years. By the way, the Columbia Falls church is now looking for a youth pastor. Why don't you write them a letter?" On his recommendation, I did.

Pastor Frank Sims from the Columbia Falls Assembly of God Church called and asked if I was coming to Hungry Horse. I told him we were, much to the surprise of me and my family. Word spread in the Bible college of my plans and some of the students asked me, "What about the rest of us? When we graduate, what will we do?" I felt sad about their questions and I didn't have a ready answer for them. But I did feel thankful for the leading of the Lord in my life. We sold everything we owned, even my deeply-beloved guitar, bought a Plymouth station wagon, and prepared to move. I had already scheduled a week of meetings with Ed Steigel at the Triangle Assembly of God Church in Virginia.

Before leaving for Triangle, Virginia, I searched diligently for a pop-up trailer and finally found one. The man accepted my offer of $300. But the next day, somebody had offered him more so the deal fell through. I asked the Lord why, but I didn't seem to get an answer. We went to Triangle with everything we owned in the station wagon.

At the end of a 7-day revival meeting at the church in Triangle, they took an offering for me, since I was the visiting preacher. The pastor told me it was the biggest offering they had ever received for any evangelist in the history of the church.

The pastor also said he had just bought a new camper trailer and had a two-year-old pop-up trailer for sale for only $50. He asked if I'd be interested. *Praise God, Jehovah Jira (the Lord is my provider).* Brother Butler taught me that if God sends you, He will pay your way. The Lord provided me with a $2,000 camper trailer for just $50.

We left Triangle towing our new pop-up camper behind our station wagon. About forty miles down the road, I turned to my wife and said, "Can you feel it?" She said, "Yes I can." It's hard for me to describe what happened in the car that morning, but I will try.

A strong joy came over me with that heavy pounding in my chest, like I always get when I'm being prompted to give a message in tongues or an interpretation. As we drove north on US 95, just south of Washington, DC, we received a visitation in our car.

It was one of the heaviest feelings of the presence of the Holy Spirit I have ever had. It was similar to the feeling I had in Vietnam when my second wind kicked in as we force marched across the country to the ocean.

The presence of God in the car that day reminded me of the feeling I had the day I gave my first message in tongues to a congregation. It was such a powerful utterance, my wife later told me her knees had started knocking together, and if she had not been hanging onto the pew in front of her, she would have fallen to the floor.

That day in the car, I received a powerful confirmation that we were following the perfect will of God. I have heard it said, "If you win the victory in the spiritual realm, you have won the victory—period. Let me explain. If you have needs in your life, whether physical, material, spiritual, social, problems on the job, family-related or needs for direction from the Holy Spirit, pray and seek God with all your heart and soul. This will involve giving God your tongue and your voice, and perhaps some valuable sleep.

Possibly it will also require you to do some fasting, but I promise you, if you will persevere and pray through (a term we don't hear much anymore) and take the kingdom of God by force, you will win the victory in the spiritual realm, and all these other things will simply be taken care of by God.

We had received a word from the Lord, actually two words: "Hungry Horse." Stepping out in faith and traveling toward the place that God had called us to brought tremendous joy to our lives.

✞

There is a lot to be said about knowing where you are going and exactly what you are looking for. I am reminded of a man named Taylor Texas. He went to a garage sale in Quartzsite, Arizona. There he purchased a large rock for $12, which was the asking price. It seemed like a good deal to the seller because it had been found in the desert.

When Taylor Texas carefully cut the rock, he discovered he had the largest sapphire ever recorded, and he sold it for $3.6 million. Now the question I want to ask you is this: "When you are traveling around through life, perhaps from garage sale to garage sale like the wife and I do every Saturday, will you recognize God's direction when you get it?" To a lot of people, this sapphire was just another big rock, but to the trained eyes of Taylor Texas, he saw something more.

I recall hunting in central Montana, northwest of Choteau and climbing up a large mound of dirt the size of four houses. At the top, there was a flat spot with several large stones. I sat down on one of the large stones and began to use my field glasses to check out the surrounding area, and not spotting any game, I moved on.

Sometime later, a man more knowledgeable than I, hauled those stones back to his laboratory and by using some type of sophisticated x-ray and with the help of a large chop saw, discovered that those rocks were not rocks at all, but contained the fossilized embryo of an unborn dinosaur. Had I known what I was looking at, I could have been rich and famous, but apparently that wasn't God's plan.

We need to train our ears and eyes; we need to practice listening to what the Holy Spirit has to say to us. Learn how to put on your spiritual rabbit ears to hear the still, small voice of the Holy Spirit that speaks to his people today.

I am going to share something with you that may seem a little strange. The man of God who mentored me, Brother Walter H. Butler, made this statement in class one day. He said, "Students, if you pay close attention to the Holy Spirit, you could even receive direction as to what car to buy and what car not to buy." The way Brother Butler explained it went something like this: When you look at a car, something inside you will go, "Uh huh," and with that feeling will come a peace in your heart. And he told the class just the opposite is true, that the Lord can also give you a negative feeling. The way he phrased it was, "Unt augh." [I warned you this was going to be a little strange.]

In Genesis 17:4-22, we see God carrying on a conversation with Abraham, almost as if he was sitting at the dining room table, talking about how good the pot roast was. If you will read the verses carefully, you will see the creator of the universe carrying on a conversation with a man.

However, in this conversation, we see El Shaddai (All Mighty God) not only changing Abraham's name and his wife's name, but making a covenant that would soon become one of the strongest promises in the written word.

This covenant was so strong, Moses used it to convince God to change his mind about destroying the nation of

Israel. Israel had turned from worshipping the Creator (God), and began worshipping a golden image that was in the form of a calf. Pray the Lord will help you to recognize the leading of the Holy Spirit.

✞

Let me make a side note at this time. The Scripture says we are supposed to walk by faith and not by sight. We see great examples of this in Genesis 17:1-6, 22:17, and 28:14.

Abraham received a word from God in Genesis 17:1. That word was, "Walk before me and be sincere." At ninety-nine years of age, Abraham was confronted with a fresh challenge from God. It wasn't as if he was a brand new believer. He had already walked with God for twenty-four years. God's call came to him when he was seventy-five years old. He was reaching the climax of his spiritual maturity, the place where God was going to fulfill the promises whereby he had drawn him out of Ur of the Chaldees. We see many examples in the Scriptures of men and women taking years to mature in their spiritual walk.

Moses is a good example of this. God kept the entire nation of Israel waiting for forty years while he worked on him. He taught Moses to listen and obey his voice. Thus, Moses went through the maturing process.

I feel like God has given me a word for 2008. I will first summarize it—things are going to be great in 2008. Now let me explain. God is going to pour out a fresh blessing on his people. We are going to see great and mighty things accomplished in the kingdom of God.

Many people have gone through the maturing process. They no longer live on the sincere milk of the word, but they have graduated on to strong meat. If you desire to be a warrior for the kingdom, sooner or later you will have to come into spiritual maturity, and hearing God's voice will be a part of the maturing process. Know this one thing: God is surely saying to you, "Church, it's time to grow up!" It's time for a fresh revelation of the Holy Spirit.

In Genesis 17:3, it says Abraham fell on his face and God talked to him. Could it be Abraham was slain in the Spirit? That is something we don't see a lot of these days.

✞

I am going to share a humorous story with you that perhaps some will not understand. It involves an older man that everybody called Brother John. This fellow had a serious prayer life, and God's anointing and power was on him so great that when he would stand in the midst of a congregation and raise his hands in worship, the people around him would fall down. They call it "Being slain in the spirit." After many services with this same thing happening, the pastor finally asked Brother John, politely, not to raise his hands during the worship service.

✞

Another example of a man maturing in the Lord is found in a pastor named David Hogan, who ministers in the mountains of Mexico. It is reported to me by very credible people that David Hogan is being used repeatedly to raise people from the dead.

In the New Testament, we see Jesus calling to a man who had been dead for three days and life coming back to his body. In the book of Acts, Paul was preaching late one night in a barn when a young man sitting, on a beam high above the floor, drifted off to sleep. After falling to the floor, he was pronounced dead, but the apostle Paul laid his hands on him and the boy was brought back to life.

Are these things for us today or are these things just of the Bible days? The answer is found in the words of Jesus, who said, "Things that I do ye shall do also." It's exciting for me to think someone out there reading this book could catch the vision and accept a fresh challenge to become a modern day man of God or woman of God. I promise, it is an exciting life full of joy and peace, just to mention a few items of God's pay package.

Are you a candidate to receive a fresh challenge from God? Abram was, and as a result, his name was changed to Abraham. Jacob matured to the place where he could hear God's voice and his name was changed to Israel. The same happened to Sari—her name was changed to Sarah.

Peter, in the New Testament, became a changed man when he matured in God. Even Saul's name was changed to Paul when he heard the voice of God. Any man who's had a sincere meeting with the Holy Spirit becomes a changed person. Maybe you are reading this and thinking you want to mature in God and you want to become changed. It can happen to you through hearing and obeying the voice of God.

✝

I am reminded of a young pastor who felt challenged by the Holy Spirit to pray for one hour every day. He chose the hour from ten to eleven in the morning, as he was home alone at that time. As he walked around the apartment praying, he seemed to feel a stronger presence of the Holy Spirit when he prayed at the end of the kitchen table with his back against the wall. Often he would use his prayer language and it seemed every time he stood in this certain spot, he would feel that same closeness of God's presence.

A month went by and there came a knock on the door; it was the lady from the apartment next to his. She asked if he and his wife could come to lunch the following day. Somewhat surprised, the young pastor said, "Yes," and the following day he heard this incredible story.

It seems this lady had a sixteen-year-old daughter who had been contemplating suicide. The daughter told the Pastor when she would go in her room and lay on her bed she could hear the young pastor praying through the wall that separated her bedroom from his dining room. When she heard him praying, the awful feeling to commit suicide would go away.

The young girl said, "I would even go to my room early, before ten o'clock, because I knew when I heard you praying in this strange language, it would help me not to think about hurting myself. Before their meeting was over, the pastor was able to lead the mother and daughter to the Lord. They were born again that day while sitting around the kitchen table, and the sixteen-year-old girl was delivered from the spirit of suicide. Praise God for His grace!

Lives were changed because one man, by faith, said yes to the voice of the Holy Spirit, giving him a fresh challenge.

✞

The Hungry Horse church building had been sitting empty for nine years. The old parsonage behind it was used as a rental. As part of our pay at the Columbia Falls church, we were granted free use of the old Hungry Horse parsonage, and it was in terrible condition. The first morning we moved in, I put on some gloves and tore out the old carpet. I didn't even want to touch the carpet with my bare hands, it was that bad. When I lifted up the old carpet, I discovered there were hardwood floors underneath.

One of the ladies from the church named Lynn Gilder came over with some cleaning supplies and helped us get the house ready to move into. What a job—the place was an absolute mess, unfit for even a dog.

I was in the garage working, when twelve neighborhood kids showed up. Most of them were eight to twelve years old. I introduced myself and each one told me their name. They began to ask me questions, mostly out of curiosity.

The Lord spoke to me and said, "Jack, you have taught Sunday school classes with fewer pupils." I took the hint and began sharing with them the Gospel of Jesus. I began telling them how I was saved, and during my testimony, I quoted the Scriptures dealing with salvation. I concluded my testimony with the story of Nicodemus coming to Jesus (John 3:3). Jesus said, "Except a man be born again, he cannot enter the kingdom of God." I explained a second time how you can be born again. I told them it was the greatest decision that I had ever made in my life and the very same thing could happen to them.

So standing there in the middle of a very dirty garage, I asked twelve kids to bow their heads and pray with me. At the end of my prayer, with every head bowed and every eye closed, I asked them, "How many would like Jesus to come into your heart and be your Savior, cleansing your sins and making you ready to go to heaven. If you really want to know Christ as your personal Savior, raise your hand." Twelve kids raised their hands. Twelve kids prayed the sinner's prayer with me on my first day in Hungry Horse.

One of those twelve is in the ministry today. Some received encouragement from their parents, and some the very opposite. I believe God will hold those parents accountable for their negative influence toward the things of God in their child's life.

There was a couple who lived down the road ten miles—Pat Lee and her husband, Al. They owned and operated a general store at the mouth of Glacier National Park. It was my practice to visit every home in the Bad Rock Canyon area where I lived. When I met the Lee family, it wasn't very long before she told me she had cancer. They had been to the very best doctors in the nation and had several opinions, but the doctors had concluded she was terminally ill. I shared with her the healing power of God and how I had seen many others healed. I also told her how God had miraculously healed me of malaria and a gunshot wound that I received in Vietnam. Pat and her husband were Lutheran and had never heard about divine healing. We soon started having Bible studies in their home.

At the second meeting, Pat received the baptism of the Holy Spirit. Along with my wife, our two children and her husband, we anointed her with oil and prayed God would heal her from the cancer.

We continued having these weekly meetings all winter long. During that time, she went back to the doctors and they discovered her cancer was completely gone. The doctor showed Pat the two sets of x-rays and told her it was an absolute miracle. Needless to say, Pat became a very active witness of the Gospel of Jesus Christ, which included the doctrine of divine healing.

We prayed several times for her husband, Al, to receive the baptism of the Holy Spirit. He did finally get his prayer language in a very unusual way. He was driving to town one day and as he drove by our church, he looked at the sign on the front of the building that said Hungry Horse Chapel; he burst out speaking in tongues. I tell you, God has his own advertising program.

There was a lady who was a thorn in my flesh; she didn't miss an opportunity to cast aspersions of the work of the Hungry Horse Chapel. She was also Pat Lee's good friend, and when she had a stroke, she began to talk to Pat about spiritual things. This is when Pat introduced her to the plan of salvation and I lost my thorn in the flesh.

It is a ten-mile drive to have weekly Bible studies at the Lee's house. I never once asked for any gas money and never took up an offering, but Al insisted on filling up my gas tank, and inviting me and my wife to shop at his store for groceries, free of charge. What a blessing.

I recall the Scripture Isaiah 55:1, "Ye that have no money come buy and eat." At that time, we had absolutely no salary, no steady income of any kind. Every now and then, people from other states would send us checks in the mail. What a blessing from God that would be. Often I thought to myself, "This is how it must have felt for Elijah, living in a cave and having the ravens bring him meat on a daily basis." I encourage you to read it for yourself in 1 King 17:6.

It seems God's plan involved the right man being in the right place at the right time. Bob Hope once said, "Timing is everything," and I have to agree there is a lot of truth to that. Being at the right campground at the right time, stopping and talking to a man on a logging road, meeting a little Jewish man from vine street, and the list goes on and on. I guess this book seems to center on God's timing.

We went to the Valley Forge military base, and just as we drove in, the guard was taking some sort of break. I can tell you from my experiences, military guards don't do that on a regular basis.

✞

Philip, meeting with the Ethiopian eunuch in Acts 8, still has an impact today. Many years ago, missionaries from America journeyed into the deepest part of Ethiopia, where people had never seen a white man before. These same missionaries found small groups of Christians. When asked how they heard about the Gospel, their reply was, "Our ancient ancestors have passed down a story about a eunuch who traveled to a far country and brought back with him revelations of the Gospel."

I don't know about you, but that sounds like Acts 8:27-31 to me. *Amen.*

✞

In the six years of being a pastor in Hungry Horse, we averaged about $2,900 per year. Somebody once said, "You don't go into the ministry for the money," but nonetheless, the blessing of the Lord made us rich with things money could not buy.

My family and I wanted for nothing and we were totally debt free. We ate elk, moose, antelope, pheasant, grouse, Canadian geese, Mallard duck, deer, fish, and black bear every night of the year.

We also housed and fed several guests who lived in the church basement. We called them our church mice. These guests were mostly in their 20s, men from all over the United States. They were hippies who had been saved on their journey through Hungry Horse. When they decided to stay, we offered them living quarters in the huge church basement. We jokingly would say we were growing Christians in the church basement.

✝

CHAPTER 23

Three Forks, Montana

I need to say that I felt called to leave Hungry Horse and go to Three Forks, Montana to start a church there, but things were going so well and God's blessings seemed to flow so richly among us, that I disobeyed God's Voice and I stayed in Hungry Horse longer than I was supposed to.

However, we did make a trip to Three Forks once, and camped one night on the edge of town, which happened to be the very night my number two daughter, Scottie Beth, was conceived. After driving around the small town of Three Forks and visiting some of the businesses, someone told us to go visit the Madison Buffalo Jump, which was southeast of town about fifteen miles.

We arrived there very early the next morning and drove into this large area to park. There was a pavilion on a knoll about a hundred yards east of the parking lot with a three-foot-wide path leading up to it. As we walked up the path,

I noticed a prankster had stretched a dead bull snake across the path that led to the pavilion. The bull snake was about three feet long and as big around as a tangerine.

As we were reading the signs that told the history of the sight, about the Indians of old, and the stampede of the buffalo over this huge cliff, a tour bus pulled in, and about fifty Asian ladies got out. I couldn't understand a word they were saying, but they were laughing and having a good time. Eventually, the whole group began walking together toward the pavilion. I turned and said to my son, Jake, "Watch, this is going to make you laugh."

It seemed as if half of the ladies group stepped over the snake without ever seeing it. Then all of a sudden, there was a scream like I had never heard before, and right after that a second scream, and a third, and then a fourth—they all began yelling one word in a foreign language.

I couldn't understand what the word was, but I have a strong feeling fifty women were all yelling, "Snake," jumping around not knowing where to go.

Apparently one of the ladies had caught the snake with her toe and had thrown its corpse up in the air, and of course, it landed on another lady, who in turn threw it up in the air again. Well, it was a very humorous sight to see all these ladies trampling each other and knocking each other down. trying to get in that skinny bus door, all the while screaming at the top of their lungs.

My first guess was that the local ranch kids knew the schedule of the tour buses and this was some form of country kid's entertainment. I have never seen my family laugh so hard in all my life.

✝

CHAPTER 24

Hungry Horse Revival

The years we were in Hungry Horse were like a six-year revival. People were constantly being saved, healed, and filled with the Holy Spirit. The young men married our Christian girls, got jobs, and bought homes to live in.

During our first winter there, my license plates came due on February 15. I went on February 14 and stood in a line that was a block long. After about a three-hour wait in line, it was finally my turn, I found out my car license plates were assessed at $62.18 for the year, and that was more money than I had. I went home to pray to the Lord, telling him I had only one more day, February 15, to get plates for my car without paying a heavy late charge.

The next morning, I went to the post office and found three letters, one from Pennsylvania, one from New York, and one from Illinois. That was all the mail for that day. In each letter was a check; two of the checks were for $25 and one check was from my adopted brother, Steve Brimmer. He said he had felt led to give me his income tax return, which was $12.18. The Lord provided $62.18 on the very last day my plates were due. *Jehovah Jira (my provider his grace is sufficient for me).*

Hungry Horse was one miracle after another! I took the job as youth pastor for the Columbia Falls Church seven miles west of Hungry Horse. There was no pay, but they did give me $25 for Christmas and God provided me an elk in November. I was also given a Volkswagen van to drive, but it had no heater and when it was 20 degrees below 0, it was an adventure to drive.

I was praying at noon for the Wednesday night service when God laid it on my heart to go hunting. I had previously been to the sporting goods store and told them I had lived in the state for five and a half months. The hunting regulation said you had to live there for six months before you could get an elk license, but the girl said I was close enough. She gave me a resident hunting license.

Meanwhile, back in my prayer closet, I felt led to go up the Columbia Mountain trail and hunt elk. I argued with God, saying I didn't want to leave at one p.m. to go elk hunting. Ninety-nine percent of the hunters would get up long before daylight and be high in the mountains before sunup. This was accepted operating procedures, but I finally gave in, put on my boots, grabbed my rifle, and drove over to the Columbia Mountain trailhead. As I started up the forest service trail, it was very much like Dorothy following the yellow brick road in the *Wizard of Oz*. It was like a light leading me up that trail.

Halfway up the mountain, I saw a slightly used path going off to the left, straight up the mountain. The Lord told me to go up the game trail.

Pretty soon, I was in a foot of snow that had thawed and re-froze. Each step I took was crunch, crunch, making it very noisy every step I took. I stood there bewildered about what to do. Never having hunted elk in my life, I just stood there and prayed, asking the Lord for guidance. It wasn't very long before I heard antlers rattling on branches. It sounded as if it was in a very deep canyon right in front of me that was clogged with thick trees. I figured that the only way I could see down there was to go around to the head end of it and look down, but every step I took, there was a very loud crunch.

As I stood there pondering what to do, the Lord spoke to me and said, "Sit down." Again, I argued with God, telling him we only had about one hour of daylight left, and I didn't have time to sit down. But there was a big tree laying there that had fallen over, so I brushed the snow off of it and sat down. I kept hearing the noise of antlers rattling on brush. After about five minutes, a large bull elk stepped into a clearing straight across the canyon from me. It was all of three hundred yards away. I slid off the log, got in a good sitting position, took careful aim, and shot. The bull just stood there, not knowing where the shot came from, so I shot again.

He turned and ran away, and I shot again as he went into the brush. I ran over to where the bull was standing and it was very obvious that I had hit the elk. I started following his tracks in the snow and before I could get another shot off, he bolted down the hill. I continued following his tracks down the mountain, and about a quarter of the way down, I managed to shoot him again in the neck as he was standing on a cliff.

The elk fell about a hundred feet down a cliff and landed upside down, wedged in an eighteen-inch tree that was growing straight out of the cliff about halfway up. I put my rifle down and inched my way over to the elk on a twelve-inch ledge that was covered with snow and ice. What a job it was, dislodging that 800-pound elk from that tree.

When it finally fell, one of its long horns hooked my pant leg and jerked me off my feet. Fortunately, I had time to grab the tree; otherwise, I would have taken a long, nasty fall.

After the elk fell the rest of the way down the cliff, it slid in the snow for a long way down the mountain. I had my winter's meat. *Jehovah Jira!*

After dressing the elk out and propping it open, I headed back to the car. I made it home in time to shower, change, and make it to church by 7:00 p.m. I shared the testimony with the people how God provided me with an elk; it would feed my family for the winter. I later learned that an older church member called up my district superintendent and tattle-tailed on me. Getting a resident hunting license and being two weeks short of the six months apparently was the problem; I didn't know what to say. Was the girl wrong that sold me the license? Or was I wrong for buying it? Or was God wrong for sending me up the Columbian Mountain trail? There isn't one single doubt in my mind that God spoke to me to go up that trail and hunt elk.

✝

CHAPTER 25

Having a Poised Heart

Sometimes God's ways are contrary to human reasoning and maybe we make the leading of the Holy Spirit too complicated when it's really quite simple. All we need to do is learn to listen. Often, that means quieting our spirit and getting all of the junk out of our thought life so our soul can be poised toward God. Many of us have known people in our lifetime that were extremely poised. It is the little things you notice—how straight they stand without slouching, how clean their shoes are, how squared away they look.

I think it is a lot of little things in their spiritual life that makes a believer's heart poised toward God, (for example, daily prayer, fasting, faithfully tithing, daily worship, spending time in the scriptures, Christian fellowship and sharing Christ with others). Without a doubt, these things will help your spiritual ears to be poised toward hearing God's voice.

We do know this: God promises if we will call on Him, He will answer us and show us great and mighty things we know not of (Jeremiah 33:3).

In the New Testament, 1 John 1:9, it teaches us that if we confess our sins, He is faithful and just to forgive us our sins and to cleanse us from all unrighteousness.

Once you have confessed your sins, you will experience a spiritual rebirth, often referred to in the New Testament as being saved. The word *saved* in the Greek language is *sozo*, which means redeemed, healed, made right with God, just to mention a few of its attributes. When we find Christ, we enter into the household of faith, which has many, benefits.

Where once you had sorrow, you will receive joy and gladness, trading your anxiety and strife for peace that passes all understanding. If you need healing, God will heal you; fill you with His Holy Spirit, and give you the ability to speak another language that you have never studied.

He will give you peace, joy, and a more fulfilled life than you have ever had, and much more. All this is yours because you confessed your sins, believed in the Lord Jesus Christ, and accepted him as your Lord and Savior.

Talk about a good deal, and we all love good deals. That has to be the best offer you have had all day. The fact of the matter is, it's the best offer you will ever get in your entire life!

Some say there is no God. I remember my friend, a highly intelligent man, champion country dancer, and extremely successful businessman, telling me he was an atheist. I said to him, "Do you know the experts tell us that mankind has learned only 2 percent of the total knowledge that is out there to be learned, leaving 98 percent undiscovered?"

Back in the days of the depression, they closed down the patent offices. We had discovered the automobile, electricity, telephone, radio, and the airplane. They thought surely there is nothing left to be invented. Well, they were wrong; they have since reopened the patent offices. Man has continued discovering new things. The experts and scientists in this field conclude our discoveries and inventions have pushed us up to the learning level of 2 percent of total knowledge. In other words, we have only learned 2 percent of what lies out there waiting to be learned.

I said to my friend, "Suppose you were the smartest man on the earth and you knew half of everything ever learned or discovered. This alone would make you, without question, the most intelligent man in the entire world. You would know one-half of the 2 percent of everything man has learned thus far in the history of the earth. Don't you think that in that 99 percent of total knowledge you still have not learned, there is a possibility there is a God?" He said, "No." I couldn't believe my ears. My friend was dying of cancer at the time. The doctor had given him a short time to live, and he still refused to embrace God. I would like to think, in the last minute of his life, he changed his mind; but honestly, that wouldn't be my first guess.

The Bible is an in-your-face book; it's alive. It proclaims only a fool says there is no God. My friend died, and before he died, he sent word that he did not want to see me if I was going to talk about God. I was very sad when he passed away, a sadness that lingered in my mind for six months. I guess it's impossible to pray with everybody in the world; perhaps even to pray with everybody in your town.

I can't help but think of one minister, I don't remember if it was Smith Wigglesworth or D.L. Moody, but he would go and stand on the street corner and pray that the Holy Spirit would send him to the right person who was ready to listen and receive the Gospel. Sometimes, he would stand there for hours and finally the Holy Spirit would say, "That's the one."

In the book of Acts, there is a story about a man named Philip who preached a mighty revival and all of Samaria was saved. In the middle of his revival meetings, the Holy Spirit spoke to Philip and told him to go down to Gaza. So he left his meeting and went down there.

I understand it was a very long walk—I have heard up to ninety miles. There he saw a chariot with a black man reading the Scriptures. He was known as the Ethiopian eunuch. Philip ran up beside the chariot and asked, "Do you understand what you are reading?" And the eunuch ordered the chariot to halt. Then he replied, "How can I understand, except for a man to show me?" (Acts 8:27-35). You might say Philip interrupted the black man's reading.

✝

We could talk a lot about divine interruptions. Joseph had one when he was sold into slavery by his own brothers and forced to go to Egypt, only later to become vice president of the country. Daniel had one that got him thrown into a lion's den and he experienced a miracle from God. Shadrach, Meshach, and Abednego had one that landed them in a fiery furnace, which brought them face to face with the son of God. A man named Saul had a divine interruption experiencing a light so bright that it not only made him blind, but threw him off his horse. Right in the middle of this interruption, he literally heard the audible voice of God.

Each of us has had interruptions in our lives, and if we could only learn to look on them with the right prospective, often we will see the hand of God and hear his voice directing our lives.

The apostle Paul had many divine interruptions. Some of them landed him in prison, where he had lots of time on his hands to seek God and write much of the New Testament. Even John had a divine interruption, and he was exiled to the isle of Patmos where he had one of the most profound visions in the history of man.

Maybe you are experiencing an interruption right now in your life. A treasured job suddenly went away, a crisis in your marriage, perhaps your health has taken a turn for the worse. Mary, the mother of Jesus, had a divine interruption in her life—a much unexpected pregnancy. All these experiences can either make you bitter or better. It really depends on how your soul is poised toward God.

I would like to give you a Scripture to write down on a piece of paper. Stick it to your refrigerator door, memorize it until it becomes a revelation to your heart. It's found in Romans 8:28 and says that "we know that all things work together for good to them that love God, to them who are called to his purpose." Perhaps you have already memorized this verse but it has not become a revelation.

Did you know that God gives growth in adversity? But more often than not, the Creator knows what's best to help us be conformed to his image.

Let me share with you a true story of a lady missionary who spoke at a church service and told how, when in Africa, she became very sick; it was a lack of proper food. She stated what her disease was and felt when her supplies came, she would use the fruit and vegetables to restore her health. The crate came with the food for the entire month, and nothing was in it but oatmeal. So she ate oatmeal gruel for the next thirty days. After the church service, a doctor said that oatmeal gruel is exactly what he would have prescribed if she were his patient.

Always remember this, dear reader; you can never go wrong by putting your trust in the word of God. Keep this in mind: if God interrupts your life, He will surely have a good reason for doing so. It's when we can learn to trust the sovereignty of God, that we are able to find true rest in the Lord.

It's possible some Christians are not acquainted with the sovereignty of God. Let's see if I can help you understand. *Webster* says, "It is a status dominion, power, having all authority, a supreme ruler, having supreme rank, having independent and self-governing power."

An example of this is found in Genesis 2:9, where God placed a special tree in the middle of the garden where Adam lived. This tree was called the knowledge of good and evil.

Here is the picture: everything was spoken into existence, except for man, who was formed by the hands of God. God's plan was for Adam to be a caretaker of someone else's property. He had countless other trees to eat from, but this one tree, the owner said, "Thou shall not eat from it."

Later on, when Adam was showing his friend, Eve, around the garden, he would be compelled to acknowledge to her who the owner was. Perhaps Eve said to him she thought it was his garden, but when Adam showed

Eve the tree of good and evil, he would be obligated to acknowledge the sovereignty of God.

As believers today, we need to acknowledge God's sovereignty in our lives. And the way I see it, there is only one way according to the Scriptures, and it is by bringing the tithe and offerings into the house where you are being spiritually fed. We can say with our words that God is sovereign in our life, but the proof is in your tithe. I can say I am the strongest man in the world, but it is only when I pick up 583 pounds and lift it over my head that it really makes it so.

✝

Meanwhile, back in the desert, here was Philip interrupting a black man reading the Scriptures. To make a long story short, Philip led the man to Jesus, and told him about water baptism. The chariot came to a pool of water. Philip and the black man walked into the water and there Philip baptized him (in the Greek language it is *baptismo*), which means to be immersed under the water, not sprinkled.

When Philip was done baptizing the black man, the Holy Spirit caught up with Philip, and the black man saw him no more. I tell you, that excites me. Just to know there is such a Holy Ghost ride that possibly I could go on someday—that would be so awesome. I would even settle for a fiery chariot ride off into the sky, like the one that happened to Elijah.

It happened to Enoch, a man of God in the Old Testament, who one day was praying in the spirit and got so close to the throne of God, the Lord took him and the people saw him no more.

✝

CHAPTER 26

How Intercessory Prayer Works

I can't help but think about a story in a book called *High Adventure in Tibet,* by Victor Playmer. Victor and two of his associates were in the high mountains of Tibet doing missionary work when they were captured by head hunters. They were tied hand and foot and placed in a round mud hut with a center post in the middle that held up the roof; a broken piece of pottery was lying by the doorway of the hut. A man stood at the door with a spear in his hand guarding Victor Playmer and his two associates. They were sentenced to be boiled alive at sunup and then eaten by the entire tribe.

Meanwhile, in Tacoma, Washington, a godly woman awoke in the night and felt a call to pray. She got up and knelt by her bed, and then began to pray in her heavenly language. While she was praying, she had a vision of three men tied up in a circular mud hut with a post in the middle, holding up the roof, and there was a broken piece of pottery at the door, with a man holding a spear standing guard.

She recognized the man tied up in the middle as Victor Playmer, a missionary who had itinerated at her church some time earlier. She prayed in her heavenly language until the burden lifted and then she went back to sleep.

The next day, she drew a sketch of what she saw in the vision and showed it to her pastor. He mailed it to Victor Playmer. Victor later said if she had a camera, she could not have taken a more accurate picture of the scene in the mud hut.

Meanwhile, back in the jungle, a runner came to the village with a message from a higher chieftain who had heard of the capture. He ordered the release and safe conduct of the missionaries. The message was, "If you touch a hair on Victor Playmer's head, you will answer with your life."

I recall another incident of intercessory praying that took place in my office. As I was praying, a message in tongues came to me with the interpretation. It was just one word, Kaladaachec. The more I spoke that word, the louder my voice got. After repeating the word a half dozen times, I felt the spirit lift. I thought to myself that surely some missionary in Poland needed a special prayer. So I just let it go at that.

My Greek lexicon was lying open and for some unknown reason, I wrote Kaladaachec on the margin of the page. That was the middle of January, 1976, in Hungry Horse, Montana. That summer, the town threw a big celebration for the 200th year anniversary of our country. There were thousands of people playing horseshoes, softball games, archery shoots, sack races, karaoke, and oh yes, don't forget the pie eating contest. They had a different event going on every hour, with loudspeakers all over the grounds letting people know what event was next.

I was admiring the beautiful quilts in the sewing contest when I heard a voice come over the PA system saying, "Mr. Kaladaachec, would you please report to the concession stand, you have a phone call." I couldn't resist the urge to meet a man named Kaladaachec after my experience that past winter. I waited by the concession stand and a middle-aged man showed up and said, "I'm Mr. Kaladacahec, did you call me?" I approached him and told him of my experience in January of 1976.

The man looked at me with tears running down his face and he told me his story. He was in a hospital dying of cancer. The doctors had given him no hope to live, when an angel walked into his room and stood at the foot of his bed and touched him. The angel said nothing, just turned around and left. He said, "I immediately felt strength come back into my body and later, the x-rays proved my cancer was completely gone. This happened in the middle of January of 1976. The man raised his hands and closed his eyes and quoted the verse, "Call unto me and I will answer you and show you great and mighty things which you know not of" (Jeremiah 33:3).

That man was dripping with the Holy Spirit. Although that was 39 years ago, I remember it as if it was yesterday and that is what a heavy anointing of the Holy Spirit will do. It will pierce your heart like an arrow and lodge there for many years.

That kind of anointing doesn't just happen. This man had spent time with God. When his body said I want to sleep, he took authority over it and climbed out of bed in the night and prayed. You may say he took the kingdom of God by force. This man was a champion, he flew like the eagle he was called to be.

Another time, I remember being in a sectional youth meeting in Rockville, Maryland; the song leader acknowledged a man in the church and asked him if he would share a word of greeting. The man stood up and told the story of a teenage girl during the days of depression whose family had run out of coal; they had no heat in the middle of the winter. She knelt and prayed that God would send her money to buy some coal.

The next day, a railroad car derailed and spilled coal all over the backside of their property. The railroad told the local people that they could have the coal because they could not get a machine in to pick it up. This little girl knew God's phone number—Jeremiah 33:3.

Too many of us spend valuable time wallowing around in a mudhole over something that has happened to us in the past. God says to rise up out of that painful memory or it will strangle you for the rest of your life. Spread your wings; mount up as an eagle; let the wind's currents lift you up into the heavens. Wallowing around in your mistake of the past is a satanic trick to cause you to forget who you are and who you represent.

A child of the king has no business crawling around in the mudhole of a hurtful past. You are better than that. Remember, God rewards those who diligently seek Him, and for what you do in secret, God will reward you openly.

✞

CHAPTER 27

Life in Montana

To continue our story from Montana, for the next seven years, I shot seven elk. I read somewhere that only 3 percent of all Montana hunters shoot an elk every year. All I can say is that the Holy Spirit was my guide. I could indeed tell you many stories of God directing me during hunting season.

I soon learned that one black bear, eight deer, eight antelope, one elk, an assortment of pheasants, grouse, ducks, geese, and four hundred fish, all the legal limit, plus twenty gallons of huckleberries, would feed my entire family for one year. In twenty-nine years of marriage, we never had to buy one pound of meat, yet we ate fish and wild game every night of the year. *Jehovah Jira, the Lord is my provider.*

One day, in October, 1972, I was praying and the Holy Spirit spoke to me and said, "I want you to resign as youth pastor by Christmas." It was a hard thing to do since it was the only security I had for my wife and two small children, age five and six. Nonetheless, on Christmas Eve I read my resignation.

There we were, on our own, in a little logging town, population five hundred. The town of Hungry Horse is in the middle of a place they call Bad Rock Canyon, which got its name in the 1800s when the Blackfeet Indians came across the mountains to steal horses from the Flathead tribe. The Flathead Indians soon caught on and set up an ambush in a place where the trail narrowed to about ten feet between a raging river and a sheer cliff. This precarious ledge was six hundred feet long, and the horse thieves were very vulnerable as they passed through. The Flathead Indians hid in these cliffs to ambush the thieves and get their horses back; hence the name, Bad Rock Canyon.

✝

CHAPTER 28

The Christmas Tree

And so we spent our first Christmas in Hungry Horse. I took my daughter Lori, age 6, and son Jake, age 5, in the woods to cut down a Christmas tree. There were two feet of fresh snow on the ground and the going was pretty rough for the little kids, but they tackled it like troopers because they got to pick out the Christmas tree.

I remember our first Charlie Brown Christmas tree was about 7 feet tall with branches laden with fresh snow. As I crawled underneath the branches to chop it down, the snow fell down my neck. Paying more attention to the snow falling down my hooded shirt than which way the tree was going to fall, I didn't notice that the skinny little tree was going to fall on me.

I faked it, and yelled, "Help, help!" With one kid pulling on each boot and a little help from dad, they pulled me out from under the tree. That's when my boots came off, and of course, when they pulled me out, my hooded shirt came up. I was covered with snow from the top of my head to my bare feet. Those two kids laughed until they cried. I put my two boots back on, and then tackled them both and rolled them around in the powered snow.

Little did I know we had started a family tradition. Every year, the Christmas tree had to fall on dad, and even seven children later, it still got laughs. We didn't have a lot of money, but we had more than our share of good times and never once lacked for anything that God didn't provide for us.

Our first New Year's Eve in Hungry Horse, we sought out a little log cabin church in the town of Martin City, which was one mile away; as it turned out, the church was in the process of being closed down. We got there early and sat toward the back of the church. Two teenage girls came in and sat in front of us. Before too long, I felt the Holy Spirit nudge me to talk to them and ask them if they needed to be saved. I introduced myself, my wife, and my children, and began talking to them about the Lord, explaining the plan of salvation.

I started with the same story, John 3:3, as I did in Vietnam with Rick Kucera. It's a simple story about a rich man named Nicodemus, who came to Jesus by night, hungering and thirsting for the things of God, which I believe is the secret of receiving anything from the Lord.

Hungering and thirsting will cause you to do unusual things. As I told the story to the two girls, one aged sixteen and one aged seventeen, tears began to run down their faces, and I asked if they would like to pray with me and accept Jesus as their Savior. They agreed and I began to lead them in the sinner's prayer.

I noticed that not only were there tears running down their faces, but both of the girls' chins were quivering.

Somehow, I knew they were going to receive the baptism of the Holy Spirit, and they did. They both began to speak in tongues as the Holy Spirit gave them the ability to speak a language that they did not know.

That was the beginning of a youth revival, which lasted for six months. We met every Saturday night at six o'clock We would have as many as fifty-one kids sitting in our living room floor, the kitchen, and the hallway. We opened with prayer and my friend, Lloyd Fine, would tell the kids jokes. Lloyd and I made a good team together. His precious wife, Karen, not only played the guitar at the meetings, but was also a mighty prayer warrior. Several of us would play the guitar and sing worship songs, which would result in long sessions of singing in the spirit and experiencing manifestations of tongues and prophesies.

Dozens and dozens of these teenagers received a prayer language. The youngest of these was four years old. That group of people, 90 percent teenagers, sang in the spirit for an hour at a time. It was a very beautiful thing. Every Saturday night, we saw six or eight, sometimes as many as ten kids get saved. Many of them were filled with the Holy Spirit. We would go to the Crooked Tree Hotel next door, where they had an indoor swimming pool, and we would baptize six to ten kids every single week for six months.

One girl that was saved, Inez, and her best friend, Sherry, rode their bicycles seven miles to come to our house. When Inez was saved, her face shined just like a 40-watt light bulb and it stayed that way for three weeks. It was the light of the Holy Spirit inside her.

The news of our youth revival spread like wildfire. We had parents driving teenagers and their friends sixty-five miles one way to our Saturday night prayer meeting.

It was in early March that spring that I was standing in front of the bathroom sink shaving, when the Holy Spirit spoke to me and said, "When you get back from district council, go and rent the town hall and start having Sunday services."

At district council, I told my district superintendent, Brother R.L. Brant, what I was going to do. He put me on a home missions program so I could get a $50 a week salary for the next three years.

I was only making $2,400 a year, but we never lacked for anything. I never took a secular job. *Jehovah Jira (my provider, his grace is sufficient for me).*

The first service at the town hall cost me $5 to rent the room for three hours on Sunday morning. They really should have paid me the $5 for picking up all their beer bottles, sweeping and dusting off the chairs. It was a humble beginning; there were only seven of us—four adults and three children.

So began the Hungry Horse Chapel. We continued to have the Saturday night prayer meeting and the Sunday morning services right up until family Bible camp started, which is only a quarter of a mile from our house.

We discontinued the Saturday night prayer meetings and hoped everybody would go to family Bible camp, kid's camp, teen camp, Maraud camp, or the Baptist camp.

In the summer, the Hungry Horse Bible camp was a busy little place. I often wonder if I made a mistake canceling those Saturday night prayer meetings. Many of the kids did not go to camp; to this day, I think I missed God's leading by canceling those prayer meetings.

It was June of 1973 when I received word that my old friend, George Kaufman, was getting married in Boulder,

Colorado. We decided to take a week off and go to his wedding. Twenty miles down the road, something didn't feel right, so I turned into the Little Brown Church in Big Fork, Montana, where my good friend, Hal Curtis was a pastor. (He also sat under Professor Walter Butler's teaching). I went inside to pray, and after about an hour on my knees at the altar, I knew I was supposed to cancel going to the wedding and return to Hungry Horse, which I did.

As I mentioned before, there was a very large church building right next door to the parsonage. The congregation in Columbia Falls was trying to sell it in order to raise money for TV time. Our little group had tried every way we knew to raise the $15,000 to buy it, but to no avail.

A week previous to this, at our Saturday night prayer meeting, Lynn Gilder gave a word from the Lord, which said that both of these building and this land will be delivered to you debt free in the very near future by the hand of the Lord. I am not sure if I forgot the prophecy, as in those days, we would have two or three of them at almost every service, or perhaps I was busy thinking about going to George's wedding.

We were not back at the house thirty minutes when there came a knock at the door. It was Brother Brandt, my district superintendent. He handed me the keys to the building next door (the church) and said, "It seems Margaret Nash, a member of the original church in Hungry Horse back in the fifties, said she was at the meeting when they merged the two churches and she remembered in the church minutes that it stated if there was ever another Assembly of God Church started in Hungry Horse, both buildings would be handed over to the new congregation."

We knew they were trying to sell it for $15,000 and we had been praying God would send us the money to buy the building, but instead he sent us some nine-year-old church minutes. Whoever heard of saving the minutes from membership meeting for nine years after the church had shut down? It may have been a miracle; at any rate, the Hungry Horse Chapel had a new home.

The windows were broken out and boarded up, and part of the floor in the sanctuary had been burned. There were no pews and no pulpit, no songbooks, and the roof leaked. We took up the offering in a plastic peanut butter bucket.

It seemed as if we had very little, but I would soon learn a valuable lesson. Little is much when God is in it. Just like the little boy who shared his lunch. Jesus blessed a few loaves and a few fish and he fed five thousand people—he even had twelve baskets of leftovers. We saw miracle after miracle in the Hungry Horse Chapel.

A young hippie named Tom Brake was traveling through Montana from back east. As he drove by the church, he thought to himself, "I need to go there tonight." He went skiing all day in White Fish and then he returned to the Sunday evening service. He was saved and filled with the Holy Spirit. He rented a house, got a job, and spent the next six years going to church three times a week. I love to see God work.

Just to show you how good God is, let me tell you the story about the grapes. My wife, Carol, was from back east. She grew up in the middle of grape country, and in the fall, she enjoyed eating concord grapes, which she loved dearly. One day, there was a knock at the door and there stood a man named Bryon, from Helena, Montana, two hundred miles to the south of us. He had a large box of Concord grapes in his hands. He said he felt led to buy these grapes for Carol. Carol later told me that she had been secretly craving Concord grapes.

Bryon had another man with him, so we invited them in for a bit of lunch, which was our custom. Now I had never met Bryon, but immediately we had a friendship, just another example of being in the family of God. He said he had a window of free time, and asked me if I needed some help with anything. I told him as a matter of fact, I did. I had purchased two huge rolls of carpeting that probably weighted five hundred pounds a piece and I wanted to get the carpet laid in the church.

The three of us went over to the church, and four hours later, the job was completed. What a difference new carpet made in that old church building. We were ready for some seats, but I had no idea where they would come from, but I knew that the Lord would provide them. It seemed that an old movie theatre had shut down and the seats were in storage for ten years. The people were happy to give them to us. Praise God, He is awesome.

Before Bryon and his friend left, I asked if he had anything in particular that he would like us to pray for. He told me his wife had left him and she had been gone quite some time. The four of us joined hands and prayed earnestly that God would restore this marriage.

Later on that winter, Bryon showed up at church with his wife at his side. God had answered our prayer. She didn't just come back to her husband; she rededicated her life to Christ and was really on fire for God. Thank you, Jesus, for answering prayers.

I remember one miracle that seemed extra unusual. A man testified as he was driving by the Hungry Horse

Chapel. He thought he saw flames coming out of the roof of the church. The same instant he saw this, he burst out speaking in tongues. When he looked back the second time, he saw no flames. I can tell you what he did see; it was a supernatural manifestation of the Holy Spirit.

The church began to grow and pretty soon we had fifty-two regulars. One couple told me their brother-in-law from California was an evangelist. They asked if it would be OK if he came for a week of meetings. We said, "Sure."

At the end of the week of meetings, he went down the road eight miles and started his own church, taking twenty-six of our people with him. It was a hard thing to swallow. Ironically enough, he only lasted there six months, and then went back to California. Possibly the culture shock of northwestern Montana, being much different than Modesto, California, was the reason he left.

It brings to mind something Walter Butler, who was one of my mentors in Bible College, once said. "You don't need a call to go to the mission field, but you will need a call to stay there." I was 100 percent sure God called me to Hungry Horse.

At this point, I would like to tell you about a meeting in Billings, Montana where I was applying for my ministerial license. Brother Brant and his board of perpetrators were asking me questions, one of which was, "Jack, we know you feel strongly called to Hungry Horse, but we'd like to know what you'd do if we decided there was already a church seven miles down the road and we really don't feel like we want another Assembly of God Church so close."

Without hesitation, God gave me the answer and I said, "I believe all the men in this room are sincere men of God and I believe that God speaks to you as He speaks to me. I want you to know I am subservient to any decision you make on this matter. If you decide there should not be a church in Hungry Horse, I will simply move on to the next project God has for me. I will also feel released from the call that God gave me to go there and I will leave the burden of that call and the responsibility of it on your table. I will trust your wisdom in this matter. Be it right or wrong, I will submit to it." That same day, the Montana District Council decided there should be a church in Hungry Horse.

Brother Butler always used to say, if the Lord sends you, He will pick up the tab, and that was my experience in Hungry Horse. God indeed supplied our every need.

We kept on preaching and teaching the word of God, visiting homes every week. It wasn't long before the little mountain church had around 100 people, most of them young hippies, whom I called pilgrims. They came and got saved, grew in the Lord and settled down into fine citizens, whom the mayor of Hungry Horse called the mighty men of the Hungry Horse Chapel.

✞

I remember my friend Lloyd and I went to an auto parts store to buy a battery. We arrived there about 12:30 P.M., and the sign said they were closed from twelve to one for lunch. We decided to wait for the half hour. Lloyd suggested we go next door and visit his aunt. She was there by herself; we shared the Gospel with her. She knelt by the couch and prayed with us and was saved and filled with the Holy Spirit at the same time.

Just then, her 20-year-old daughter came home, walked into the room, tears began to run down her face, and she too was saved and filled with the Holy Spirit. It was a cool thing seeing the mother and daughter receiving together a fluent and audible prayer language, which the Scripture calls speaking in other tongues. It surely was a divine appointment.

✞

CHAPTER 29

Vine Street

It had been five years since we had a vacation, so we decided to go back to New York state and visit Carol's relatives. I did most of the driving, and it took us about thirty hours to get to Chicago, where we stopped and visited my spiritual adopted brother, Steve Brimmer, and his lovely wife.

I had never been to Chicago before; I had never even lived in a city before. What a time I had finding Steve's home! We got there around seven o'clock that evening and Steve graciously had dinner waiting for us, as well as a spare room for us to sleep in. Carol and the kids went to bed exhausted. Steve and I stayed up until two or three in the morning playing the guitar. (I never went anywhere without taking my new guitar.) I had sold my old guitar when I left Bible College, but during my first week in Hungry Horse, I met a man who had a music store that was going out of business. When he heard that I was going into the ministry, he sold me a Yamaha FG300 guitar for 10¢ on the dollar. It sounded every bit as good as a Guild guitar.

Steve and I were teaching each other new worship songs and catching up on old times. Finally, the thirty hours on the road caught up to me and I went to bed exhausted. It was the middle of July, and Steve had no air conditioning, but I fell asleep anyway.

I opened my eyes and looked at the clock and it was six o'clock; the sun had barely come up. I told God I was exhausted and I just couldn't get up, so I was going to pray in bed. Not two minutes went by before the Holy Spirit spoke to my heart, saying just two words, "Vine Street," and that's all he said.

I somehow knew in my heart that there was something I needed to do on Vine Street. I dragged myself out of bed, and got dressed. As I walked out the front door onto Winchester Avenue, I didn't know whether to go right or left. However, I felt like I was being led to turn right, which I assumed would lead me to Vine Street. Instead, I was led to Howard Street. Bewildered, I did not know what to do; the whole area seemed deserted. Suddenly I saw something move on the opposite side of the street. A little old man was trying to stand inconspicuously in an alcove at a storefront building. He was the only person in sight. I walked across the street directly toward him, thinking I would ask directions. When I said, "Excuse me, sir," I noticed a terrified look on his face. He backed into the corner of the alcove and put his hand on his wallet. He trembled and had great fear in his eyes. I had no idea why, but I now know this man feared being mugged, something that probably happens in Chicago every day. I asked him if he could direct me to Vine Street. He just looked at me for a minute. Finally, he asked me why I wanted to find Vine Street. I thought to myself, "I will never see this man again as long as I live, I will just tell him the truth, so I did."

The man asked me if I knew how big Chicago was; I said, "No, sir, I have never been here before." He informed me that Chicago was eighty miles long and forty miles wide. Vine Street was clear across town; and it was barely two blocks long.

Then the man told me he was there by accident, an hour early for business. He thought his appointment with the storeowner was at six o'clock, but the store didn't open until seven. Then the man said, "Perhaps you had more than one appointment this morning . . . I live on Vine Street."

With tears in his eyes, the elderly man said, "I am Jewish and I am very interested to hear more about this Holy Spirit that speaks to you." For the next hour I shared with him the Gospel of Jesus Christ. I asked him if he would like to be born again. He said he would like to think about it. However, what impressed me was that one minute the man was terrified and fearing for his own life, and the next minute, he was asking me to tell him more about God's Holy Spirit. Also, he was soaking up every word I spoke to him about the Gospel. Talk about a door flying open to share God's love.

I would like to tell you I prayed the sinner's prayer with the man, but it didn't happen. It's an exciting thing to be led by the Holy Spirit—if only the Lord could order my steps more often, such as they were that hot July morning in the city of Chicago.

I went back to Steve's apartment no longer exhausted. My strength was renewed, and I was ready to finish the last leg of our trip to New York.

I share theses stories, and every single one is true, at the risk some would think I am bragging. With God as my witness, I do not mean it in that way, but I do mean it to glorify the Lord and encourage others to hear what the Holy Spirit would say to them. *Amen.*

✞

CHAPTER 30

A Word from God

As our church grew, it soon became evident we needed more space. The property next door to the church was for sale. They were asking $13,000, but before I knew it, the mayor had purchased it for $12,000. I went to visit him and asked if he would be willing to sell it to the church. He said he would, but he wanted $15,000 for it. We voted to buy the property, not knowing where the money was going to come from; he offered us owner financing with a low interest rate.

Two months into the contract to purchase the property, the Lord spoke to me very clearly and said, "This Sunday, I want you to ask the people to give their entire next paycheck to pay for the mortgage on the property." I told God, "I just can't do that; many of these people live paycheck to paycheck. They wouldn't have money for food or for their children."

God reminded me of the children of Israel picking up manna and the thousands of quail flying three feet off the ground, which were easily clubbed and taken for food. He reminded me of the sparrow flying into the picture window, breaking its neck, landing on the slanted ledge, and not rolling off; this happened within one foot from where I was sitting.

God spoke to me and said, "Jack, what about you? Are you willing to give your entire next paycheck?" I said, "Lord, that is the easy part. Of course, I am willing. Lord, you can have my whole paycheck, but I just can't ask these people to do the same thing."

I prepared my own little message for the Sunday morning service, and that was exactly what it was, my own little message. When it came time to preach, I stepped up to the pulpit and the tears began to run down my face; it wasn't planned, it just happened, but I surely had their attention.

I held up my notes and said, "Church, I have in this hand a message I had prepared to preach this morning, but I am struggling with it because I also have a word from the Lord. It is a hard word and I have argued with God over and over all week that I didn't want to give it." One of our older members named Oddy Hethcock, a career logger, stood up and said, "Pastor, we came to hear from God, so go for it."

It seemed as if everybody in the church shouted, "Amen!" So I gave them what God spoke to me. I also told them I believed God was going to show us a series of miracles that would eliminate our church's debt, and during this process, our faith will grow, making us stronger believers.

I told my congregation that when I argued with the Lord, he asked if I was willing to give my next paycheck, and I told God that was the easy part. Of course, I was willing to give my next paycheck. The Scripture that came to me was, "Stand still and see the salvation of the Lord," give and it shall be given to you, pressed down, shaken together, and running over. I told them to take the week and pray about it, and next Sunday, let's see what happens.

That week, some of the people called me and said they got paid every two weeks, so should they give only one week of the paycheck or the whole two-week paycheck. Another family called me and said they are paid once a month. "We fall timber in the woods and it takes that long to skid out and load it up to haul it to the saw mill, get it measured and then they pay us by the board foot. Do we give the entire month's paycheck or a week's worth?" I told them they were asking the wrong person; this wass a question for God.

The following Sunday, every single employed person and family in church stood and said, "We feel God wants us to give our entire paycheck toward the mortgage on the property we have next door." The family that was paid once a month, even though they had five children, pledged and paid their entire paycheck for the month, as did the familys that were paid every two weeks, and so on. To make a long story short, we miraculously paid off the entire $15,000 debt in six months. But the story didn't end there.

One by one, each one of those people gave a testimony of how God gloriously supplied their needs. I don't remember them all, but here is an example of what happened. The family who gave their month's paycheck testified the following week they had received an inheritance from a relative they didn't even know they had. It was three times the amount of their monthly paycheck.

On and on each one testified how God had supplied their needs; talk about a boost of faith and a sense of adventure and excitement. The joy of the Lord flowed like milk and honey in our little mountain church; I just love to see the Lord work.

The people were experiencing first hand, up close and personal, what it is like to be led by the Holy Spirit. I am convinced God has something for us, new and fresh, to experience every morning if we will only learn to listen, trust, and obey God. *Amen.*

✞

CHAPTER 31

Home Meetings

Some of the people in the church wanted to have Bible study in their homes, so every Tuesday and Friday night we would go to different homes and have a Bible study. One home belonged to a man named John Bowles, and when his wife heard John wanted to have home meetings in the living room, she began to pray for some carpet and sheetrock on her walls, as her house was unfinished and had been that way for a very long time.

Within days, her father-in-law unexpectedly showed up with a truck full of sheetrock, paint, and carpet. Within a week, he had finished off the whole inside of her house.

They had a little girl (about seven years old, named Carla), and they had been trying for a second child unsuccessfully for five or six years. During one of the meetings in their home, God gave me this prophecy for them. "God the Father is going to bless this home with a little one, and you'll name him John. He will do the work of an evangelist." Nine months to the day, Liz gave birth to a baby boy and they named him John. It was a great source of spiritual encouragement to that young family. That was in 1976.

✝

CHAPTER 32

Visions

At this point, I want to share something very exciting with you. If you want, you can hear from God today. You can get directions from God, comfort from God, wisdom and knowledge from God, and even more faith. Now here is the good news that I am talking about—70 or 80 percent of the time that God communicates with mankind, He will do it through his word, which is called the *Holy Bible*.

Adam, the first man who walked the earth, heard God's voice. Samuel, as a young boy, living with the priest Eli, heard an audible voice. Moses heard an audible voice, and Paul heard an audible voice, but that is not the only way God communicates with us.

In the Bible, you will read about a young man named Timothy, and how he heard the voice of God. It was through his mother and grandmother. Mamas, I tell you the truth, you can be the audible voice of God. So mamas, raise up your babies to be believers in Jesus.

I have often said there is no higher calling in the world than to be a mother and raise a child for Jesus. Inspire that child at a young age to become a lover of books and to memorize Scriptures. For all you know, you could be raising the next Moses, or the next Queen Esther. So take heart, mothers. There is a bright light at the end of the tunnel, and diaper season will soon be over.

God communicates with us in many different ways. Joseph had a dream, and when he told his dream, it made his brothers so mad at him that they sold him into slavery.

My wife and I sat in a marriage seminar and heard the speaker ask if we had a vision for our marriage. At that point, my wife felt that God had given her a vision to write this book.

Visions are meant to change things, motivate us, direct our lives, and the lives of others. The Bible says that where there is no vision, people parish. Have you ever envisioned the kid next door going to Sunday school? Have you ever had a vision to write a book? If you have, I am here to tell you, it will involve some effort and energy on your part to pursue that vision.

Abraham had a vision and because of it, he moved his entire family over a thousand miles; Nehemiah had a vision; it was a little scary, it moved him to a job site that was bigger than one man could ever do in his lifetime. Nehemiah's vision involved others standing by his side, willing to help to fulfill that vision.

I have heard it said that my pastor, Tommy Barnett, of the Phoenix First Assembly of God Church, has unlimited vision. I do not doubt this for a minute. Perhaps Tommy Barnett is a modern-day Nehemiah. In order for his visions to be fulfilled, he needs help, a lot of help. Just one of his many visions is to have a world-class Christmas Pageant.

In December of 2007, my wife and I took my brother and sister-in-law, Dick and Earlene Nelson, to see one of these productions. Suspended from cables, there were five or six white-robed angels flying around in the air, one of which was the most poised five-year-old girl you have ever seen in your life. She was suspended from a cable fifty feet up in the air, going back and forth across the auditorium. There were live horses, an elephant, a camel, and one of the biggest Bengal tigers I have ever seen. The cast for the production had over six hundred people and I understand that the entire workforce consisted of over four thousand precious volunteers. The result was a sold-out church for fourteen performances, with hundreds responding to the altar call each time. Pastor Barnett could not have done that by himself, but when the whole church joined hands and pulled together, they got the job done. This is something that they do every Christmas, and it all started with a vision.

The Bible says that in the last days, God's people are going to have dreams and visions. How much confidence do we have in God's ability to enable us to climb spiritual mountains or to even wait and find the gold mine at the base?

Years ago in California, a pastor of a small church felt he had received a word from the Lord to buy a piece of land. A year later, oil was found in the area. A decision was made to drill an oil well on the pastor's land and he became wealthy practically overnight. God has three answers to our prayers: yes, no, and wait a while. That is what I mean when I encourage you to wait at the base of the mountain to have God show you your gold mine. God's gold mines come in different forms. Perhaps you cannot handle great riches, but you can handle befriending your next door neighbor, and thus influencing them for Jesus. Go ahead, try getting up in the night and sitting in your armchair without saying a word; just wait on God. However, be forewarned, it is quite possible He will speak to you.

If we are to experience the precious and rich things in God, that is what is required of us. Study about waiting on the Lord and make an appointment in the middle of the night to get up and practice waiting on the Lord.

Sometimes it requires courage to have confidence in God's ability. Surely, it will require us to get excited about the positive, and crowd out the negative thoughts so we can cultivate positive faith.

There is a verse in Philippians 4:8 that we all learned in Sunday school that says, "Finally brethren, whatsoever things are true, whatsoever things are honest, whatsoever things are just, whatsoever things are pure, whatsoever things are lovely, whatsoever are of good report, if there be any virtue, and if there be any praise, think on these things."

Every deed is started by a thought. It might be a good idea to put this verse on your refrigerator and from time to time, submit yourself to an attitude adjustment. Our mental attitude can be a springboard to our faith and can surely enrich your worship. You may say that's pretty elementary, and I would agree, it is very elementary. But just as there are nuts and bolts in a space shuttle and the lack of an 85¢ washer can cause a billion dollar space shuttle to explode before our very eyes, so it is with the government of God. We dare not stray away from the basics. There are also little nuts and bolts type verses in the Gospel and this is one of them, but if neglected, it could cause our spirit to become anemic

Having the right mental attitude is somewhat like the little train going up the steep hill, saying, "I think I can, I think I can," and as he reached the summit he said, "I know I can, I know I can." Often we need to have a positive outlook on things, and it may require an attitude adjustment. Jesus said, "Anything is possible with God." So we must have a vision, we must have a dream for the future.

Getting back to Joseph's dream in Genesis 37: 1–7, it was obvious Joseph had setbacks, but a great quality he had was bounce-back ability. Even when things looked bad, Joseph would say to himself, "I still have breath to praise God."

Setbacks, failures, and slaps in the face are just a part of life. Don't think for a minute you are going to venture out into the supernatural without giving away your position, and believe you me, the devil has snipers that will shoot at you at every opportunity that they get, and there is a real chance that you will be wounded. Joseph, David, Daniel, Peter, and Paul, just to name a few, were all seriously wounded. Hear this, dear reader; when God has an impossible mission to do, He chooses an impossible person and crushes them and makes them into a vessel that He can use. Remember this; even if a man dies, he can live again, and even if he is seriously wounded in the spiritual realm, he can minister again.

On December 31, 1980, a farmer was walking in his field in central Iowa and found an eagle whose wing was broken by a bullet. He sent the eagle to a medical center in

Minnesota and the wing was put into a cast. One year later, in February 1981, this same eagle was sent to Washington, DC to be a part of the reception for the return of the hostages from Iran, and part of a memorial service for Vietnam MIAs.

Thirty days later, back in Wisconsin, in front of four hundred medical students, this same eagle was publicly released back into the wild to fly the wind currents again. Someone took a picture of it and someone else transposed the picture onto a canvas; this famous painting is now called *freedom*. A major setback for that eagle became the very springboard to stardom. It can happen to us, if we will allow God to give us bounce-back ability.

Can we really believe our life is ordered of God? God has a goal for us, and even though we think we may have many reasons to sit the rest of our life out, the Holy Spirit is saying to take a stand for the Gospel.

Jeff Keith had a setback, but he also had a dream to run across America coast-to-coast with one leg. Jeff made it, raising thousands of dollars for cancer research, and he said yes to faith. A solution to a problem is always a positive thought. Dare to believe God to give you a ministry and I promise you, no matter who you are or where you live, God will use you.

The Scripture says we are many members but one body. Some of us are called to be feet, hands, or ears. Did you know there is such a thing as having a ministry of listening as your neighbors share their burdens with you? We could go on and on about fitting into the body of Christ, but suffice to say, God has a divine plan with your name on it.

Tommy Barnett needed help from others in order to accomplish his many projects, and soon others caught the same vision. Walls began going up; where there was once the site of a city dump now stands Phoenix First Assembly Church, one of the most beautiful, active, and efficient Christian campuses in America. Like Nehemiah, he had his Sanballats and Tobiahs, and often he had to work with a shovel in one hand and a sword in the other.

Perhaps I should explain about Mr. Sanballat and Mr. Tobiah. They were two Jewish men in the book of Nehemiah 4. They lived in the midst of the rubble in Jerusalem for many years. These men were used to seeing the walls lying in ruins and they were very much opposed to change.

Too many churches today are used to putting God on a time clock and being happy with three songs, an offering, and a twenty-nine minute sermon. Dear saints, remember this: if you ever want to build a wall, you must deal with the rubbish first. No one has ever gone to a church service and had a neutral effect on it. Either we lift a service with our spirit of praise or we depress it with our negative attitude. Today, the family of God has been commissioned to build God's temple and if we read Galatians, Philippians, and Ephesians, you will discover exactly how to build the temple of God in your own heart.

The Holy Spirit desires to play a major part in this project. Picture yourself lost in the deep mountains of the Alaska Range. You have gone thirteen days without food and you are wandering around in twenty-four inches of fresh snow and one day an airplane lands and a person says, "Hello, I am an Alaskan Guide, I know the way back to town. Can I give you a ride?"

This happened to me and my son, Jake. We gladly accepted the ride. We put all of our trust in that pilot to guide us out of there, even though we were two hundred miles from the closest town. When God's children become hungry enough and tired enough of trying to walk the Christian walk on their own strength, that's when the Holy Spirit comes alongside and becomes our guide through the wilderness of life.

These two men, Tobiah and Sanballat, not only had a critical spirit, but also a spirit of ridicule. I assure you, if you pick up the bat and step up to the plate with a dream of hitting the ball for God, eventually the devil will send you your own personal Tobiahs and Sanballats. They will try an assortment of tricks to keep you from a place of worship, from having a prayer life, from reading the word, having Christian fellowship, and tithing.

Nehemiah had a vision to rebuild Jerusalem's walls that were twenty to one hundred feet thick and sixty to one hundred feet high. One hundred and twenty-five years earlier, Nebuchadnezzar had torn every stone off the wall while looking for Solomon's gold. Can you imagine what a pile of rubble that must have been? Nevertheless, Nehemiah was not a quitter; he was a man who showed up on the scene with a word from God, and not only that, he was called by God to do a work.

Let me tell you something about a calling. You do not have to have one to go into the ministry, but you will have to have a call from God to stay. It is important that we learn to listen to that still, small voice that will speak to our hearts often. But this can only happen when we learn to listen.

Not all the Jews were cooperating with the work. It seemed a little doubt and a pessimistic spirit poisoned their attitude. Remember this, these two things will go a long way to taint your spirit, your family's spirit, and go as far as affect an entire church.

✞

Too often, an entire family will come home from church to sit down at the dinner table and have "roast preacher. "Parents, this is a sure way to poison your kids toward the Gospel, but wait—there's more. Criticizing the office of the pastor is taken very seriously in the Scriptures and I urge you, before you even think about doing it, read about Moses' sister, Miriam. When she criticized Moses, God's chosen one, it almost cost her her life.

We could get into a deep study on this subject at this time and find many verses in the Old and New Testament to back up what I am saying to you, but that could make another book, so let's let it go at this time.

In Proverbs, it lists six things that God really hates. Just one of these things God hates is a critical spirit; it is extremely contagious and can become fatal to the spiritual man. My advice is avoiding it and all of its relatives, or it can surely take over your life. You may want to read for yourself the other five things that God hates in Proverbs 6:16-19. Please note as you read this Scripture that one of the things God hates is repeated twice. This particular Scripture is also one of the Ten Commandments.

Are you a candidate to catch a vision, or hear from God? Do you hunger for a closer connection with the supernatural? This book is here to tell you, not only do these things happen to people today, they can happen to you.

When I was 16, I went to the altar and did this, this, and this (confessed, repented, and received), and the creator of the universe in turn, did this, this, and this (heard me, forgave me, cleansed me, healed me, recorded my name in the Lamb's Book of Life, and led me into the family of

God, just to name a few things). He even promised not to forsake me, even if I go to the uttermost parts of the earth. We read in the Scriptures that most of God's promises are conditional. Some would even strongly argue that all God's promises are conditional. What I would like you to grasp today is the fact that God is still a prayer-hearing and prayer-answering God.

✞

CHAPTER 33

Another Guided Elk Hunt

The pastor's office at the Hungry Horse Chapel was approximately six feet wide and eight feet long. There was just enough room for some bookshelves, a very old over-stuffed chair with a quilt over it for a chair cover, and one small chair next to the desk. There was a small gas heater in the room that I tried not to use any more than I had too, in order to keep the gas bill as low as possible.

I used a blanket to cover up with when I prayed. On Thursday morning, I was in my office kneeling by my overstuffed chair seeking the Lord for the Sunday morning message, singing in the spirit, and praying in tongues. Finally, I got up and sat in the chair. There was a four foot by three foot window I could look out of and see the Columbia Mountains to the west. As I was sitting there waiting on the Lord, I felt the Holy Spirit speak to me, and this is what he said. "Jack, do you see the outcrop of rocks three quarters of the way up the mountain?" I looked up and said, "Yes," and again the Lord spoke to me and said, "There is a bull elk up there I want you to have."

Usually when I go elk hunting, I like to leave at three or four in the morning and climb for several hours in the dark so I am close to the top of the mountain at first light. It was already noon, but over the years, I have learned to trust the still, small voice that speaks to me on a regular basis. So I went over to the house and changed clothes and away I went.

There's a small, narrow road that goes a quarter of the way up the mountain, but I could only drive partway up the road because of a rockslide. I grabbed my rifle and started walking. It took me about four hours to get to the outcropping. It was very steep with a foot of snow on the ground, but when I arrived at the top of the cliff, sure enough, there were fresh elk tracks in the snow.

I could tell by the rounded tips of the toes it was a bull elk. A cow elk is very dainty; they pick their feet up and set them straight down. Their hoofs are pointed, but a bull elk drags his feet, perhaps like a lazy kid, and then he rounds the front part of his hoof off. I also noticed his droppings went in a straight line for about fifteen feet. A cow elk is a little more sophisticated. Her droppings will be in one pile about the size of a Frisbee.

I began to track this bull in the crunchy snow, but I was very noisy. I don't think I had gone a hundred yards before I surprised the bull. The brush was too thick to get a shot. The bull soon disappeared, running down the hill, but I did get a look at his horns; on one side were six long, heavy tines and the main beam was bigger around than your arm. On the other side, there was a lone brow tine. I had never seen a rack quite like it in my life.

It was getting dark fast and I didn't want to be stuck on those high cliffs after dark. Going down was harder than coming up. On the trip back down the mountain, I came to a big shale slide with a foot of hard snow on it. I reached into my back pouch and pulled out a garbage bag, which I always carried for an emergency raincoat. I sat on the garbage bag and started to slide down the chute, steering myself with my heels and one free hand.

"This is going well," I thought to myself, but by this time it was almost dark and I didn't see the cliff coming up in front of me. You guessed it. I went airborne, something I don't recommend when you are by yourself.

I landed right in some rocks—feet first, fortunately. I landed so hard that I broke the plastic butt plate on my rifle in half. My wool pants caught on a snag and ripped the full length of the leg, and I kept sliding uncontrollably. Several other snags caught my clothes, which ripped my jacket in a dozen places. I ripped the seat out of my pants and scratched my cheek until it bled. The chute went all the way down to the main road. I was so tired, I took the easy way out and kept sliding.

When I got to the road, I started walking. The first car that came along stopped and gave me a ride. The driver of the car was an extremely attractive woman with long chestnut hair past her shoulders. What happened next convinced me without a shadow of a doubt that she was sent my way by the devil himself.

She asked me what happened, since my clothes were in shreds. When I told her, she said she felt sorry for me and put her hand on my leg. She went on and on about how I could have been killed, and she gave me a tissue to wipe the blood off my cheek.

She told me her husband had abandoned her and left behind a whole dresser of expensive hunting clothes, and if I had time, she would be happy to fix me a hot cup of coffee and give me the hunting clothes. I have to admit, I did think about it, but only for a minute. Then I told her my wife was expecting me, and it would fine if she would just drop me off at the Hungry Horse Chapel, which was right on US2. I tell you, this elk hunting can be dangerous.

I had no more than walked in the door when my friend, Craig Renfro, called and asked me if I wanted to go hunting in the morning. I had been trying to get Craig to go to church for a year, so I thought perhaps this was an opportunity to cultivate our relationship. Even though I was bruised and battered, I decided to go. I also told him I knew where a bull was.

There we were again, at first light in the morning, walking up the road where I had parked my car overnight. We came to a hogback ridge that went up the mountain. I explained to Craig there were two ways to get to the top. We could follow this hogback ridge we were standing on or take another ridge a quarter of a mile from this one. I gave him his choice, and I told him the one he didn't want to take, I would take. Of course, he chose the first one. I told him to give me twenty minutes and we'd work up the mountainside together.

I continued on the logging road, which came to a dead end after another quarter of a mile. I had only walked ten minutes after leaving Craig, and as I came around a bend, there stood the same bull I had jumped the night before. We both saw each other at the same time and the elk bolted for the woods. I had just enough time to pull my rifle up, aim, and shoot just as he entered the timber.

I followed his tracks in the snow for about fifty yards and there he lay, stone dead, with a bullet through his heart; two feet lower than the point where I had aimed. That fall off the cliff had knocked my scope off and I had forgotten to check it, which isn't like me.

I usually hand-loaded a hundred rounds of ammunition for hunting season and used eighty of them to periodically check the zero of my scope to ensure it was sighted in correctly. I had already told Craig about Holy Spirit bullets, and I definitely knew I had just used one of them.

Let me explain the term Holy Spirit bullet. It is used to describe an extremely hard shot we manage to make. For example, twice, my teenage daughter, Lori, age fourteen, killed an elk with one shot in 30 degrees below zero weather. One of them was at five hundred fifty yards. Another time, I killed an antelope at nine hundred yards. It is shots like this these when you realize you are getting some extra help from the Holy Spirit. You might ask if God is really interested in these small facets of your life. My answer is simple—God is interested in everything we do. The Bible says He knows the count of every hair on our head. Why wouldn't He be interested in every success of an Elk hunt?

I figured the bull would be easy to get out and I really didn't need any help, so I decided not to fire a signal shot to Craig. Now let me explain to you what a signal shot is. I really believe it was an idea that the Holy Spirit had dropped into my heart. The NRA teaches if you are in trouble, shoot three shots in a row up in the air, but we had a different signal shot which goes like this: First thing in the morning we set our watches so they all tell the exact same time, and then during the course of the day, if we need help or direction, we fire one shot exactly on the quarter hour and then your partner hears this shot and looks at his watch and immediately fires one shot back. Then we start walking toward each other, until we join up, but we only do this in an emergency.

It just wasn't necessary for him to miss a day of hunting, but nonetheless, thirty minutes later, here he comes. He told me he heard the shot and knew I wouldn't miss. I was so embarrassed about the scope being out of adjustment I didn't tell him about my rifle being bumped the night before.

I knew it was the same bull the Lord pointed out to me three quarters of the way up the mountain on top of the cliff. He had a five-foot beam on one side with six points, and an eighteen-inch brow tine on the other side. It was the biggest body elk I had ever seen. Well, God had directed me again, but the story doesn't end there.

Craig decided to stay and look around for some more elk. I walked back to where my car was parked and drove back home. I hoped to find my neighbor, Elvin Nash, home so I could use his truck to bring out the elk. Elvin was getting ready to leave the house when I pulled in his driveway. He and his son, Rod, were going east of the mountains on an antelope hunt. They were scheduled to leave an hour before, but they kept running into delays.

His son, Elvin, and I were able to cross the rockslide in his four-wheel-drive pickup and drive within fifty yards of the elk. Elvin had an eight thousand pound winch on his truck, which easily drug the elk out so we could load it, but when we started back out, his brand new pickup truck stalled.

The battery was stone dead and wouldn't turn over again. I don't say this to brag, but this is a true story. We laid hands on that battery and prayed. Elvin turned the key and it started right up. Craig just looked at me and shook his head. The year before we had prayed for some light in the middle of the mountains. Craig thought we were asking for a little much when we miraculously received four flashlights. You would think that with all this, I would be able to lead Craig to the Lord, but I never did. Lord knows we sowed enough seeds in his life. Hopefully, they were watered and somebody else will lead him to the Lord.

✞

CHAPTER 34

A Prophecy Comes True

In 1982 at the Thompson Falls Christian Center, the same prophecy I received in John Bowles' living room came back to me a second time. There were fifteen or twenty of us praying for a lady named Joan Finley, who had been married for some time, but had no children. In the midst of prayer time, I found myself saying to her, "God is going to bless you with a little one, and he will do the work of an evangelist." The only difference is this time I did not hear a name for the child. Nine months later, Joan had a little boy. This has only happened to me three times in my life. The last one occurred in October, 1984, in McGrath, Alaska, which is deep in the interior of the state.

There were three of us moose hunting up the Roam River in central Alaska. I had tried crossing the river by walking on a tree that had fallen into the water, when I slipped off the tree and fell into the water, injuring my knee.

The same day, a plane flew over our camp. I signaled for them to land, and wouldn't you know, it was a plane from the Alaska Emergency Rescue Association. They were out looking for a downed aircraft. They gave me a free ride to McGrath, a native community on the Kuskokwim River.

There, a lady showed up on a three-wheeler and gently squeezed my knee, had me get onto the three-wheeler bike behind her, and took me to the hospital. She gently squeezed my knee again, gave me some aspirin, and then sent me out the door. I received a bill for $500 for medical attention. The cost of living in central Alaska is very high.

After being discharged from the hospital, I found myself wandering around the streets of the town trying to inconspicuously carry my .300 Winchester rifle when, by chance, I happened upon the Assembly of God Church. There, I met the pastor and his wife, who graciously invited me for dinner. He told me the church bylaws were against hunters sleeping in the church, but there was nothing said about who he could have as guest in his house.

So here I was, again meeting another fellow brother in Christ, in the household of faith known as the family of God. I was a perfect stranger with no money in my pocket. Yet they took me in and showed me gracious hospitality. I tell you, being a child of God is wonderful.

So the pastor (I think his name was Tom Thumb), asked me to stay the night. We visited for a time after dinner, read some Scriptures, and had prayer time. When it was my turn to pray, I had a message in tongues and also gave the interpretation. I told him God was going to bless them with a little one, who will bring great joy into your home, and who will do the work of an evangelist.

It was fifteen years later when I saw this pastor again, who was now ministering in Palmer, Alaska. I shook his hand and asked if he remembered me. That's when he said, "How could I forget the man who prophesied the birth of my son?" Then he shared something that I thought was interesting.

He told me after the prayer meeting that night in McGrath, he and his wife were walking up the stairs to their bedroom when he said to himself, "I will have something to say about this, I do not want a child." On the other hand, his wife was ecstatic; she wanted a child very badly.

As we continued to talk in Palmer, I asked him what happened. He said, "Let me introduce you to what happened." He called a teenage boy over to us and introduced me to his fourteen-year-old son. The pastor said "He has been the greatest joy to me and his mother. More than I could have ever imagined, and he has told me he wants to go into the ministry." It was a boost to this pastor's faith. I think that's what the gifts of the Spirit are supposed to be; to give us direction, knowledge, understanding, and certainly it adds a little spice to a Christian's life.

It concerns me that I see the gifts of the Holy Spirit not only fading out of the church, but in some cases, pushed out. In my opinion, that's a tragedy. Some say they don't have to speak in tongues to be a Christian, and that's when I ask them if an elephant can be an elephant without a trunk. Of course, the answer is yes, and the elephant can be an elephant without a trunk, but he won't be able to do the things his brother and sister elephants do who have trunks; he will be greatly limited and somewhat anemic.

Many churches believe in the gifts of the Holy Spirit, but they do not practice what they believe. I have read about many revivals, such as those in Topeka, Kansas; Azusa Street in California; Brownsville, Florida; and even Hungry Horse, Montana. They all have a few things in common; lots of prayer and worship, the teaching of the Word of God, and the manifestation of the gifts of the Holy Spirit.

An angel of the Lord appeared to Zacharias in the Gospel of Luke 1:8-25, and told him that Elizabeth was going to have a baby, although she was well stricken in years. The child would have the spirit of Elijah. Before this incident, it had been 400 years since God's people had heard from an angel in this way.

I pray my children and grandchildren do not have to wait a lifetime to see and experience the exciting faith-building, mind-boggling, exciting gifts of the Holy Spirit. These gifts can be so adventurous; it will force you to smile. God knows we need more smiles in the church.

I write about my journey with the leading of the Holy Spirit at the risk of some of you thinking Jack MacDonald is trying to toot his own horn, but this is the last thing that I want to do. I remember well the hole in the pit from whence I was dug. In fact, writing this book was my wife's idea. She talked me into it after I had shared these stories with her over the years, convincing me these stories would be of help to other people as they sought the leading of the Holy Spirit in their own lives.

✝

CHAPTER 35

Fasting and Praise

My real desire is to give you a glance of what you can have in God and inspire you to press in and do whatever it takes to have these experiences for yourself. I should warn you, it may require fasting, it may require radical prayer, and it may compel you to spend extra time with God.

Let me ask you this question: Have you ever fasted for a 24-hour period in your whole life? Perhaps many of you will say no, I have never done a fast. Going without food for spiritual reasons is found throughout the Bible. Jesus did it, Paul did it often; in fact, as we examine the Scriptures and do a character sketch of the many men and woman of God that we find there, fasting seems to be a normal function.

What happens is our flesh does not like fasting; many times, it scares us. But Jesus says *when* you fast, not *if*. He absolutely assumes that His followers practice this type of communication with God.

Jesus said some things only happen with fasting and prayer. So if we need real power in our lives, part of the answer is fasting and prayer. When our spirit rules our body, it causes our faith to grow, but when intellect rules the spiritual man, it has a tendency to dissipate our faith. Fasting seems to raise our spiritual antennas, enabling us to better hear the still, small voice of God.

The apostle Paul, certainly a mighty man of God, tells us this about himself. He practiced fasting often, and another thing that we definitely know about Paul is that many, many times, he heard the voice of God.

Another point that I would like to make is that Jesus taught his followers that when you pray, say, "Our Father, who art in heaven." Praying is best done with our voice; speaking to God with our voice, bringing under submission the most unruly member of our body, the tongue.

In Hosea 14:2, it says, "Take with you words, and turn to the Lord, and say unto him, take away all sin and receive us graciously, so we will render the calves of our lips."

It doesn't say to tell the Lord in your heart, which is a form of meditation. No, it says, "Say words, confession and praise is done with the mouth. In Hebrews 13, it tells us about bulls and goats being a form of sacrifice in the Old Testament. Today, the sacrificial system is still here; it hasn't been done away with, but it has been fulfilled.

There has been a change in the priesthood and a change in the sacrifice. Once it was bulls and lambs, now it is the calves of our lips, which is the sacrifice of praise.

God is after a man or a woman who stands in his presence and says, "I love you, Lord." Sometimes this is very hard to do; often our problems get so big that we can't see God. Praise is the mechanism that gets us out of our shell, so we can see how big God really is. Let us function as a New Testament priest, lifting our hands in God's presence, until we get that subjective assurance that we are truly worshipping God in spirit and truth.

The Bible tells us we are priests, but we need that assurance. Don't go to bed until you have offered the evening sacrifice of praise, and when you get up in the morning, don't do anything until you have offered the morning sacrifice of praise. Pretty soon, you will be giving the offering of the sacrifice of praise at your coffee break, at lunch, and at dinner. That's when we understand Hebrews 13:15, "Giving the sacrifice of praise to God continually, which is our reasonable service."

In all things, give thanks, and this is something we must learn to do ourselves. I can lead you to Christ, but I cannot love him for you. God does not need our praise but we need to give it. We need some mechanism to bring us out of our little world. We see an example of this in Acts 16:19-25, where Paul began to praise God because he was feeling low.

Let me elaborate a little bit. Paul had just cast a demon out of a girl. Her pimps then turned on Paul and Silas, dragged them into the marketplace, and after lying to a judge, they had all their clothes ripped off. They were beaten with a whip and cast into the inner prison, their feet clamped between two iron bars. You might be tempted to ask why God allowed this to happen; Acts 16:30-31 answers this question.

Surely Paul could have cried to God, and perhaps it was at this time God spoke to him, Romans 8:28, where he later wrote, "All things work together for good to them that love God and to them who are called according to his purpose."

This Scripture gives me comfort about being sent to Vietnam and only seeing one marine accept Christ. But the point that I want to make here is that Paul and Silas prayed, sang praises to God, and the Scriptures say the prisoners heard them.

Evidently, these prayers were a little on the loud side and actually disturbed those around them. No doubt, the prisoners had seen them brought in naked and bloody, and surely they realized Paul was in prison, but prison wasn't in Paul. Although their backs were bleeding, they still had a song in their hearts. Please note exactly what praying and praise accomplished.

Doors were barred, backs were bleeding, but they still had a song. All over the world today, we see people bound with the shackles of sin with no song in their hearts. It seems singing praises to God changes things. It can change things for you just as miraculously as it did for Paul.

Acts 16:26 says, "And suddenly, there was a great earthquake and all the doors flew open, and everyone's handcuffs fell off." I don't know about you, but I see that as a miracle! Perhaps you are in prison today. Let's use the prison of cancer, for example. Without prayer and praise, this prison can seem unbearable. The prison of cancer may seem like it is as big as the ocean, drowning all your hopes, steering up all your fears, which in turn disputes your faith. Please read this next line carefully. The more we learn to worship, the bigger and bigger God becomes, while the cancer gets smaller and smaller.

Today we can be in prison, but prison does not have to be in us. TheBible teaches us that laughter doeth good, like a medicine.

As a result of a half of a night's stay in prison Paul started a church in the city of Philippi. Always remember this folks—when we offer the sacrifice of praise, things happen. Perhaps we don't realize it at the time, but we can see from God's word that it has a profound effect, not only for the one who offers the sacrifice of praise, but for the people around him. When you are touched by the spirit of God, other people see it and it becomes contagious.

God said that the praise isn't for us. It helps poise our soul toward God. In Psalm 51:15-17, David says, "Oh Lord, open my lips; and my mouth will declare your praise. You do not delight in sacrifice; or I would bring it: you do not take pleasure in burnt offerings. The sacrifices of God are a broken spirit: a broken and contrite heart, oh God, you will not despise."

Psalm 51 is a plea from David that God wouldn't take away the anointing of the Holy Spirit from his life. In verse 10 it says, "Renew a right spirit in me." David was very earnestly praying, "Give me back that which I once had." This was an extremely dark chapter in David's life. His heart and mind are full of failure and guilt.

If you study the Bible, you will find more than a few men and women who failed God; for example, Jonah, Sampson, Peter, Adam, Abraham, King Saul, and Moses, just to name a few. Rahab, the harlot, failed, but went on to become the grandmother of David.

If the truth were known, most of us have failed God at one time or another; but a major hurdle in making a come-back is genuine repentance, asking God's forgiveness, and offering the sacrifice of praise Maybe your problem to-day seems as big as Mount McKinley in central Alaska, 21,000 feet high. But if you will begin to offer the sacrifice of praise, I assure you, that problem, no matter what it is, will begin to shrink, and God the father will become bigger than your problem.

David had a great fear of losing the touch of God that he had on his life. Paul shared the same fear.

The world today is craving to see a man or a woman with a touch of God on their life. We don't care what color their skin is, we don't care what country they are from. What we really care about is someone, anyone, coming into our midst, obeying the voice of God.

David knew a secret, and it wasn't offering bulls and goats to the Lord; it was the sacrifice of praise to God from our lips. Words of praise are what God really wants. We definitely need to give the morning and evening sacrifice, and we need to pay attention to the little man in our heart, and trust me, we all have one.

For example, a little three-year-old named Johnny was standing up in his highchair and his mother said, "Johnny, sit down." Little Johnny said, "No mommy, I am not going to sit down and you can't make me."

She turned and looked at Johnny with one of those stern looks that parents need to use more often and she spoke in a calm voice. "Johnny, sit down in your highchair, or I will sit you down myself." Little Johnny said to his mother, "I will sit down mommy, but the little man in my heart is still standing up."

We have to be careful that when we offer the sacrifice of praise with our eyes closed and our hands in the air that the little man in our heart has his eyes closed and his hands in the air also. We are taught this in 1 Timothy 2:8.

"I want men everywhere to lift up Holy hands in prayer, without anger or disputing."

That being said, Let's look at this from a different perspective. If you study the men of God in times past, and discover their characteristics, customs, and habits, you surely will come up with a list that contains these words: paying tithes, having the praises of God continually on their lips, and having a spirit of meekness, which should not be confused with weakness.

✞

CHAPTER 36

Alaska

Alaska has always been a place I was fascinated with; little did I know that a day would come when I would sell everything I owned, buy a newer diesel pickup truck, and an older Jeep Waggoner, two large camper trailers, and head north.

What an adventure; we had four licensed drivers, so we switched off driving. Halfway through Alberta, Canada, my sixteen-year-old son, Jake, was driving the pickup truck that had a 25-cubic-foot freezer in the back, full to the top with wild meat and huckleberries. As he was pulling the twenty-six foot trailer, the rear tire on the pickup had a blow out. I was driving the Jeep at the time, and I had just started to pass him on a long straightaway, so I saw the whole thing up close.

He handled the critical situation like a seasoned trucker—I was very proud of him. A lot of people would have jammed on the brakes, which is exactly what you are not supposed to do; instead he used the trailer brakes to stop him, which immediately straightened out the pickup. I could not have done a better job myself.

Some may say sixteen is too young to be driving a pickup pulling a trailer, but I have always believed in teaching my kids to drive while they are young. Jake sat on my lap when he was seven years old and steered the car. We did a lot of driving deep in the mountains on forest service roads where there was hardly any traffic. I guess that is one of the benefits of rural living.

The family rule was that you had to have five thousand miles of driving experience under your belt before you could get your driver's license. Half of those miles had to be in snow and ice. I made it a point to teach my kids how to control a vehicle when it went into a slide on slippery roads.

I can remember once when we had a near mishap. My nine-year-old son, Dave, and I went on a three-day caribou hunt. We were about two hundred fifty miles north of Anchorage on a very desolate road called the Denali Highway. This part of the road was so desolate, people would get stuck in the winter and actually freeze to death trying to walk out. Alaska can be a very harsh place to live. It is definitely not for the faint-hearted.

I was driving a Toyota four-wheel drive pickup, pulling a very small flatbed trailer, just big enough for my little Suzuki 250 quad. We were deep in the mountains with no other cars around, when I ask Dave if he wanted to try driving the pickup. He jumped at the opportunity. Dave had sat on my lap and had steered the car before, and often did the shifting from the passenger side, but he did not have a lot of solo experience behind the wheel, but I felt like he was ready to get started. A ranch kid in Montana back in the 70s could get a driver's license when he was twelve years old.

Meanwhile, back in the mountains, Dave was doing great working the clutch, shifting the gears, going along about twenty-five miles an hour. I was enjoying the day until I looked in the rearview mirror and wouldn't you know it, right on my tailgate was the game warden waiting to pass. We came to a straightaway and I had Dave pull over to the shoulder as far as he could and slow down.

The game warden took the hint and passed us. I saw him do a double-take as he drove by; he didn't stop, he just kept going. Dave was sitting on a pillow so he could see over the steering wheel. I didn't think there was any problem, but Mr. Game Warden didn't see it that way.

We traveled along another two miles and came up over the top of a hill and there stood the game warden right in the middle of the road, waving his arms over his head. I guess that was some sort of modern day mountain traffic stop. We didn't see him until we crested the hill. He wasn't more than a hundred feet in front of us.

Dave was going about twenty miles an hour. I told Dave with an emphatic voice to take his foot off the gas, push in the clutch, and put on the brake. Dave, with eyes as big as saucers, froze up on me. We were getting closer and closer to the game warden, standing in the middle of the road, waving his arms. Again, I told Dave in my most emphatic voice, only much louder, to take his foot off the gas, push in the clutch, and put the brake on. No good; son David was still frozen solid.

Now, I guess this game warden was into playing chicken, because he wasn't moving. We were getting closer and closer, probably going ten miles an hour, and the game warden was standing about twenty feet in front of us, still frantically waving his arms. I reached over, turned off the key, and turned the steering wheel to the left. At the same time, this tall, lanky game warden sprang to the right and dove head first, right into the ditch. It was a deep ditch, and wouldn't you know, it was full of water three feet deep with another foot of soft mud.

The Toyota came to a stop. I looked over and saw the game warden swimming over to the side of the ditch. That's when I envisioned myself going to jail and leaving poor Dave there to freeze to death.

I braced myself and told Dave to roll down his window. The poor man was covered with mud from head to toe. He had his duty belt on and all his leather was muddy and wet. His pistol was caked with mud, his uniform was caked with mud, and even his hair was covered with mud.

As he stepped up to the window, I mustered up my most cheerful voice and said," Good morning, sir." His face was beet red as he replied, "Get that kid out from behind that wheel or I will give you a ticket and ruin your hunt." All I said was, "Yes, sir," and got out of the truck. By the time I got my door closed, he had walked back to his pickup truck, which was quite a ways down the road.

I don't know why he picked that spot to stop us. It was definitely an ambush. Maybe he thought that Dave might try to outrun him; I don't know. I switched places with Dave and we continued our drive. I didn't see another car for two days.

That particular hunting trip had some memorable moments. For example, that night, Dave and I slept on a mattress in the back of the truck underneath the waterproof topper, camping out. We ate peanut butter and jelly sandwiches, drank Pepsis, and had potato chips for dessert. After supper, we had a time of prayer and we thanked God for protecting us, asking his blessing on the hunt.

When Dave prayed, he asked God to bless the family, naming them one by one. It made me very proud; he didn't even forget to ask God to bless Mac, our black lab. I suspect we had the most blessed dog in the neighborhood. For some reason, all the kids ended their prayer at night with, "God bless Mac."

We fell asleep having father-son talks. Surely this was the good life. The next morning, we had a bowl of cereal with bananas and a bottle of orange juice for breakfast. We unloaded the four-wheeler and then headed off for the deep woods. We had not gone more than a mile when I saw two large bull caribou, about five hundred yards away. I pulled my rifle out of the scabbard that was mounted on the quad; we left the bike there and continued on foot.

At about two hundred yards, I made a perfect shot. One bull fell dead in his tracks and the other bull ran off. Dave and I walked up to inspect our work, and after dressing it out, I told Dave to stay there while I went to get the bike.

The bike was a considerable distance away over rough terrain and I didn't think both of us needed to make the hike. Upon retrieving the bike, I rode back to where Dave was. As I rode up over a knoll on the tundra, I could see Dave about one hundred yards away sitting on a log next to the dead Caribou.

The other bull was standing five feet away, sniffing David. For a full five seconds, I panicked. I stopped the bike and jacked a shell in the chamber of my .300 Winchester Magnum.

I had developed an extremely accurate load of 77.7 grains of Hodgdon 4831 powder with a CCI 250 Magnum primer behind a 180-grain nozzle partition bullet. I put the crosshairs on the Caribou's neck, knowing that I could hit a dime at a hundred yards. I was confident that if he took one more step closer to Dave, I could drop him in his tracks.

That bull must have stood there for five minutes. I was very relieved when he turned and walked away. I asked Dave if he was scared. He told me he was until he saw me take aim at the bull; then he knew he was going to be OK. We quartered up the animal and went home. We had had enough excitement for one day.

✞

CHAPTER 37

Little House in Alaska

My family and I had arrived in Wasilla, Alaska on Saturday, the first week of June, 1985. The next day we went to church, as was our custom. It was there that we met the Wayne Brockman family, who extended to us their northern hospitality. We parked our camper trailers at Wayne and Margaret's house; I don't think you could find a finer example of a Christian home, or more godly parents than my precious Brother and Sister Wayne and Margaret.

We plugged in the freezers to keep our meat frozen, unhooked the vehicles, and began searching for a home to buy. At that time, property was very expensive in Alaska. We wound up buying one acre of land. The land had no septic system, just an outhouse. There was a two-room cabin that was barely livable, but it was all we could afford.

We purchased it for $55,000 using our smaller camper trailer as a downpayment. We immediately started building an addition onto the cabin. At that time of year, it didn't get dark until two o'clock in the morning, and was light again at four. I decided to add six bedrooms, a large living room, and two bathrooms with septic system that summer.

I couldn't afford to hire help, so we had to do it all ourselves. One of our hobbies was going to garage sales. I couldn't believe the truckloads of lumber I could buy at garage sales; I even found a brand new keg of 16-penny nails in the dump one day.

I had brought along my carpenter's tools in anticipation of a building project. By the time we reached Alaska, my family had grown to six children, ages three to seventeen. I had enough helpers for two shifts. The morning shifts were from six o'clock in the morning till two o'clock in the afternoon, and the swing shift was from two until ten o'clock in the evening. My son, Jake, and two of the smaller kids would join me for the first shift, and my oldest daughter and the remaining little kids would be the helpers for the swing shift—away we went, six days a week.

In three months, that little crew had remodeled that cabin, adding six bedrooms, a living room, and two bathrooms, completely finished with a septic system. It was a sight to behold. I am so proud of my children and my wife. They never complained; they all worked like beavers.

In the middle of the project, I noticed that two of my sawhorses were missing, and a full sheet of half-inch plywood was gone. I was too busy to think that much about it. But a week later, after picking up a copy of the *Anchorage Daily News*, which was the largest newspaper in Alaska, the picture on the front page told me where my sawhorses and my sheet of plywood went.

There was a picture of my daughter, Scottie Beth, and her friend, Alice, holding up a glass of Kool-Aid. They were standing in front of their little makeshift Kool-Aid stand, with a little sign that read "Kool-Aid, 5¢ a glass." It seems the editor of the newspaper just happened to be driving by this remote part of the Matanuska Valley, when he saw the girls with their Kool-Aid stand.

The intersection where they set up their stand just happened to be named Hollywood Road and Vine Road, which was a half block from my house. The editor who wrote the article also included pictures. The title of the article was "Young Entrepreneurs move to Alaska from Montana."

The mystery of my sawhorses was solved. My daughter, Scottie, after working eight hours a day helping her dad do carpentry work, had her own second job running a Kool-Aid stand, trying to raise money to help support the large family. Although she didn't bring a lot of nickels to the table, the boost in the moral was worth a million dollars, not to mention making her father very proud. She was nine years old.

That first summer in Alaska was a very busy one. My second daughter, Scottie Beth, working her second job at the Kool-Aid stand, inspired her father to work a third shift, but I couldn't get any volunteers since the third shift started at ten o'clock in the evening. Everyone was tired and wanted to go to bed. But often old Dad would work until midnight or later since it didn't get dark until two in the morning.

I would be back on the job at six o'clock the next morning with my three helpers. I need to say my hardworking wife, who was the acting general superintendent, kept the nails, lumber, sandwiches, and drinking water flowing smoothly.

Since Saturday is the very best time to go garage saleing, and is one of our favorite hobbies, week after week we went out for a couple of hours to see miracle after miracle, finding items that we needed.

It seemed whatever we needed, we found at a garage sale, for pennies on the dollar. There were a lot of garage sales back then, and when people decided to leave Alaska, things were sold very reasonably. For example, a whole pickup load of 2 × 6s, twelve feet long, would be $20.

I got to the point where I needed plywood, and one guy had a whole stack of 4 × 8 × 1/2-inch, well over fifty sheets, for $50. I remember getting to the place where I needed 12-2 electric wire. I bought five boxes for $5 at a garage sale. These people were leaving Alaska the very next day and they didn't seem to care what amount they sold things for. Their mind was already down the Alcan Highway heading back to Oklahoma.

I recall getting to the point where I needed more insulation and discovered that the lumberyards, which were extremely busy, would sell any broken bale of insulation they had for 10¢ a foot. What a great deal. It seemed like every time I turned around, God was blessing me.

At one point, I needed sheetrock. One lumberyard had a whole unit of sheetrock that had been scraped by a forklift, nothing more than a quarter inch deep. After it was taped, you would never tell that the scrapes were there. A 4 × 12 × 1/2 inch sheet of sheetrock for $1 was an extreme bargain, to say the least. I bought fifty sheets.

✞

Some may ask, "Why doesn't God bless me this way?" I don't pretend to have all the answers, but the first question you need to ask yourself is, "Do I give my 10 percent to God and the work of His Kingdom?" In other words, do you tithe?

✞

Back in Alaska, we were working two and a half shifts and things were coming along fine. It seemed whenever we needed something, we'd find it on our Saturday hunt at garage sales. Going to garage sales is definitely a way of life for those who are conservative in nature and want to be a good steward of God's money.

This reminds me of another house I was working on; I needed about thirty gallons of paint. Every weekend, my wife and I would set out on the garage sale trail, looking for paint, spending 50¢ a gallon or $2 for a five-gallon bucket.

We had collected a couple dozen buckets of paint, all of it exterior latex. We needed to paint seven or eight of the uprights (used telephone poles that served as pillars for the outside deck). On top of the telephone poles, we installed 4 × 12 beams, which served as a resting plate for our floor joists. We bought a large truckload of 2 × 8s, mostly sixteen feet long, for $150.

When the outside deck was completely framed, it was over nine hundred square feet. It was a very large deck and all the used lumber needed was a coat of paint. First we used a wire brush to brush it down, and then we pressure washed it. After letting the deck dry for two days, we mixed all these buckets of paint together to make one color and wouldn't you know, the color we wound up with exactly matched the gray stucco on the house.

To tell you the truth, it's an awesome thing to be able to rejoice in the small blessings of life. When you add them all up together, you come up with a whole book.

It took us twelve weeks to the day to finish the building project in Alaska. Our meat supply had dwindled over the summer, and I was hoping to get a moose to see us through the winter.

In the area where we lived, the last day of hunting season was September 30. At that time, I was not a seasoned moose hunter, nor did I know the country that I was hoping to hunt. I told myself I would not go hunting until the house was finished. I finished it on September 29.

It had been a hard twelve weeks. At least half of those days, it rained, but I discovered if I could keep my skill saw under a piece of plywood so it wouldn't get wet, I could keep working, even in the rain.

When it rained, I made the little ones stay inside and I told the bigger kids they didn't have to work in the rain. However, they decided on their own to help their Dad. I know many full grown men that were not man enough to work in the rain, but here were four kids, ages 8–17, handing me lumber and finding me different tools I needed. They were learning valuable skills about being a carpenter's helper. Again, I am very proud of my children. They all turned out to be hard workers and very resourceful, with a great ability to make something out of nothing. They discovered hard work would not hurt them. In fact, it can be enjoyable.

✝

CHAPTER 38

Tithing Works

Tithing works, but we must first bring it into the storehouse. Some have a problem figuring out where the storehouse is. I heard about two neighboring preachers once, who decided to pay their tithes to each other. Somehow, I don't think this is the way God intended it.

Back in the Bible days, the storehouse was the place where you obtained food. It seems tithing is the way we acknowledge the source of our spiritual food and seed. You can read more about this in Corinthians 9:7-11.

I've heard it said that tithing is the only way we can acknowledge the sovereignty of God in our life. Way back on day one, man was placed in this beautiful garden God had prepared for him, and there were dozens of different fruits he could eat. Yet, in the middle of the garden sat one tree God told Adam he was not allowed to eat from.

Why was Adam not allowed to eat from this one tree in the middle of the beautiful garden? No doubt it was to remind Adam he really wasn't the owner, but just the caretaker of someone else's property. Later on, Adam would be compelled to tell his friends not to eat from that certain tree, because the owner said not to. When we are born again and ask Christ to come into our lives, we are no longer our own. We have been bought with a price, and we re-enter into the family of God.

Tithing is simply a believer acknowledging the sovereignty of God in his life. In Romans 12:1-2, Paul says, "I urge you, brothers, in view of God's mercy, that you present your bodies as living sacrifices, Holy and acceptable unto God, which is your spiritual act of worship. And be not conformed to this world, but be transformed by the renewing of your mind, that you may prove what is that good and acceptable and perfect will of God."

When I was pastoring in Hungry Horse, my wife went to a ladies convention, which was conducted by a mighty woman of God, Marilyn Hickey. In my opinion, she is one of the greatest expositors and teachers of the Bible of modern times. At that convention, my wife met a lady from Chouteau, Montana, who asked if we would come to their ranch and have home meetings. It was 150 miles away, but we felt God nudging us in that direction.

Her husband, Leif Larson, operated a large wheat and barley farm, and they were hungering and thirsting for the things of God. We taught them about the baptism of the Holy Spirit, divine healing, tithing, and some of the principles of faith.

It was an extremely dry year with very little rain, and Leif asked us to pray because his crops desperately needed the rain. We all joined hands and with faith and believing, asked God to send rain to his farm.

The following day, Leif was visiting with the rancher across the road and told him about the prayer meetings. The rancher laughed at him and said, "You don't really believe you can simply pray and it will rain, do you?" Leif answered, "Yes, I do."

That following week, it rained long and hard. It rained all over Leif's farm and ended at the dirt road that separated the two farms. Half of the dirt road was wet and half was dry. I never heard if the neighbor changed his mind or not, but that would be enough to change my mind about prayer.

It was a great boost of faith to that hardworking Montana wheat farmer. Both Leif and his wife, Elaine, had their own testimony to the miracle they both personally saw God do. Each of us can have our own testimony of what God can do in our lives; and even one revelation from God pays big dividends.

I can promise you this—if you will put Malachi 3:10 into practice, you will watch the following verse (3:11) blossom before your eyes. You will discover that there is a formula for blessings. It is the only place in the Scriptures that God says, "Prove me. Test me and see if I will not open the windows of heaven." God promises to give us a blessing so big that there will not be room enough to receive it.

Blessings do not just come in the form of money. In fact, God's blessings often involve things money can't buy. You may be tempted to say, "I can't afford to pay 10 percent of my gross income to God."

One man asks, "Do I pay my tithe on my net, or on my gross income?" The answer is "It depends on whether you want a gross blessing or a net blessing." I am here to tell you that it does not cost to tithe, it pays. You don't have to pay tithes, you GET to pay tithes. You don't have to breathe either, but they both pay big dividends. Thirty-five percent of Jesus' parables dealt with money and stewardship.

The first couple God ever created was placed as caretakers of a garden that belonged to someone else. They were made stewards by the creator. It seems this subject of ownership interests the Father.

I remember seeing a large black bear a quarter mile off the road on a ranch. Not wanting to trespass without permission, I drove back to the farmhouse and asked permission. There, I was told by the rancher that this was his property and I didn't have his permission to go after the bear. I drove away thinking about the Scripture, "The earth is the Lord's and the fullness there of." The cattle, the silver, and the gold were all created and owned by God.

I truly believe our creator desires us to acknowledge him as the one who made us and has given us everything we own. And that's where the rub comes. A prideful man does not acknowledge God as their Lord and master, and the creator of the entire universe.

Again, tithing is the only way we can truly acknowledge who the true owner is of everything we have. When we pay our tithes, we acknowledge God the father as owner of everything we have, and we are simply the caretaker of somebody else's property. It would take a whole book to explain to you the many facets of tithing and how it works. But let me simply say this—if I had to tell just one hard and fast truth, it is this—tithing works.

I could keep you here all day, telling you true stories of how God has blessed my life. I remember in Bible College,

I went to work for the school, building classrooms for $2 an hour. One evening, after work at the Bible College, I was in the superintendent's office, visiting with Brother Bell, my boss, when I noticed a piece of leftover carpet threshold trim sticking up out of the trash barrel. Just the day before, my wife had told me that the gold carpet going into the kid's room was becoming frayed at the threshold. Using my tape measure, I told my wife I needed some carpet trim that was 27-33/64's of an inch long.

When I ask Brother Bell what he was going to do with the leftover carpet trim, he said it was going to the dump and I could have it if I wanted it. I pulled it out of the barrel and reached in my nail apron for my tape measure.

There in my hand was a brand new piece of gold carpet trim cut squarely at 27-33/64's inches long. Again, it was the hand of God meeting my needs. To some it may seem a small thing, but when you see the big picture—the fact that the carpet was gold and the metal threshold trim was also gold—all these factors were just too much of a coincidence, not to mention that I very seldom went to Brother Bell's office. Could it have been a divine coincidence to boost my faith? I normally worked my own hours and quit whenever I wanted to. But there I was the next day with a piece of leftover gold trim in my hand exactly the length I wanted. No one can ever convince me that this was a coincidence. This was definitely a blessing from God.

✞

CHAPTER 39

Miraculous Provision

I prayed about where to go moose hunting and studied the maps. I knew I didn't have the time or gas to drive very far. On the evening of Sept 29, I chose a place called Hunter Creek, which was about thirty miles from my home.

I arrived there well before daylight on the last day of moose season, and I began to climb up the mountain in the dark. I saw a few moose tracks and a very fresh bear track. I was on a mission. Halfway up the mountain, I ran into some of the thickest brush I have ever seen in my life. The only way to get through it was to crawl on my hands and knees. It was late afternoon by the time I reached the top, and I had not even seen a cow moose; only bulls were legal to shoot.

I sat there looking at this breathtaking view and having myself a prayer meeting. I told the Lord that I needed some help and some divine guidance. I was physically exhausted; I felt like I couldn't take another step.

The past twelve weeks had caught up with me. Right about then, two men came down the ridge behind me. I said hello and we stood there talking for about ten minutes. I told them I had to leave soon since I had only forty-five minutes of daylight left, but that I was on a mission to get a moose to feed my family of eight for the winter. As I turned to leave, my eye caught movement halfway down the mountainside and, sure enough, it was a bull moose. We decided to split up and whoever got a decent shot first should take it. The route I took led me to a sheer cliff. I only had ten minutes left in moose season. I could see the bull chasing a cow, as the rut was in full swing. I was concerned he would disappear in the black timber, never to be seen again. I judged the distance to be five hundred yards, a shot I have made many times while antelope hunting in Montana.

I knew my .300 Winchester Magnum was capable of that shot. Right next to me was a tree with a fork in it, at just the right height for a solid rest for my rifle, which is a must for long distance shooting. I decided it was now or never. If I didn't leave soon, I would never get down the cliff before it got dark. I turned my Leopold variable scope up to six powers and placed the pointed part of my duplex crosshair on the moose's lung and fired one shot. He immediately disappeared out of sight; I knew I only had a little daylight left to go find him. I went around the left side of the cliff and found a place where it was all shale. It was almost like downhill skiing, or like riding an avalanche of shale under your feet at a very steep incline; it is just something we mountainmen do.

I found the bull stone dead. A few minutes later, my two new friends showed up, slapping me on the back, telling me that was the longest shot they had ever seen. I took the opportunity to share with them about Holy Spirit bullets.

They decided they would help me dress the bull. I pulled out my four-inch long jack knife. They both laughed and asked if that was my knife. Then they reached in their backpack and pulled out a sixteen-inch long homemade knife that used to be a chainsaw bar. It was the sharpest thing I had ever seen. In no time, the three of us had the moose dressed out, and quartered up. It would have taken me hours to do it by myself.

We followed each other down the mountain in the pitch-black dark, snapping limbs as we went so I could find my way back the next day. I offered to give them some moose meat, but they declined. It took us about an hour to get on the road. My truck was on the left and they went to the right, where the road came to a deadend; there were no houses in that area at all. I had to walk two miles down that road in the dark to get to my pickup truck. I kept expecting these two men to drive by on their way back to the highway but they never came. I have to admit, I toyed with the idea they were angels. I did notice one of the men was wearing a heavy wool hunting jacket that was red with black plaid on it, the same kind of jacket that a person wore who helped me when I was stuck on another hunting trip in the mountains.

They came along just when I needed help. I'm pretty sure it was one of those divine appointments. I was one happy camper when I got back to the pickup truck.

The next morning my oldest son, Jake, and Tom Cook (who would become my son-in-law in ten years), plus my dear friend, Levy Ratsloft, and I climbed back up to get the moose. Levy and Tom grabbed the two hindquarters, which was a very smart move. Jake grabbed the front quarter, and dear old dad got the other front quarter, head, horns and neck. What a chore dragging that moose down the mountainside. I gave Levy and Tom some moose meat and the rest of it went into my freezers. All I had left to do was cut ten cords of wood and we were set for winter.

Speaking of divine appointments, I can't help but think of an experience I had while I was in the mountains on a hunting trip, forty miles up the south fork of the Flat Head River and ten miles up Sullivan Creek, the same area where I had met and ministered to a grieving father a year earlier. My associate pastor, Lloyd Fine, and Craig Renfro drove up there with me to go elk hunting. We decided to split up and meet at the pickup after dark.

All three of us were seasoned hunters. We hunted best alone. I had gone all day without seeing a thing; I arrived back at the truck a little before dark. Craig was already there, but no Lloyd Fine. We noticed, hanging on the pickup, a plaid shirt all drenched in blood; it was Lloyd's shirt. Our first guess was that Lloyd had shot an elk, gotten all bloody dressing it out, and then had gone back to bring the elk out. I had devised a signal that the Holy Spirit inspired me with. It was our way of communicating. Craig and I heard one shot exactly on the quarter hour. It was Lloyd. He had shot an elk way back in the mountains and needed help. Pretty soon, Lloyd showed up at the truck; even though it was almost dark, we decided to go back and try to retrieve the elk.

All I can say is you do crazy things when you are young. Luckily, the elk was lying on an old logging road, so it was easy to find, even in the dark. Even though the road was full of fallen trees and saplings, it was better than no trail at all. We had no flashlights and no rope. The very best we could do was to have one guy grab an ear, and the other two grab a hoof, and then on the count of three, all pull together. We could only move the bull about two feet at a time. It turned into one of those pitch-black nights where you couldn't see your hand in front of your face, and in the process, Lloyd had poked a stick in his eye.

We stopped right there and prayed. We were exhausted, but we had only moved the bull about a half a mile and it was already after midnight. After we finished praying for Lloyd's eye, I asked God to give us strength to get the elk out of the woods. When I finished praying, I said, "Amen." Lloyd immediately prayed, "Lord, would you please send us light—we can't even see where we are going."

Now, Craig did not even go to church. His wife and kids would go without him. When Lloyd made his request for light, Craig turned to Lloyd and said, "You're asking for a little much, aren't you? We're fifty miles into the mountains and two miles from the nearest road." Lloyd simply said, "I believe in miracles." We talked for a few minutes and then we decided we would pull on the elk some more, but after a couple of tries, I could see it was getting harder and harder.

Just then, I heard a noise and some muffled sounds that were coming from down below us. We thought it was a grizzly bear that had smelled our kill and it was coming to take it away from us. We braced ourselves for the worst, but then we heard human voices. We yelled, "Hey, up here, we need help!" And wouldn't you know it, they shined a flashlight in our direction. Craig looked at Lloyd and told him he would believe anything that he told him after that.

Four grown men showed up with four flashlights and two pieces of rope. They were out looking for a friend who was lost. They had given up looking and were on their way back to their camp. I shared with them my invention involving a single shot exactly on the quarter hour; they liked it.

To make a long story short, we tied the rope around the elk's head, and with all seven of us pulling on the rope, the elk slid out of there like a log behind a team of horses. We were at the pickup in no time. We shared with them how we had prayed and asked God for a light. The men agreed that prayer changes things, and in my mind, it was a divine appointment, just like many others I have had.

✞

CHAPTER 40

Wilderness Angels

Alaska is a very big state, three times the size of Texas—two thousand miles from one corner to the other; 99 and 19/20ths percent of Alaska is completely unaltered by man. In other words, all the private property, all the towns and the cities, roads and railroads, trails and power lines, make up 1/20th of 1 percent of Alaska.

The population of the whole state is a little over 600,000. It seems like half of that population is made up of hunters and fisherman, so what few roads there are, those are the areas that are hunted a lot.

My friend, Kurt West, introduced me to the idea of making a mud buggy. Kurt is one of those guys who can make something out of nothing. Joined with the fact that he was a master mechanic and could fabricate his own designs, it was amazing how efficient the transportation was he invented for getting around in the deep interior of Alaska.

My oldest son, Jake, and I decided to try our hand at building a mud buggy. I bought a one ton, four-wheel-drive 1967 Dodge extended cab pickup. We took the box off, the cab off, and the front clip off, and began welding our own frame on it for a cab. To this, we bolted one-half-inch plywood for the floors, walls, and ceiling. We used wood so it would be as light as possible. We also mounted three thirty gallon gas tanks to it. We made the windshield out of a rear side window from a Chevy suburban. We bolted a bench seat behind the steering wheel and built another bench seat behind that, which converted into a very comfortable bed.

We could haul six people inside the cab of the buggy. Where the cab bolted onto the frame, we ran the bolts through hockey pucks to cut down the vibration. In front of the radiator, we built an elaborate heavy-duty screen system to protect the radiator from sticks and brush. We found a piece of drilling pipe which was two inches across and extremely strong, so we used it for our front and rear bumper.

Then we mounted an eight thousand pound winch on the front with one hundred feet of cable and an eight thousand pound on the back. We welded a small frame on the back (four feet by six feet) for a box to haul cargo. Then we put forty-four inch tractor tires on the front and back that were eighteen inches wide. We had a roof rack on the top that was ten inches high. We utilized the entire roof for cargo. Next, we bought a tandem axle trailer, put new tires on it, and built heavy duty fenders that we could drive over.

There were seven of us on our maiden voyage. Forty miles back off the road, we found moose everywhere. The first day we were there, we shot two bull moose five minutes apart. The next two days, we shot two more bulls, and then we decided that we had better quit if we wanted to drive back out. I can't tell you how much four bull moose and seven men weigh, but it was all the mud buggy could handle.

We got stuck a dozen times, but with that many men to help, we did manage to get back out. I say all this to tell you a true story that happened the following year.

Just two of us went in on the same trail and shot two moose and we were on our way back out. Now, this forty-mile trail had about a half dozen bad spots; the worst of the worst we named Jericho Slew, after my youngest daughter, Jericho.

We were trying to cross Jericho Slew when we slipped into a black hole that had no bottom to it. The buggy was tilted at almost a 45 degree angle and the more we rocked it back and forth, the deeper it got. The two of us had worked two hours straight to get unstuck, but to no avail.

I was beginning to consider a twenty mile walk to go get help. Those twenty miles had no sidewalks or even a gravel road. It was a muddy trail, often with water up past your knees, and mudholes as deep as four feet.

I was discouraged and prayed the Lord would give me strength because I was so exhausted. Just then, two men walked up. Both men looked like they were in their thirties; they asked if I needed any help. With a bit of encouragement in my voice, I told them I certainly could use some help and I would be very obliged for any assistance that they could give us.

These two men worked like slaves for five hours, but they didn't seem to get muddy. I didn't think much about it at the time. Two tires of the buggy were completely under mud and water, and two tires were completely out. It was a very precarious situation. We managed to get some logs under the tires so we could finish winching ourselves out. I offered these two guys some food and something to drink but they said they were fine. All the time they worked, they seemed to enjoy what they were doing. Neither one of them smoked or used bad language. During the course of the project, my friend took a picture of me and these two guys. (I since have had it blown up to an 8 x 10 picture.)

Finally, with the help we received, we were able to get the buggy unstuck. By then it was dark, and I didn't want to try to make the rest of the journey without daylight, even though I had a dozen lights I could use to see the trail. The swamps were very hard to read in the dark, and I was physically exhausted. We had our sleeping bags, so we just folded the seats down and decided to leave in the morning after a good night's sleep.

The two guys said that they needed to get back; I didn't think of it then, but back to where? We were twenty miles from the nearest road. They simply replied "We're glad we could help you get out, nice to meet you, God Bless," and walked away.

I listened and listened, but I heard no four-wheeler, no mud buggy, or no helicopter. Where had they come from? After five hours of hard work, they didn't want anything to drink and wouldn't even take a sandwich or a candy bar. I was covered with mud from head to toe; I had to take a bath in the swamp. I changed into some dry clothes, yet these two guys were barely dirty. In my opinion, I had been visited by two angels. They were always laughing, never got tired, didn't even get thirsty after five hours of hard work, didn't even want a Snickers bar—they did not even seem human. They came and went out of nowhere!

There were no houses or cabins in that part of the country and nobody in their right mind would try to walk out of there after dark, not in twenty miles of wilderness and swamp. The swamp we were in was six miles long. There is no other creditable explanation; God had sent two angels to help me. I have shown their picture around the closest towns, but nobody had ever seen them before.

I would like to make an observation. One of these men had on a red plaid hunting jacket, boots that went up to his knees, and funny-looking pants. I remember a pastor named John Weaver, back in Montana, who was elk hunting in the mountains near the Ruby River, when a man walked up to him and said, "Hello John," and he began to talk to John about things that John was sure that only he and God knew about. Then he began to tell John about things that were going to happen in the future.

John was amazed at the wisdom of this man walking around in the mountains, carrying no gun. As he said goodbye and turned to leave, John noticed that the man left no tracks in the two feet of fresh snow and he was wearing a hunter's red plaid coat, boots that went up to his knees, wearing what John described as funny-looking pants.

My good friend, John Weaver, whom I have known for many years, rates in the top 5 percent of all the people I have met in my lifetime who has great credibility. There is not one trace of doubt in my mind that John met an angel that day in the middle of hunting season, deep in the mountains, not carrying a gun.

Neither one of these two men that I met carried a gun or a backpack, and one of them was dressed in the exact same way that John's angel was dressed 25 years earlier. That's my angel story and I'm sticking to it. I don't think anybody will ever convince me otherwise. If you want to see a picture of two angels, just give me a call. *Jehovah Jira is my provider, his grace is sufficient for me. Amen.*

✝

CHAPTER 41

Family

To some, Sunday school may seem like a little thing, and maybe the teachers that teach our children don't have degrees, but I believe if you will give your time faithfully to God every Sunday morning, God will bless you for it. It takes time and effort to get seven kids out of bed, fed, dressed, and loaded in the car 52 Sunday mornings a year. God will smile on you and you will be positioning yourself, not only to receive blessings from the Lord, but to be a blessing to the Lord.

As I said before, my adopted Christian parents, the Brimmers, taught me about being faithful in attending God's house three times a week, come rain, sleet, snow, or hail. And in turn, I don't think my seven children have missed going to church more than a half dozen Sundays the entire time they were growing up. To make it to church, we often drove through deep snow and icy roads. It took a lot of planning and preparation to get seven children ready for church, but most of all, it took resolve and "want to."

No one ever asked if we were going to church. The MacDonald family always attended Sunday school; it was our way of life. In the New Testament we read that Jesus went to the synagogue on the Sabbath Day as was his custom.

Another thing we did was send our kids to Bible camp. Some of the most powerful services I have ever attended were at camp meetings. I remember one year, I was drafted to be a Bible camp kid's counselor. There were two of us in charge of thirty kids, ages nine to twelve. The first day did not go well; they were very rowdy and unruly.

At the counselor's meeting, I told the staff about our problem. They asked me if I had any ideas and I told them I did. I told them that we would like to create an atmosphere of a military boot camp for our group. The other pastor that was working with me was an ex-airborne ranger, so he liked the idea.

Breakfast was at seven, so at six o'clock, we threw on the lights and started yelling, "Get up, get up." We got them all dressed and stood them in line out on the road, and away we went on an early morning run. It was a touch of boot camp all right. Some of them thought they were going to die. Once we assured them that we were the bosses and wouldn't take no for an answer, things went very smoothly. Some of them had to do extra pushups, but it proved to be an anointed idea by the end of the week. Our kids would sit through the service and were much more attentive than the other groups.

Our dorm was the first to attend chapel in the morning and the last to leave. There is nothing like seeing a ten-year-old praying and touching God. Night after night, they would fill the altars; many were saved and their life showed it. Dozens were filled with the Holy Spirit and spoke fluently in another language that they had never spoken before, and some said that they felt called to the ministry.

I think if we had been soft with their misbehavior that first day, they would have talked and laughed and punched each other throughout the week; they knew if they did that, it would be extra pushups.

I later received several letters from parents, thanking me for counseling their child. The report they got was that the counselors were really hard on them. "They made us do exercises every morning and go on long runs, and every day we had to clean the dorms until they were spotless," but every single child also told their parents it was a lot of fun and they couldn't wait to go back next year.

Several parents told me they saw a great change in their child for the better. I wrote the parents back and said the natural order of things will produce good fruit every time. By that, I mean the mother and the father are suppose to rule their children and not the other way around. That first day of Bible camp was sheer chaos. When you told the kids to do something, they looked at you like they had never been told to do something in their lives. When John and I let them know that we were the bosses, they accepted it, and things began to improve.

Kids growing up these days are not stupid; they have made manipulating their parents a sophisticated science. There's a lot to be said about the natural order of things. I like what Wayne Jensen, a friend of mine, said. He told me his family lives by the golden rule: he who has the gold, rules. Parents, teach your children to be respectful and obedient at an early age.

In many homes today, our youth have become way out of control. Last week on the news, I heard of an eleven-year-old boy stabbing his twelve-year-old brother in the chest with a knife during an argument over which channel to watch on TV. What I am about to present to you is time-tested and it works, if you will do it right. It probably won't work if you only do it half-right. It involves the father, if at all possible, to instill family values in these very young children.

Let me share with you something I have proven to work for me. It started out when my daughter, Lori, was nine months old, and she didn't want to go to sleep at night. She wasn't sick, her diaper was dry, and her tummy was full. She wasn't cold or hot, she was just testing the waters.

I was stationed at Quantico, Virginia at the time, training second lieutenants on how to survive in the jungles of Vietnam. It was a very demanding and exhausting job, and having a child keep me up all night was not an option.

I told Lori Joy to go night-night, but she kept fussing. I told her again, telling her what the consequences would be. Still, she kept fussing, so I rolled up a newspaper, and I went in and started spanking on her crib, hitting the wall with the newspaper, all the while saying "Lori Joy go night-night right now." I never once hurt my child, but she got the message that I really meant what I said.

With Lori Joy, it took two different episodes; with my other six children, it only took one run-in for some of them. I got so I would even plan the so-called *run-in with dad*. It was usually when the kids were around 10 or 11 months old when I would put a rolled-up newspaper by their bed, with stuffed animals that I could throw on the floor for more drama, and different things that would make a lot of noise when hit with a newspaper, but each and every time we performed this initiation scene, the reaction was always the same. During the initiation process, they were not allowed to stand up in their crib.

Yes, it was a bad scene and I did not enjoy it, but listen carefully to what I have to say next. Every night after that, when they would fuss and not go to sleep, all I had to do was say in a stern voice, and here I want to emphasis the *stern voice*. At first it may have to be louder than usual, but later on down the road, you can convert it into a stern look. I called them by name, and would say "go night-night," and once in a while I would have to speak to them twice. I did not have to speak a second time to them very often.

Seven children in 29 years, and never once did any one of them ever talk back to their parents. When they were told to do something, they did it. Never once did I ever hear a swear word out of any of my kids. They knew what their mother and father expected out of them, and that is simply the way it would be.

Even as teenagers, they would obey their parents, and in my opinion, I had seven wonderful kids who I am extremely proud of. I really believe the early family initiation laid a strong foundation for those kids to build a lifestyle on. There is a saying that goes like this: you cannot argue with success, but I know Dr. Spock would disagree with my family tradition.

The reason my traditional "run-in with dad" episode worked so well is because the Word of God works. Proverbs 22:6: "Train up a child in the way he should go and when he is old he will not depart from it." Proverbs 13:24 says, "He that spares his rod hates his son, but he that loves him disciplines him diligently." Do not reject the discipline of the Lord or be weary of his correction, for whom the Lord loves, he reproves; even as a father corrects the son in whom he delights." It is obvious the Lord wants us to teach our children discipline and He teaches us how in His Word. I cannot emphasize enough—the word works—that's why my system works. I am not bragging on me as a father. I am bragging on my heavenly Father.

Please don't misunderstand me and think I am telling you I was the picture-perfect parent, because I wasn't. I do want you to understand when Christ comes into your heart, God's blessing comes with it and that one blessing (the Bible teaches) can flow to thousands of generations.

Just the opposite is true if we refuse to serve God. The Scripture teaches us our children can have a curse on them for up to four generations. Perhaps you are thinking to yourself, does Jack believe in curses? I would have to say to you that I do, because the Bible teaches we can have spiritual and physical curses that can be passed down from generation to generation in our family.

A good example of this is King Ahab and his wife, Jezebel, two very evil people. If you will take the time to study the life of their daughter, you will soon find out she was even more evil than her parents. No doubt, a generational curse was handed down to her by her parents. It could have been broken by calling on the Lord, but that didn't happen. Read about it yourself in the last half of the first book of Kings.

I believe in curses—in Deuteronomy 30:19, it says "I call heaven and earth to record this day against you, that I have set before you life and death, blessing and cursing: therefore choose life, that both thou and thy seed (children) may live;" Verse 20 is what this book is about. "Thou may love the Lord thy God, and thou may obey his voice." So we see there is a choice between two opposites, blessing or cursing, life or death. The Bible encourages us to choose life and blessing. Right now, today, there is an election going on. Will you vote for the way of life? If you do, it will flow down on your family.

In Deuteronomy 29:29, it says "The secret things belong to the Lord, but those things that are revealed belong to us and our children." One of the things revealed to us is that when Christ died on the cross, "he bore all our pain, he carried our sorrows, he was bruised for our iniquities, and the chastisement of our peace was upon him and with his stripes we are healed" (Isaiah 53:5).

There is an amazing story of a girl who was born crippled, laid in bed for fifteen years, and got worse and worse. One day, Jesus came into her room, bent over, and looked her in the eyes. At that moment, she felt her spine move, and for the first time in her life, she got out of bed and walked. Scripture says, "with his stripes, we are healed."

I could easily talk about divine healing here, and go on for another four hundred pages, but the point that I want you to understand is this. When Jesus died on the cross, He broke the curse. He made many, many things available to us. Salvation and healing are at the top of this list, but I want to explain to you that we can have a godly family legacy because of what Jesus did on the cross.

In my family tree, diabetes is more than evident. My grandfather, my grandmother, my Uncle Albert, and Uncle Jack all died losing one limb at a time from diabetes. I truly believe that when I got saved at the age of sixteen, that curse was broken. I purposely have been tested dozens and dozens of times in the past forty-six years. There is no trace of diabetes in my life or in any of my seven children's lives, or any of my twelve grandchildren's lives.

What a deal God offers us. You, too, can be under this blessing. It is not just spiritual, but financial and physical as well. The Bible says God will quicken our mortal body here on earth today. This provision comes through Christ, who has set us free from the curse. In Isaiah 54:13-14, it teaches us that all our children shall be taught of the Holy Spirit and great shall be their peace. In righteousness, they shall be established and shall be far from oppression; they shall not fear and terror will be far from them.

✞

CHAPTER 42

Slave Labor

I have always taught my kids to work. It was something I learned at a young age and I believe it to be a good thing. I have heard it said that we have a generation of laziness. Young people today not only boast about being a couch potato, but they are proud of it. I wonder if some of our kids actually think that work will hurt them. I heard a story about a girl going on a date, and she asked this young man, who was in his mid-20s, what he did for a living. He told her he did nothing but stay at home and watch TV. Then he told her he didn't have any money. (I can't imagine why, except maybe he was hinting for her to pay for the date.)

If I were asked to give a piece of advice to a young person seeking a date, the first thing I would say is to seek a born-again Christian. If you are a born-again Christian and seeking a date, allow me to offer a few guidelines. If they don't have a job, forget it. If they drink or smoke or do drugs, forget it. You may think that sounds a little strong, but I promise you, you won't regret it.

I raised my children to be workers. There were many things on my child rearing list that I felt were super important, and not being afraid to work was one of them. I really believe that hard work builds character.

For several years, we heated our home with wood. One year I gathered several hundred lodgepole pine trees in eight to twelve foot lengths. They were six to eight inches in diameter. I threw them in a big pile behind the house, handed my son a double-bladed axe, told him to chop them up in sixteen-inch lengths, and then stack the pieces against the house for firewood.

My creative son, Jake, who, by the age of twelve, was already showing muscles in his biceps, told some of his friends that they could get muscles too. He invited them over to the house to work on their muscles by chopping wood. The next thing I knew, we had a wood-chopping contest out behind the house.

I have never seen ten cords of wood cut by hand so fast in my life, but the plot thickens. They stacked the wood up against the house six feet tall and seventy feet long. The pieces that you could see sticking out had a point on them. It looked like the log had been chewed down by a beaver.

One day, a friend and I were in the backyard and he said, "Look at all that firewood. How did you get it all to be pointed like that?" I told him I had a pet beaver and I put a little salt every sixteen inches on a log, and I trained him to chew the log in firewood lengths for me.

The guy said that this was the most amazing story he had ever heard. He wanted to know how I had caught the beaver. When I realized that this guy believed me, I laughed until I cried. He could not figure out why I was laughing. Then I showed him how the wood was cut with the axe, not with beaver teeth.

We finally graduated from an axe to a chain saw. After dinner each night, I told my second daughter, Scottie Beth, to get her crew together and fill up the wood box, which was about five feet long, three feet wide, and three feet deep. When it was cold, one box only lasted about a day. It was our only source of heat. I have to smile every time I remember ten-year-old Scottie Beth asking me, "Daddy, why does it have to be my crew?" I told her it was because she was a leader. And she is.

She'd get a trail of kids carrying in firewood; her older brother, Jake, would go out with them. He'd split the chunks of wood into pieces about the size of a loaf of bread, and the younger kids carried them in. It was rather funny to see four-year-old Dave, all bundled up in his snowsuit, carrying one small piece of firewood. Usually the firewood would be about the size of a roll of saran wrap, but he was a part of the crew at age four.

Dave is twenty-six now, and he has been installing chainlink fence for about five years. His boss tells me he is the hardest working employee he has ever seen. When I ask Dave how the job is going, he tells me he loves what he is doing, even though it is very hard work.

All four of my girls are hard workers, very resourceful, and successful. They have five or six college degrees between them; they make a father very proud. My point is I think that hard work is good for a kid.

My friend, Pat Lamb, tells the story of when he was a young boy. If he was sick and stayed home from school, his father's remedy for being sick was splitting wood. If you stayed home from school, you were out splitting wood. Pat is now one of the hardest working, successful guys I know.

In Alaska, wild meat was our staple. Every year we would shoot a moose, which weighed well over one thousand pounds. We would quarter the moose and hang it up in the barn. After it hung there for about a week or so, depending on the weather, we would pick a Saturday and finish butchering it.

Jake and I would skin the quarters and then place a piece of plywood on the tailgate of the pickup so we could debone the rest of the meat. We had three big pans, one for steaks, one for roasts, and one for hamburger meat.

A couple of the kids would carry the pans into the garage where there was an assembly line. One kid would scrape it, and then throw it on a piece of saran wrap where it was tightly wrapped. We would then put it on a piece of freezer paper, where it was tightly wrapped again and firmly taped.

Another kid would label it with the year it was wrapped and then initial it, MS for moose steak or MR for moose roast. We ground our own hamburger with 10 percent beef suet. These packages would be labeled MH for moose hamburger.

Another person would have the job of packing the meat in the freezer. We would keep two extra freezers in the garage and one large freezer in the shop. We would always share our bounty with our neighbors.

I can promise you this; if you will put these next two verses into practice, you will discover the formula for blessings. Malachi 3:10 says, "Bring the whole tithe into the storehouse, that there may be food in my house. Test me in this says the Lord God Almighty, and see if I will not throw open the floodgates of heaven, and pour out so much blessing, that you will not have room enough to receive it." Verse 11 says, "And I will prevent pests from devouring your crops, and the vine in your fields shall not destroy the fruits before the time in the field, says the Lord of hosts."

I know that I have brought the subject of tithing up several times in this book and perhaps you are asking, what does this have to do with obeying the voice of God? First, it will increase your ability to perceive God's voice if you are a mature Christian. I have never seen a mature Christian who didn't tithe.

Second, obeying the voice of God involves revelation and I would like you to write this next statement down in the margin of your Bible. (If your Bible is too expensive to write in, I suggest giving it to someone else and buying yourself a less expensive one that you can write in.) Perhaps you would like to write these words with a red pen—revelation from the Holy Spirit is increased when you tithe to God.

✝

CHAPTER 43

Why the Church?

I brought in 99 percent of the family's income; my wife would babysit once in a while and often she would work in the church for free. She worked hard in the home, cooking, sewing, and keeping that big tribe clean, which was a full time job in itself.

I knew a man who said to his father-in-law, "We just can't make it on one income." The father-in-law said to him, "I guess you need to get a second job, then." My opinion is, if we could raise seven children on one blue-collar income, then others could do the same. I do have a word for the parents who read this book; there is no higher calling in the world than to be a mother.

God has placed in her hands a brand new life to mold and to shape, to inspire, and to pray for. I know this is not a popular word in the new millennium, and it's OK if you want to call me old-fashioned. But I can tell you, it worked for me, and it is a real possibility it can work for you, too. It all depends on how resourceful you are.

As a child, watching my mother making a dime when she should have made a dollar, helped me to become resourceful as an adult.

It would do us all well to read again about the life of Susan Wesley. She took large blocks of time out of her day and spent that time one-on-one with each of her 12 children. If mothers would only get back to that, we would see a great improvement in our society. I can't help but think of Brad Baker and his son, Brock. Brock is a teenager, but he is also an anointed man of God. That doesn't just happen, but is a result of godly parents sharing God with their children on a daily basis.

In the Old Testament, there is a book called Ruth, where we see Elimelech and Naomi, leaving the Promised Land and journeying into Egypt with their two sons, Mahlon (which means sick) and Chilion (which means pining). *Why in the world would anyone name their sons sick and pining is beyond me.*

The two boys took wives from the women of the Moab tribe and within ten years, Naomi's husband died and her two sons died; all this quiet woman of God had left were her two daughters-in-law. Naomi made a decision to go back to Bethlehem, so she instructed her two daughters-in-law to return to their mother's house. After some debate, one daughter-in-law, Orpah, kissed Naomi and left, but Ruth stayed by Naomi's side. It was Ruth who returned to Bethlehem with Naomi. If only each of us could influence just one person, like Naomi influenced Ruth, even if it takes us ten years or even a lifetime. We need to recognize that this is the will of the Lord.

God is still in the business of crossing our paths with people today that He has ordained to be influenced by us.

We need to be watchful for these people and realize that it won't be every single acquaintance you make.

Naomi and her family left Bethlehem, a place chosen by God, destined for great things. This is the place where David killed Goliath, the place where Jesus was born, a place where wise men experienced a revelation for the son of the living God. Bethlehem means a house of bread and praise.

Naomi and her family soldiered down into Moab, a non-spiritual place, and there they took a family beating. Her husband and two sons all died within ten years in a far country. I wouldn't exactly say that was the blessing of the Lord following them around. God's love is not soft; God's path is great, but it is not easy. Never, ever forget—God is more interested in our character than He is our comfort, and through it all, we are not to despise the chastening of the Lord.

Elimelech and his wife Naomi were trying to better themselves, but they went from bad to worse. Today we have modern-day sojourners that would leave Bethlehem, a place where wise men experienced a revelation of the Christ Child. I have given these people the nickname of church hoppers—they hop from church to church, trying to better themselves and find the perfect church. Perhaps there are some who won't like this name.

Now hear this—if you ever find a perfect church, please do not join it, because then it will no longer be perfect. You are not perfect, I am not perfect; there is no such thing as a perfect church. But as we rub shoulders with our brothers and sisters, we become polished vessels, fit for the master's use.

We must learn to keep our eyes on Jesus, and not on our brothers and sisters or even on the pastor, because man will fail you. Christ is the author and finisher of our faith. What God is saying is find one church that preaches the word of God and worships him in spirit and truth. Be faithful to Sunday school and know that faith and faithfulness go hand in hand.

Jesus himself had a custom, and his custom was this: to go to the synagogue on the Sabbath day. If our children see us being faithful to God's house, they will have a much easier time doing the same later in life when they become adults.

Now the other side of the coin is also true. If they see us hopping from church to church, attending a couple months here and a couple months there, we will be in danger of raising a family of church hoppers. Not only that, the news get worse. After a while, there are no new churches to hop to, and the devil comes along and says, "You really don't need the church. You can pray and study the Bible at home."

The Bible says a threefold cord is not easily broken. This is so important that I want to go slow and try to fully explain. A quality, strong rope is not made up of one big thread, but of many little threads twisted together to make a cord, and then several cords are twisted together to form a rope. The Scripture also says iron sharpens iron, and so man sharpens the countenance of his friend.

Throughout the Scriptures, we see different terms such as "The Family of God," "The Household of Faith," "Brothers and Sisters," "The Church," and, oh yes, let's not forget "The Bride of Christ."

In First Corinthians 12:1, Paul began a very important teaching saying, "Now concerning spiritual gifts brethren, I would not have you ignorant." It seems God has designed the church as a place of education and a place of on-the-job training so we can experience supernatural happenings as well as the operation of spiritual gifts in our lives.

A whole book could be written on the extreme importance of being active in the Household of Faith; 85 percent of the people who find Christ are sixteen and under. I would dare say 95 percent of those young people got saved in some sort of a Gospel meeting, no doubt largely in Sunday school.

There are thousands of lessons to be learned about being a member of the body of Christ. And there is no better way to learn them than to sink your roots in one church and allow yourself to be fed, watered, stretched, and pruned. This is the way we become fruitful Christians, which is the will of God for our lives. I strongly suggest that this is a key ingredient in poising yourselves toward hearing and obeying the voice of God.

Satan specializes in half truths, and this can confuse us easily if we are not careful. He tried to tell Jesus to cast himself off the cliff, because the Scripture says, "God will give angels charge over you." But Christ answered with some additional scripture, "Thou shall not tempt the Lord thy God."

It is true that we can pray and study our Bibles at home, every day, and we should. But that is not meant to take the place of being fitly joined together to the body of Christ. Put down your roots (in a church) and stay there. Hard times will come, but they are designed to make you strong.

Naomi and her family didn't intend to stay in Moab; they just wanted to travel around for a while. Sometimes people want to leave the things of God and drift around for a week or two, or even a year or two and not shoulder any responsibility. We must find our place in the body of Christ and be jointly fitted together (just like one bone fits into another bone) if we are ever to become an exceedingly great army.

If you insist on going to Moab, the devil will give you plenty of reasons to go. Be warned, your sons may marry heathen wives and you too could take a whipping in a far country and experience a time of hardship and testing.

We read about the children of Israel wandering around in the wilderness, visiting place after place with names of no consequence. The Israelites already had their marching orders, but they constantly broke them.

The church has their marching orders. They are to take the Gospel to the entire world and that doesn't necessarily mean that we have to travel to Africa. Sometimes the mission field can be as close as your next door neighbor.

God is still giving directives to his church today for us to follow. For forty years the children of Israel wandered aimlessly, visiting place after place with names we can't pronounce; they were of little or no consequence. But once they crossed into the Promised Land they began to visit exciting places like Jericho, Jerusalem, and Bethlehem—places full of excitement, history, and victory.

Ruth saw something in Naomi's life that she wanted to have and she made a decision to go back to Bethlehem with her mother-in-law, and she even said "Your people will be my people and your God will be my God," and from that point on, Ruth began a very exciting journey.

What does your daughter-in-law see in your life? How does she see you handling hard problems? Do you blame

God for hardships or do you see God's hand shaping your life.

Naomi inspired Ruth to go to a place where she found a kinsman redeemer. If you will read Ruth 1, you will see the scriptural foundation for this teaching and it will act as a springboard to help you understand the ways of the Lord.

I read once that the hand that rocks the cradle rules the world, and in my opinion, there are few things on earth more powerful than a godly mother raising her children for Jesus. Give credit where credit is due to the many Christian homes that have led their children in the ways of the Lord.

I think of my pastor, Tommy Barnett, at Phoenix First Assembly Church; all three of his children are working for the Lord. The list goes on and on; each of us could name families that are glowing examples of a Christian home. There is a saying that goes like this: you can't argue with success.

✞

CHAPTER 44

Sunday School

I have met some unsaved parents in my day that left me scratching my head. I would go to their house and tell them personally about our Sunday school program and what it has to offer. Then I would invite them and their children to come. I would even stop by Sunday morning and give them a ride if need be. The part that baffles me is that these adults would actually ask a six- or seven-year-old if they wanted to go to Sunday school. Part of the time, the child would say they didn't want to go and that would be the final say-so.

Often, I would drive away wondering if the parents left it up to the child whether or not the child wanted to go to grade school, or whether or not they wanted to take a bath. Or, did the child decide whether or not he wanted to play in the middle of the road?

There is nobody in the world that can dispute the great benefit of a Sunday school education. It is more than being entertained by puppets. Sunday school teaches a child the Scriptures, things like the Ten Commandments, foundational stones that this whole country was established on. But the greatest benefit was brought to my attention back in East Greenville, Pennsylvania, where Reverend Mayeski was the pastor.

He hosted a group called *The Sunday School Caravan,* which brought fresh statistics from the Assembly of God headquarters in Springfield, Missouri. Here it is, thirty-eight years later, and I still remember this interesting fact. 85 percent of the people that get saved, born again, and experience a revelation of Jesus Christ in their life, do so at age sixteen and under, and the lion's share of those kids find Christ in Sunday school, and, oh yes, did I mention that it was free, no tuition.

I have seven children of my own and I honestly think I can count on one hand the number of times they missed Sunday school in twenty-nine years. On Sunday night and Wednesday night, we would take our small children with us and camp them out on a blanket on the floor between the pews.

They were taught to play quietly with some quiet toys. I don't ever remember any screaming or fighting, and maybe once a year we had to take them out of the service. I am very proud of my children. They learned at a very young age to mind, and now that they are adults, they tell me that I had a way of looking at them, and they knew by that look that it was time to be quiet and good.

Now this wasn't true for just one or two of our children, but for all seven. I very rarely had to spank any of them. I do remember on one rare occasion I was going to spank my oldest son, Jake, who was then about four or five. In the middle of the spanking, he cried out, "Lord God of Israel, please deliver me."

He had learned about David being delivered out of the hands of Goliath and King Saul. He had learned about the children of Israel being delivered out of Egypt and Daniel delivered out of the lion's den.

Well, I am here to tell you, it is hard to spank a kid when he is praying prayers like that. So you see, kids, it pays to go to Sunday school, and I have a word for you parents. Do not send those kids to Sunday school; get out of that bed and take them, and if by chance you have an extra space in your car, find a neighbor kid that will go with you.

I cannot say enough about Sunday school. But let me give you a personal prophecy. It is absolutely God's will for you to take your family to Sunday school next Sunday morning and if you will do that, you will reap great benefits, not only in this life, but in the next one also.

I remember while I was in Bible College, I was watching my two oldest children while my wife took piano lessons. I was in the back part of our 14x70 mobile home doing homework and my two oldest children, then ages three and four, were playing in the living room.

They were being rather quiet so I thought I would go check on them. As I peaked around the corner I saw a sight that I shall never forget as long as I live.

There was Jake, age three, kneeling at a footstool, head bowed, hands folded, and my daughter, Lori Joy, age four, standing over him, one hand on his head, and one hand in the air, saying, "Jesus, come into Jake's heart, forgive him of his sins, and heal his body. Amen."

That scene touched my heart. These two little kids were playing church. Lori was the preacher and Jake was the sinner; come to think of it, they had it pretty close to being right.

It is a lot of hard work raising a large family, a lot of sweat and a lot of tears, not to mention ten million sandwiches. Every once in a while kids will do the funniest things that will force you to smile and simply forget a multitude of sins. For example, one night it was time to tuck my youngest son Mathew into bed, and it was his custom that he had to have a story read to him before he went to sleep.

Usually there is a stack of books a foot tall beside his bed, so I grabbed one of the books and read him a story. Ten minutes later after I finished, four-year-old Mathew says to me, "Dad, that was a great story. I really liked it. Would you please read me another one?" How do you say no to a four-year-old that says please? So I said OK. I had just closed the book after reading book number two, and Mathew says to me, "I really liked that story, Dad. That was better than the first one. That was a great story. Could you read me one more?" I said, "Mathew, it is time to go night-night." Mathew said, "I know Dad, but I have been good, and I really like it when you read me stories."

After much debate I said, "OK, but this is the last story." So I read him the shortest story that I could find, and again he said to me, "Dad, that was a great story, I really liked it. You are a good story reader; could you read me just one more story? I promise to be good and I will go right to sleep." I said, "Mathew, you little bird (Mathew's nickname), I have already read you three stories and Dad is tired and needs to go night-night, too," so I tucked him in. We said our little prayers and Mathew asked me, "How about just one more story, Dad?" I told him "No, Dad is going to bed."

I kissed him good night and turned the light off and said, "Good night, Daddy will see you in the morning." I had no more than shut the door and I heard him say in a very loud voice, "OK fine, I will read my own story. " In an extra loud voice, I heard, "ONCE UPON A TIME, IN A FAR AWAY LAND, LIVED A LITTLE BOY IN A BIG RED HOUSE. I went to my room and I laughed until I cried.

My kids have always been the joy of my life. One time, my sixteen-year-old daughter, Charity, who was one of the most beautiful teenagers that you have ever laid eyes on, with hair down to her waist, decided that she wanted to go deer hunting with me. I called a friend of mine, named Wayne Jensen, and together we made arrangements to go out on a hunting trip in his brother's forty-foot boat out of Cordova, Alaska.

Two hours before we were to leave to catch the ferry, Wayne called and canceled; we went on by ourselves. Once in Cordova, Skip Jensen had us load our gear on the boat. We were getting ready to set sail and I heard him talking on the telephone to his seventeen-year-old son, trying to get him to go hunting with us, but to no avail. Finally Skip said, "OK, we will just have fun without you, and by the way, would you bring me a gallon of milk? I forgot and left it in the refrigerator."

Five minutes later, his son showed up with a gallon of milk, took one look at my daughter, Charity, and told his father that he would be right back. Ten minutes later he showed up with a sleeping bag and decided that he would go hunting with us after all. I did notice that he had forgotten his rifle. I can't imagine what changed his mind so fast.

I am very proud of my daughter, Charity. She took first place in the statewide Home Economics sewing contest her freshman, sophomore, and junior years. We are talking three-time state champion. In her senior year, she made a western shirt with hand-sewn sequins. She remade it several times until it was flawless, but she took second place that year. A boy won first place for making a pair of sweatpants. Perhaps they were trying to encourage boys to take Home Economics.

Once we took the family to Seattle on a little mini vacation. As Jake and I walked on one of the docks, a panhandler asked us for money. He was dressed in some of the dirtiest clothes I have ever seen and his breath smelled like a brewery. I asked the man if it was alright if I told him about Jesus.

When he agreed, the three of us sat down on a bench. I explained to him how God loved him and that Christ died for him on the cross, and about the brand new life that awaited him if he would surrender his heart to Christ.

Then I turned to my son, Jake, who was nine years old at that time, and I asked if he had anything he would like to add. The next words that I heard made my mouth fall open. Jake preached a nine-year-old version of Jesus' dying on the cross and how the blood of Jesus could wash away his sins, and if he would accept Jesus as his Savior, he could go to heaven.

And then my nine-year-old son led this man in the sinner's prayer. As this man prayed, tears ran down his face. I really think that Jake's sermon got through to him.

As I walked back to the car with my hand on Jake's shoulder, I told him how very proud I was of him. Where do you think these kids got the directions to hold divine healing services in the living room, kneeling at a footstool? Where do you think Jake got the words to say to the man on skid row, who was in the midst of throwing his life away? I tell you, it was at Sunday school; Sunday morning worship service; children's church; Sunday night service; listening to people stand up and testify; seeing the gifts of the Holy Spirit in operation; going to church on Wednesday night; Bible camp for a week in the summer; and vacation Bible school in the fall.

This is just one more big reason we all need the church, the Household of Faith; a body of believers to fellowship with, share Scriptures with, and be there when we need somebody to pray for us.

I have often said the greatest calling in the world is to be a mother. Mothers, you have a golden opportunity to influence your young child toward spiritual things. Many times Dad is out working and comes home tired and hungry. Perhaps he does not have the same opportunity that you do. I know he should, but too often in the real world, it is the mother who reads the stories and says the good night prayers.

Mothers, we need another Billy Graham, another Charles Wesley, we need another R.L. Brandt and we are long overdue for another Bob Ross and Tommy Barnett, to mention a few.

And believe me when I tell you, you can give them to us. It will require some of your time, perhaps a lot of your time, but there isn't a shadow of a doubt in my mind that you can do it. Just in case you are earnestly seeking to hear the voice of God and you have not heard him speak to you yet, perhaps I can be of some assistance. One thing the Holy Spirit is saying to you today, loud and clear, is this: Raise your child for Jesus, train a child when he is young, and when he is old, he will not depart from it. *Amen*.

Now I would like to tell you a couple of stories about Sunday school. I was in Hungry Horse, Montana back in the '70s, when I met a Blackfoot Indian named Hank. He was from Browning, Montana, and his wife had just run off and left him with their four-year-old son named Butch.

I met Hank on my daily visitation rounds. He was a broken, broken man. We had some things in common—we both liked to hunt and fish, and we both served in Vietnam at the same time. We didn't talk more than an hour before I led him in the sinner's prayer.

When I went to leave, Hank said to me, "It's the first time in a month that I feel like I have hope." With tears running down his face, he said, "I know now that everything is going to be OK."

Hank started coming to church with his young son, Butch. During our Sunday morning worship service, my wife held children's church downstairs in the basement. She soon found out that Butch was a handful. He would not mind at all, and he was always punching the other kids and walking around disturbing them, being a major distraction. My wife was at her wit's end as to what to do with this unruly four-year-old. We didn't want to tattle to his father for fear that he might get discouraged and not come to church anymore. We prayed earnestly for wisdom on how to handle this little guy.

Now Butch was as cute as a button. He had jet black hair that stuck straight up in the air two inches, with cold, black eyes full of mischief. Whenever you caught him red-handed doing something wrong, and he knew he had been caught, he had this unique way of getting out of trouble. He would look you straight in the eye and come up with this manufactured laugh and say, "Just kidding."

The ladies told me it was impossible to stay mad at him. We had ourselves a dilemma. God must have heard our prayers, because the answer came the following Sunday. Butch was acting up during the puppet show. On one hand, Sister Mac had a bear puppet that had big white teeth and on the other hand was an alligator that also had big white teeth.

It had to have been the Holy Spirit that inspired Sister Mac, because all of sudden the alligator was talking to Butch. He said, "Butch, you better be good. Do you want me to bite you?" And the bear said," Maybe he wants me to bite him too." The ladies told me later that little Butch's eyes got as big as saucers, and he sat there for the rest of the service as good as gold. Now the Scripture says, "If any man lack wisdom let him ask of God, who gives to all men liberally." From that Sunday on, we had no more trouble with Butch.

We prayed for Butch's mother and she did finally come back, and prayed the sinner's prayer with us. But it wasn't very long before something happened and they felt like they needed to move back to Browning where the Indian reservation was. It broke my heart to see them go. I think it was a trick of the devil to get them to move.

I read an article by Bob Munford, and he said something like this: if the devil sees that he can't stand in front of you and stop you, he will get behind you and push and get you going so fast you can't negotiate the curves. And believe me, there are curves in life. I have personally experienced more than a tragic few.

Life seems to be full of twists and turns; many times we need extra wisdom to recognize black ice. (A term you hear up north describing a transparent layer of ice on top of pavement that can be extremely slippery and dangerous. It is hard to distinguish from dry payment.) It takes a trained eye and years of experience to recognize the conditions that cause black ice. As a parent, I taught my children about black ice beginning at a very young age, because in this case, ignorance can be fatal.

So parents, teach your kids what to do in a spiritual emergency. Help them to apply the principles you have read in this book, such as the importance of daily prayer, reading and memorizing the Scriptures, being faithful to God's house, and the importance of going to Sunday school.

If they make $1 at the lemonade stand, teach them to put 10¢ in the offering. Let them see Mom and Dad with their eyes closed and their hands in the air worshipping God, and you will be very blessed when you observe them seeking the Lord on their own.

✝

CHAPTER 45

How to Be a Witness

The last thing Jesus said to his followers before He ascended into heaven is found in Acts 1:8: "But you shall receive power after that the Holy Ghost will come upon you and you shall be witnesses unto me both in Judaea and Smyrna and to the under most parts of the earth."

I know that I have repeated this verse more than once. That's because I want to emphasize the extreme importance of the word, the Holy Spirit and its power, because it is the main source of our ability to be a witness. And we must not lose sight of the great commission that is given to all of us; that is, to spread the Gospel to our next door neighbor, our mailman, the people we work with, and to the whole world.

In case you are wondering what this chapter has to do with obeying the voice of God, which is the theme of this whole book, let me give you a quick summary. There are certain things that we can do to help poise our heart and our soul so that obeying the voice of God comes easier. These are things like tithing; cultivating unity with the brethren; developing a spirit of praise and worship in your heart; maintaining a disciplined life of prayer and fasting; most definitely, being faithful in witnessing to others, not in your own strength, but relying on and trusting the Holy Spirit to give you the ability to be a witness;and last and certainly not least, being faithful in attending God's house, where you hear the word of God preached by a man of God, known as the pastor.

By the way, we all need a pastor. Let me make a quick note here. One of the devil's tricks is to lead you to believe that you don't need a pastor or a home church. This will often lead you to developing an independent spirit, which can strangle the spiritual man.

Listening to Christian TV and radio is a good thing, but according to the Scriptures, they are not meant to take the place of a home church and a pastor. I will share just one of these Scriptures with you that will sum up this thought—Hebrews 10:25 says, "Not forsaking the assembling of ourselves together, as the manner of some is; but exhorting one another: and so much more, as you see the day approaching."

There are many different ways to hear the voice of God and I truly believe one of them is through the voice of a Sunday school teacher and pastor. I want to conclude this chapter by telling you a true story about a young man named Dean Forest, who had a heavy Sunday school and church background.

At age 21, he was attending Rock Pile College in Virginia. (They have changed the name of this college so many times I'm not sure what the name of it is today.) It seems this college brought in a speaker who proclaimed to be an agnostic. Five thousand students came to hear this man, noted for his extremely high education.

He began to speak and said, "I don't know if there is a God or not; some people are dumb enough to believe the blood of Jesus can wash away sins. I don't believe the blood of Jesus can wash away my sins anymore than that water fountain out on this campus can."

At that time, Dean Forest felt the Holy Spirit well up inside him and right in the middle of the guest speaker's message, Dean stood to his feet and began to sing, "There is a fountain filled with blood, drawn from Emanuel's veins and sinners plunge beneath that flood, lose all their guilty stains." Before Dean got to the chorus, the speaker screamed in the microphone, "Someone put that man in a straitjacket, he is crazy." But soon another student stood and joined in the song.

The speaker began to scream at them to stop, but soon five, then ten, and then twenty stood and joined in the second verse. By the time they got to the fourth verse, five thousand students stood to their feet and were singing along with Dean Forest. "For since by faith I saw the stream thy flowing wounds supply."

Five thousand students, some Baptist, some Nazarene, some Missionary Alliance, and some Assembly of God, did that because the blood of Christ had touched their lives. They had no songbook in their hand, they had no choir director, but there they were, five thousand strong, drowning out a speaker who was very much against the things of God.

Finally, the speaker threw up his hands and walked off the stage. Where do you think Dean Forest learned all the words to the old hymn "There is a Fountain Filled with Blood?" I'll tell you where—it was the same place that I learned all four verses by heart, on Sunday morning, Sunday night, and Wednesday night, singing them over and over, hundreds of times. And they never seem to get old. Where do you think Dean Forest and five thousand other Christian students secured such passion for a principle that compelled them to stop a man blaspheming the blood of Christ?

I can tell you from experience, years of Sunday school and church can give a person that kind of passion for a principle. I would love to have been there that day and stood next to Dean with my hands in the air, singing "The dying thief rejoice, to see that fountain in his day, and there may I, though vile is he, wash all my sins away." I wasn't there that day but I can still enjoy the thrill, the excitement, the sense of adventure, and the blessing vicariously.

I am sure I have sat through over five thousand Sunday school lessons and church sermons. I would like to take the time here to thank each and every teacher and pastor for unselfishly sharing their time and energy, sowing the word of God in my life. I don't remember all their names, but God does. Moms and Dads, please don't let your babies grow up without Sunday school. It truly brings them to the place where they can hear the voice of God.

✞

CHAPTER 46

Baptism of the Holy Spirit

One reason it is so important to seek the Baptism of the Holy Spirit (and that is exactly what Jesus is talking about in Acts 1:8) is because we often need supernatural help in witnessing to people and that is exactly what you get—the Holy Spirit of God walking alongside you, lending a helping hand whenever you need it.

The Baptism of the Holy Spirit is often misunderstood, mostly due to the lack of Biblical teaching. I think most people would realize its availability if they would simply read the New Testament. I often wonder if God's people are spending more time reading other books than the Bible, which can prove to be detrimental to your spiritual health. There are many good books out there that will inspire you to push deeper into the things of God, and even motivate you to be a better Christian, but the bottom line is this:

there is no other book given among man that is equal to the divine-inspired word of God.

And we can expect to receive more from memorizing and reading the Bible than we can in any other book. You might ask yourself the question, have I spent more time reading the Bible this week than I have reading a recreational book? Just for fun, you might even keep track of the time and compare it at the end of the week.

It would be difficult to read the book of Acts and not realize the first church experienced this phenomenon called the *Baptism of the Holy Spirit*.

Jesus himself taught it in Acts 1:8 and in the Gospels. We find it stressed in the Epistles and the first church practiced it; surely that is enough to make the Baptism of the Holy Spirit a doctrine for any church.

Reading the New Testament is something we can do on our journey to discovering the deeper things in God. And there *are* deeper things in God. I am not sure if any man has experienced all of them.

In studying the Baptism of the Holy Spirit, we will eventually come to 1 Corinthians 12 where we find nine gifts of the Holy Spirit listed.

Please do not misunderstand me—speaking in tongues, which is evidence of being filled with the Holy Spirit, is not a sign that you have arrived at God's highest level, but it is often called the *kindergarten of gifts*. It can springboard you into many other gifts, but first we must use what God has given us.

You might be sitting there thinking you don't have anything to give to God, but I would suggest to you that you do. For example, your tongue and your voice can be used to give the sacrifice of praise and if you will allow your intellect to take a backseat to the Holy Spirit, your tongue can also be used to speak in a prayer language that you have never studied, which, by the way, is a language that the devil doesn't understand. In addition, this new, exciting language can be used to gain additional faith; it is a good deal for the believer.

When God called Moses to lead Israel out of Egypt, he argued with God and said, "I am not eloquent;" it seemed that Moses stuttered. At one point God ask Moses what he had in his hand and Moses said "a rod," which is little more than a stick four or five feet long. But when God asked Moses to throw it down, that is exactly what he did, and the rod turned into a serpent. I don't know about you, but I think it would be kind of cool to see a rod turn into a snake.

As Moses was obedient in the little act of throwing the rod down on the ground, it was only then that he saw the miracle of the rod turning into the serpent, and we know Moses kept graduating onto bigger and greater things, even the miracle of the Red Sea parting and the entire nation of Israel crossing over onto dry land.

By the way, did you know that some skeptics say that the point where Moses crossed was only knee deep? When I heard that, I said to myself, "If that were really so, it's still a miracle, because that means God drowned the entire Egyptian army in only two feet of water.

Last night at the prayer meeting, we had a man who was complaining about the inconvenience of picking up another brother who needed a ride to church; he even told the man he couldn't do it anymore. The Holy Spirit spoke to him and asked him what was in his hand and his answer was plain and simple—a steering wheel to a pickup truck.

The Scripture says as we are faithful in the little things, God will give us more. Maybe you have only one word in your prayer language or perhaps even two words, but if you will use those words and in doing so, give God your tongue, I assure you, God will give you more. And next you are instructed to pray for the interpretation of your tongue, and so on and so on. God has more gifts for us than we realize.

The natural mind says, in order for me to speak in an unknown language, I must study and practice as required. But in this case, it simply isn't so. God's ways are often contrary to human reasoning, which is evidenced in the anointing of Jessie's youngest son, David, to be the next king.

The prophet Samuel himself, holding the vessel of oil in his hand, knowing he was there to anoint the next king, took one look at Eliab, Jessie's oldest son, and said, "Surely this is the next king." I picture Eliab as one of those tall, muscular, suntanned farm kids with the curly hair and snow-white teeth. But outwards appearances can be deceiving. I would like to have seen Samuel's eyes when the Lord said to him," No, this is not the one I have chosen."

One by one, seven of Jessie's sons passed before Samuel and the voice of God instructed Samuel not to anoint any of them. Eventually Jessie's youngest son, David, was called to present himself in front of the prophet; no doubt David had not had a bath in a week. He appeared to be a very rough farm boy, yet he was the one that God had chosen (1 Samual 16). David being anointed by the prophet Samuel to become the next king was truly contrary to human reasoning. More often than not, the moving of the Holy Spirit will confound the wise.

No doubt the first church did not fully understand what was happening to them on the day of Pentecost, but they simple accepted it by faith as being the very thing that the Lord had promised them. We today not only have the benefit of reading about the Baptism of the Holy Spirit in the New Testament; many of us have personally witnessed the gifts in operation.

On the day of Pentecost, the first church had been in one place and one accord for ten days. I tell you, it takes some real desire to pray and wait on God for ten days. When we seek the Baptism of the Holy Spirit, desire is the key factor. If we are hungry and thirsting after spiritual things, God will not deny us.

I am reminded of a story told by Billy Graham on how the Beatles of England went on a pilgrimage to India, possibly nothing more than a publicity stunt.

They were told that along the banks of the Ganges River they would find elders, known as Holy men, and these elders could tell them how to find God. John Lennon was walking along the shores of the Ganges River. When he came to an older man, John Lennon asked him if he was a man of God and the man replied, "Why do you want to know, son?" Then John replied, "I am one of the Beatles from London and we are here trying to find God. We were told that there were men along this river that could help us on our quest."

As quick as a cat, the old man put John in a whizzer pin and flipped him into the water. No matter how hard he struggled, he could not get free. After a few minutes of thrashing around, John could hold his breath no longer and bubbles began to come up as he exhaled his air. Just as he was about to inhale water and die, the old man brought him up out of the water and he inhaled air and lived. The old man said to him, "Son, when you desire to find God as much as you desired that breath of air that you just took, then you will find Him. And He will be just as real and life-giving as that breath of air was."

Jesus said, "Blessed are they that hunger and thirst after righteousness for they shall be filled"; surely this is one of the secrets of receiving the Baptism of the Holy Spirit.

When Paul talked about spiritual gifts in 1 Corinthians 12:1, he said, "Now concerning spiritual gifts, brothers, I would not have you ignorant." In the original Greek language, the word *ignorant* means *without desire.*

You may be thinking to yourself, what does receiving the Baptism of the Holy Spirit and speaking in tongues have to do with hearing the voice of God? Speaking in tongues is not only designed to be the natural state of a Christian, or should I say the supernatural state, but gives us a wider range of capabilities. One of them is the fine tuning of our spiritual rabbit ears, which helps us to have divine reception. This, in turn, assists us in hearing the voice of God.

God desires to anoint our lives in such a way that we can be witnesses. In Acts 1:8, you will read about the main purposes of receiving the Baptism of the Holy Spirit. Without question God gives us this power (ability) to be an effective witness. It is also an introduction to the many other gifts; for example, the gift of wisdom, faith, words of knowledge (please note this is not the gift of suspicion), the discernment of spirits, miracles, healing, prophetic utterances, the interpretation of tongues, and diverse kinds of tongues. All of these are available to us in the very same way that they were in the early church.

Always remember, we shouldn't feel proud that we are used by the Holy Spirit. In the Bible, we find God using a mule to speak. Now, if God can do that, then He can also use us.

I have listed here nine different gifts that can be called the arsenal of the believer, but keep in mind, one of the greatest gifts that God can give to us is the ability to be changed.

Once you receive your prayer language, God has much more to give you. Please do not feel that you have arrived, because you have only just begun. Not everyone will have a flowing, fluent prayer language. God is a God of variety. If He wasn't, the symphony would have only one note, and pictures would only have one shade of color. Perhaps you only have two words that God has given you for a prayer language. Use what you have, and no doubt, God will give you more later.

I remember taking my car to be worked on by a master mechanic one time, as the problem was too involved for me to solve. As he worked, I got to share with him Acts 1:8. Before the day was done, he and I were kneeling before a couch because he wanted to receive the Baptism of the Holy Spirit and have his very own prayer language.

After about five minutes of prayer, Irvin raised his hands and began to speak one word over and over—the word was *Adoni*. The next day, I was sitting in my office studying, and in the margin of my Schofield Bible was this same word—*Adoni*. It stated its Hebrew meaning, which was *Master*. I thought that was so cool that this non-churched man would receive a language from God and the very next day, I would receive its meaning. Talk about divine appointments.

There are 25 different gifts listed in the New Testament and every person that has been saved has at least one. The gift of righteousness and the gift of eternal life are two examples of these gifts.

If you want to hear God's voice on a regular basis, surely it will help if you speak his language. Some have asked if you need to speak in tongues to be a Christian. The best answer to that question that I have heard in my forty-six years of knowing God was given by Derrick Prince, as I mentioned in an earlier chapter: Can an elephant be an elephant without a trunk? The answer is yes, but he is very limited and destined to be anemic, not as well fed as the other elephants that have trunks.

In Acts 19, Paul was traveling through Ephesus and there he found certain disciples. The first thing he asked them was if they had received the Holy Spirit since they believed. They said, "We haven't even heard whether there is a Holy Spirit."

I would like to make a surprising note here: there are saved men today that haven't heard of the Holy Spirit right here in America.

In Acts 19, Paul asked, "Under what were you baptized?" And they answered, "John's baptism." In verse 6, it says when Paul laid his hands on them, the Holy Spirit came on them and they spoke with other tongues and prophesied.

I remember a sign I saw once in a room where pilots were trained that said, "What you do not know can kill you." This brings to mind a tragic incident that happened in the Atlantic, off the coast of New England. A well known and famous man, who had just received his pilot's license, was flying a very expensive airplane that had all the bells and whistles. He crashed and died when he flew into the ocean. One of the gauges on the airplane told him his exact elevation from sea level. If he would have simply looked at that gauge and realized that he was only a few feet from the water, that tragedy might not have happened.

God has given us a very detailed road map, making his gifts readily available to every believer. Reading and studying the Scriptures are just as important to the believer as reading and taking heed of the gauges on an airplane. What you don't know can be fatal, and the opposite is true as well.

What you learn from God's word can become food for the soul and escort you into the deeper things of God. I never met a mature Christian that was not a student of the Holy Bible, having spent many hours reading and studying God's word. God is the same yesterday, today, and forever. God is no respecter of persons. We see this fact illustrated by the words of Christ, when he said, "These things that I do, you will do also, and even greater things." It's only with the help of the Holy Spirit dwelling within us that we can poise our soul and spirit to hear and obey the voice of God.

✝

CHAPTER 47

Unity of the Brethren

In spiritual warfare, what we do not know can be our demise. For example, every time Jesus was tempted by the devil, He would say, "It is written." Christ Himself used the Scriptures to fend off the fiery darts of the enemy. If our Lord and Savior needed to memorize and use the Scriptures, so do we.

In another place in the New Testament, Paul said, "Brethren, do not bite and devour each other," which goes along with the list in Proverbs of things that God hates. One of them, "they that sow discord among the brethren," shows that gossip and having a critical spirit are things that can be deadly to the body of Christ.

In the upper room in Acts 2, it says that the early church was in one accord and in one place. Some ask why it took ten days of praying for the Holy Spirit to fall. One answer might be that it took that long for 120 people to remove their discord and truly love each other.

In Psalm 133, it states how good and how pleasant it is for brethren to dwell together in unity. It is like the precious oil that ran down the head of Aaron onto his beard, even down to the skirts of his garments. Oil throughout the Bible is a symbol of the Holy Spirit, and unity among the brethren is much like the anointing of the Holy Spirit. Some desire to get choice blessings from God. Psalm 133 gives us valuable insight on how to pursue a closer walk with the Lord. So here is the bottom line. Unity is an anointing of a body of believers. This anointing is not based on doctrine, where everybody believes the exact same thing, but it is based on setting our differences and criticism aside and deciding we must have unity or we will die.

I would like to tell you a true story that happened in World War II in Czechoslovakia. The Gestapo arrested five elders from a church, and separately he charged them, telling them that their brothers "said this about you, you might as well confess." One by one they all said, "No, my brothers wouldn't say that about me, they love me." After a very long interrogation, he called all five elders together and said, "I want to know your God that gives such unity," and the Nazi soldier was saved.

Psalm 133:3 states, "When unity happens, God commands a Blessing upon it." We don't even have to ask. When a man finds Christ, he taps resources that men in the world have never even dreamed of, and the power of unity is surely one of those resources.

In Ephesians 2:19, it says we are no longer strangers after we get saved, but we are of the household of God. In July of 1969, we saw a man walking on the moon as a result of many working together in unity. But a bigger and more important project here on earth is having the household of God learn to walk with each other in unity.

There is such a thing as poising our hearts towards God's blessings. There are things that we can do to cultivate our spiritual reception of the Holy Spirit. I cannot emphasize enough the importance of worship. Another thing that is very important in this process is for believers to dwell in unity. Being in one place and one accord is surely a factor in receiving God's fullness.

If this past paragraph is true, and trusts me, it is, the opposite is also true. There are things that we can do that will block the blessing of God in our lives. Having disunity is obviously one; a critical spirit, a gossiping spirit, and a spirit of pride will definitely block the moving of the Holy Spirit in our midst.

Hopefully you will learn how to find golden nuggets in the Scriptures that are deep spiritual truths as you read the word of God for yourself. This is called *revelation*. Once you have had a true revelation of Jesus as the son of God, the Savior of the world, and your own personal redeemer, I promise you, with everything that is in me, you will never be the same again.

I remember as a teenager, seeking the Baptism of the Holy Spirit at a family Bible camp. I received several words and immediately, a voice said to me, "That's not the Holy Spirit, that is just a word that you have heard somewhere."

I believed that lie for years, and then one day in church during the worship service, I felt this great pounding in my heart and somehow I knew that God wanted me to speak in tongues. At the end of the singing, the wise song leader always paused for a minute to give the Holy Spirit an opportunity to speak. Several dozen words came to me in a loud, audible way. I found myself speaking them with great authority. My wife, who was standing next to me, told me later that if she hadn't been holding onto the back of the pew, she would have fallen down; her knees were shaking so violently.

From that time on, I have had this prayer language that I can use at will, which brings me to a true story that happened in Montana. My family and I had pitched a tent at Swan Lake campgrounds in preparation for two days of fishing, when in drove this shiny, brand new van with New York license plates. These were people who were a long way from home.

Now I had been thinking of buying a van for a long time, but I had just started doing my research, which involved talking to everybody that I saw who owned a van. I asked them questions about gas mileage, dependability, and upkeep. Don't worry about it, ladies; it is a guy thing.

I walked over and introduced myself to this couple, who were in their 60s, and in talking back and forth about their van, the lady asked what kind of work I did. I told her I was the pastor of a small church in Hungry Horse. She immediately said to me, "We are Jewish and all our meetings are in Hebrew." Without thinking about it, I said to her, "I think I speak a little Hebrew." She asked me to say a few of these words. I thought to myself, *I will never see these people again as long as I live; they have New York license plates, they are just passing through.* I explained to her about getting saved through faith in Jesus and that the Holy Spirit gives us a prayer language that we have never studied, and that was the language I received.

I bowed my head and closed my eyes, as was my custom, and I began to speak in my prayer language. I felt relaxed and comfortable doing this. I guess I spoke for two or three minutes. When I finished, I opened my eyes, only to see this lady smiling from ear to ear. She hugged me and said, "My Rabbi would be so proud of you." When I asked her why, she replied, "You have surely spent years studying the Hebrew language."

I said, "No, I have never studied Hebrew at all." She then informed me that there was an ancient Hebrew language that is extremely hard to master, and then there is the Modern Hebrew language that is a great deal easier.

Then she said something to me that I will never forget. Looking me straight in the eye, she declared to me that I had just spoken ancient Hebrew perfectly, and that I quoted an ancient Hebrew prayer. Then she said "Now please, tell me more about this Holy Spirit; you have me more than a little interested—I can hardly stand it."

So I went to the book of Acts and explained to them the characteristic of the first church, which opened the door for me to present the plan of salvation, water baptism by immersion, baptism of the Holy Spirit, and, oh yes, hearing and obeying the voice of God.

The last thing that I shared with this couple was Philip's divine appointment with the Ethiopian eunuch. I told them God wanted the Gospel in Africa so he sent one man, Philip, into the country to meet with another man. I suggested to this couple that we were having a similar experience that could be called serendipity, a divine appointment from God. And quite possibly, they were supposed to share this experience with their friends back in New York.

One minute they were total strangers living thousands of miles from where I live, and in just a few short minutes, they were asking me to share the Gospel with them. The way I understand it, the last thing that Jesus said to his followers before He ascended into heaven was, "You will receive the ability to be witnesses, after that the Holy Ghost has come upon you." And that is exactly what happened in the deep mountains of Montana, overlooking beautiful Swan Lake.

✞

CHAPTER 48

The Holy Spirit in You

In the book of Acts 2:2, it says, "they heard a sound from heaven as a mighty rushing wind that filled the entire house." It concerns me today that too few people have never heard the sound of the mighty rushing wind. It might not be an audible sound, but when your heart hears it or sees it, you will know that you have had a divine visitation.

What I mean by hearing a still small voice is this: it is a knowing in your heart that you are supposed to do something. It could be like an audible voice that you hear with your spiritual ears. Also, God will lead us by circumstances, open and close doors and through godly advice.

It might not be every day that the Holy Spirit will lead you to a divine appointment but the good news is, we can hear from God every time we read the Scriptures; the Bible is alive.

I do think God desires to speak to us every day in one form or another, and lead you into a prayer life and other facets of the Christian walk.

In Ezekiel 36:26, it says, "A new heart also will I give you, and a new spirit will I put within you; and I will take away the stony heart out of your flesh, and I will give you an heart of flesh. And I will put my spirit within you, and cause you to walk in my statutes, and you shall keep my judgments, and do them."

We see in these verses God clearly telling us his divine plan is for the Holy Spirit to abide in the heart of the redeemed. We also see how we can receive the Holy Spirit and have his leading in our lives.

In the following chapter, we see Ezekiel, a man of God, being led by the Spirit to have a vision of a battlefield of casualties. As Ezekiel walked around, he saw many, many dry bones that were once the bones of healthy men in the service of an army. The Lord then asked Ezekiel if these bones will ever live again, and Ezekiel said, "Only you know, Lord."

In Ezekiel 37:4, The Holy Spirit told the man of God to prophesy upon these bones and say unto them, "Oh dry bones, hear the word of the Lord and I will cause breath to enter into you."

Here we have a man of God carrying out the vision and hearing the voice of God, which instructed him to preach to a valley of dry bones. In my opinion, we need men today with a vision to be so obedient to God's voice, they would even preach to a graveyard.

In our day and age, these bones could very well be men and women dead in trespasses of sin. If you listen, you will hear the Holy Spirit instructing you to go forth and witness to these dead spiritual bones, that they might find new life in Christ. Often, God's voice will direct you to one individual who is ready to hear the Gospel, and you will experience the miracle that comes with a revelation of who Jesus is. And if they will truly receive the word of the Lord, they too will experience a rebirth, and new life in their dried up, dead spiritual bones.

In the past forty-six years, there have been times when I have felt led to do things that I saw no fruit from, and my conclusion was that it was nothing more than a test to see if I would be obedient. It may sound a little strange, but I think sometimes these tests make us stronger. Evidently, the prophet Ezekiel was at that point during his walk with God, and he was willing to step out by faith and do something very foolish in the natural man's eyes.

Preaching to thousands of dry bones lying in a valley seems a little foolish to the human intellect. Apparently, he did not forget who he was talking to. The creator of the Universe was telling him to preach. In the next few verses, we see Ezekiel and the Holy Spirit carrying on a conversation, somewhat similar to two men talking over lunch.

Perhaps God has directed us to write this book to help you grasp this very fact, which is this: if you will talk to God, He will talk to you.

In verse 5, we see something very important. We see a man stepping out by faith saying, "thus saith the Lord." The world today is waiting for someone to step up with a word from the Lord.

Tonight, I felt directed to go to a shoestore and talk to the owner about spiritual things. I found the owner was very sick with pneumonia. However, their daughter was there, who was just recovering from a serious sickness.

When I asked her how she was feeling, she said, "Better, thank God." I told her that was the key, thanking God for the many things He has blessed her with. She then told me this amazing story.

Her grandmother had insisted to her she could only pray and thank God in church, which is truly not Biblical teaching. The door flew wide open for me to share with this young girl about Christ the Savior. I wrote down on a piece of paper a scripture for her to read—the Gospel of John 3. She promised me she would go home and read it.

If my wife and I had not gone to that mall as directed by the Holy Spirit, no doubt this young girl would not be reading the Bible tonight, as I am writing this.

Let me tell you what happened this morning. I opened my eyes from a night's sleep and the clock was exactly on the hour so I simply thanked the Lord for another day, and after singing a worship song, I told God I was available if He had something He wanted me to do today.

My wife and I went to our office to work on this final chapter, but it just wouldn't flow. We tried three times. Finally I said, "I quit, let's go to the gym, do our workout, and come home and try it again." When we arrived at the gym there were only two treadmills open. My wife took one and I took the other one; there was a middle-aged lady between us.

I said good morning, introduced myself and my wife, and we began talking. The conversation got around to spiritual things and I finally asked her a very heavy question. It went like this: If you were to die today, do you know, without a shadow of a doubt, that you are going to heaven? The lady just looked at me for a whole minute; she said, "No one has ever asked me that question in my whole life. But to be honest with you, I don't know for sure that I would go to heaven today."

As we both walked on the treadmill I explained to her the plan of Salvation. This lady kept wiping tears from her eyes. I thought to myself, no doubt this is the reason I couldn't seem to work on the book and why we came to the gym early.

In the many years my wife and I have been working out at that gym, we had never been there that early. Our usual time was between ten o'clock and noon. I thought to myself, perhaps this is a divine appointment and, as it turned out, I was right. Standing there behind the treadmills, tucked away in a corner, I led this lady in the sinner's prayer. The tears flowed freely down her face and she said, "This feels so right." I asked her if she felt any different, and she said, "Yes, I feel like a great weight has been taken off my shoulders."

I asked her where Jesus was and she said, "He is all over the earth, but He is also in my heart." It was a cool thing seeing somebody born again.

My wife and I visited with her for some time, standing around one of the weight machines. We finally gave her our phone number and some homework; to read the Gospel of John and then Matthew, Mark, and Luke. Then I told her to read the book of Acts and be prepared for a bit of excitement because as she reads, some of the words will seem to jump right off the page and land in her heart.

Before we parted, she asked my wife and me to pray for her sister, Sonya, who was going through a very difficult time in her life. I assured her we would.

Now perhaps you are reading this and thinking to yourself, I wish I could be a missionary or a minister, or I would even settle for being a prophet. Please listen carefully when I tell you this; if you will learn just like Ezekiel learned to hear the voice of God and obey his instructions, the mission field can be as close as the nearest mall, or as soon as your next workout at the gym.

There are forty million people in America under the age of twenty-one who don't know one thing about Jesus and have never been in any church of any description. They are waiting for someone who would be bold enough to preach life to them, even though they are dead in the trespasses of sin.

Forty-six years ago, I accepted Christ as my Savior; it has been the most important decision in my whole life, thanks to Harry Brimmer, who shared the Gospel with me when I was sixteen years old. Before that, I had never heard of the plan of Salvation or any other portion of the Gospel of Jesus Christ nor had I ever set foot in a church.

When the woman at the gym was saved, she said to me, "I have three children, six, eight, and ten. I am going to start reading the Bible to them every night, starting tonight.

We pray that her children were saved and her husband finds Christ also. We will pray for her sister, Sonya; this is God's plan for us—to be witnesses to the entire earth. It all starts with a word from the Lord, a revelation, a listening ear, a hungry heart, hearing the voice of God, and being a candidate to be led by the Holy Spirit.

What America needs today is to have her spiritual leaders climb into the pulpit with a "thus saith the Lord," a word from God, a fresh revelation from the Lord. That is exactly what Ezekiel did. He preached life to those who were dead in trespasses of sin and what followed next was a miracle from the supernatural. And this is what we too can expect when we hear and obey the voice of God.

Are we willing to be moved by the Holy Spirit or do we have our own agenda? Are we caught up in our own time schedule? Are we leaving room for the Holy Spirit to work in our midst?

✞

CHAPTER 49

A Mighty Rushing Wind

With the moving of the Holy Spirit, there are a lot of things made available to us. I can't help but think about the prophet Ezekiel 37:1-10 in the Old Testament, when God led him down in the midst of a valley. It was the site of a big battle where thousands of warriors were slain. Their bodies were left there to rot and feed the animals, and all that was left were dry bones. And the Lord asks him, "Can these bones live?" Ezekiel answered and said, "Lord God you know."

In man's eyes, it was a valley full of dry bones, but in God's eyes, it was a mighty army. What they lacked was a word from the Lord, a mighty rushing wind, which is the moving of the Holy Spirit in their midst, and these two things set the stage for a miracle.

America today is seeing too many churches closing their doors. My wife and I drove by one last month in south Phoenix. A beautiful, large worship center with close to a dozen annex buildings, sitting on over ten acres, with boarded windows and doors. A chainlink fence was all around it, complete with keep out signs.

Dry bones with a fence around it sounds a little like a modern day graveyard. I tell you, there is still a mighty rushing wind that is strong enough to blow down that fence and blow open those doors. One man could make a difference; one man listening to the Holy Spirit could turn that boneyard into a might army, winning souls for Jesus, singing the praises of Zion, letting their voice be heard.

God help America if we lose sight of the principles that our country was founded on. We need men and women hungering for God, not satisfied with the graveyard, wanting more, seeking the wind of the Holy Spirit. Will you be the one? Billy Graham says, "America is yet to see what can be accomplished by one man of God fully yielded to the leading of the Holy Spirit."

Indeed, Ezekiel was a man of God. When the Lord spoke to him and told him to do a seemingly foolish thing, like prophecy to a valley of dry bones, he was obedient.

Keith Green used to sing a song that was also a Scripture; "To obey is better than sacrifice."

There was a great noise in that valley of dry bones; bone came to bone as a result of one man who was obedient to the voice of God. Because of one man's prophesy, by the power of the Holy Spirit, flesh came upon the bones. And in Ezekiel 37:9, "the wind entered the dead bodies and they stood on their feet, an exceeding great army."

You say, "I am only one person, what can I do?" Well, Ezekiel was one person, and you can do the things he did through the power of the Holy Spirit. Pray for a wind, a mighty rushing wind and cloven tongues, like as of fire. Seek God with all your heart, all your soul, and your entire mind. Call on the Lord and He will answer you. I tell you indeed, you will see great and mighty things that you know not of.

I have no corner on God. I am no giant Christian, I am just an ordinary guy, but I have learned one thing—to listen to what the Holy Spirit says. It's nothing new—there are thousands of verses in the Bible that speak of the Lord talking to man, and there are thousands of verses that tell us that man listens and hears the voice of God.

I promise you, that has not changed. Jesus is the same yesterday, today, and forever. In the book of Genesis, God said, "Let us make man." Who do you suppose *us* was? I will tell you—God the father, God the Son, and God the Holy Spirit was us, known as the *Trinity*.

A lot of people have problems with understanding the Triune Godhead. A long time ago, it was explained to me like this. We see a ray of sunlight shining through a window, but what we really are seeing are three different properties. One property allows us to see different colors. Another property, allows us to feel heat, and the third property allows us to extract energy from the sun. Yet it seems like one ray of sunlight, when really, it is three in one.

It's very important to grasp God the Father, God the Son, and God the Holy Spirit—three separate facets of God having three separate job descriptions. What we have tried to do in this book is help you better understand the Holy Spirit and some of the ways He works.

From that time until now, God has not changed. He took a handful of dirt and He breathed life into it. God's breath made the difference, a big difference, and hearing the wind of the Holy Spirit can make a big difference in your life, a difference that can be compared to night and day, a difference that can be compared to life and death.

In Bible College, I drove 50 miles to attend a praise and prayer meeting that I had heard was experiencing a mighty moving of the Holy Spirit. Their meetings were on Saturday nights, in a huge Presbyterian church. There I experienced one of the greatest worship services that I had ever been in. When I asked what the Sunday morning services were like, I was shocked to hear the people tell me this. The Sunday morning services are very flat, and mechanical, and extremely scheduled.

Those people on Saturday night chose to hunger and thirst after righteousness; they chose to worship God in Spirit and in truth. They would stand on their feet with their hands in the air and sing in their prayer language for twenty minutes at a time. The power of God was so heavy in the air, you were almost stunned, yet full of awe. Little did I know that I would experience this exact phenomena for six straight years in Hungry Horse, Montana.

In Deuteronomy 30:19, God says, "I have set before you life and death, blessing and cursing, *therefore* choose life, that both thou and thy offspring may live." (Remember, whenever you see the word *therefore* in the Scriptures, it is important that you find out what it is *there for*).

At this point, let me make a comment about this verse. It seems we have a choice to make between two opposites. Jesus says, "I have come that you may have life more abundantly and on the other side of the coin; Satan has come to steal, kill and destroy."

Verse 15 and 16 help us to understand. They say, "I have set before this day life and good, death and evil." It seems this Scripture indicates life and good go hand-in-hand, and death and evil go hand-in-hand.

Now here is a heavy question: Do you think it is possible to choose to be sick? Is it possible to go around saying, "I don't feel good, I don't feel good," or "I am sick, I am sick, I need medicine," until you actually *are* sick and you *do* need medicine? And here is another question: Can we choose to be healthy? In my opinion, not enough of God's people choose life and blessing on a daily basis.

These people on Saturday night were experiencing a great blessing as a result of a divine visitation to a group of people from a dozen different dominations who had made a decision to pray. They made a decision not to go bowling, but to give God their Saturday night. They made a decision to love each other, and we can do the same today. They would stand there for twenty minutes at a time with their hands in the air, singing in the spirit. If you have never heard people worshipping God in this way, I assure you, you are in for a great treat.

There are times when we see ourselves as nothing more than dry bones, slain in a spiritual battle and rotting away, but God does not see it that way. He sees us as an exceeding great army. All we lack is the sound of a mighty rushing wind and the moving of the Holy Spirit in our lives, and we too can see this type of miracle. God does have an army that is marching through this land doing great things for Jesus, acting as his mighty hand.

Perhaps you are viewing your life today as all but ruined. You are a little more than dry bones, possibly you have even heard the voice of the devil saying "humpty dumpty sat on a wall, humpty dumpty took a great fall, all the king's horses and all the king's men, couldn't put humpty back together again."

My precious reader, I guarantee you, Satan is a liar and whatever he tells you, the opposite is true. The king of kings can put you back together again and you can rise stronger. You can fly higher with God than you ever have before, if you will position yourself to feel the mighty rushing wind of the Holy Spirit stirring in your heart.

I read a sign one time posted in front of a junkyard—Wanted: Late Model Wrecks. Do you view your life as a late model wreck, having had a head-on collision with no insurance? Do you feel like your life has been totaled? If you will carefully follow the principles outlined in this book, you too, my friend, will rise again and navigate the road that leads to eternal life.

God will use you again, because He is still in the restoration business. Receive the breath of the Holy Spirit, and God will give you the ability to hear his voice again. I promise that you are not without hope.

Perhaps you see your life in shambles even similar to the valley of dry bones, but remember that God sees an exceeding great army. Are you a candidate to be joined up with the body of Christ, working together with the master?

Many times, the natural man sees things and experiences things that make him feel hopeless; even his friends don't seem to have answers that work. There are a lot of people in the world today who desperately need to hear the sound of the rushing mighty wind.

Please understand, the rushing mighty wind in the Scriptures represents the moving of the Holy Spirit and with it comes the still, small voice of God. Once you hear it, you will never be the same.

If we as individuals will allow the word of the Lord to lodge in our hearts, we will become a candidate to be a witness. Our job is to discover where we fit in; are you a prophet, a teacher, or perhaps an administrator? It might even be that God has called you to take the neighbor's kids to Sunday school.

The body of Christ is made up of many hands, many feet, and many tongues. What God likes is when many members come together in unity and form what is known as the *body of Christ*.

Let me illustrate with a true story. In 1967, there was a seven-day war. Israel had strung barbed wire to keep their border secure. However, the enemy tanks simply crossed over. Two boys, one aged twelve and one aged thirteen, came out of the brush, climbed on the back of the tank, and each one dropped one molotov cocktail into the hatch and thus, blew up the two tanks. When the other tanks saw it, a whole battalion turned back.

At the time that this happened, which was June 9, 1967, there were 240 million people in Russia and three million in Israel.

Although Israel was outnumbered eight to one, they had a deciding factor, which was this—they had heard the voice of God. They had won the victory in the spiritual realm and if we today will win the victory in the spiritual realm, even though we are outnumbered, we will have won the victory, period.

In the book of Acts, they not only heard the sound, but they saw cloven tongues of fire. I have heard some say that was just for back then, but I vehemently disagree.

This generation today needs desperately to hear the voice of the Holy Spirit.

In Ezekiel 3:12, it says that the spirit took him up and he heard a voice of great rushing. I tell you, we can come to the place where we can hear God's voice speak to us. If we need direction, He will give us wise direction; if we need wisdom, He will give us wisdom; if we need knowledge, He will give us knowledge.

In Ezekiel 2:1, God said, "Son of man, stand upon your feet and I will speak to you." Often there are things that we must do to poise ourselves to hear God's voice. Some may find it difficult to hear God's voice when they have had a fight with their wife ten minutes before leaving for church. If your mind is on the football game you're missing or the casserole in the oven, you will not be able to feed your soul quite like you could if you've gone into it prepared.

You may not realize that you are being distracted from hearing the word of the Lord. When I was a teenager, people used to meet a half hour early to pray and seek God before the service started, but for some reason, you don't see that very much anymore.

No doubt, this was a valuable time for those dear saints; to calm their spirits and to clear their heads of the many ups and downs of the day. This allowed them to concentrate on some very important events that were about to take place. Namely this was a time of singing and worshipping, which I can't say enough about, as it is extremely important in a believer's life. They also quieted their hearts to be led in the testimony service, which I also feel has a valid place in the gathering of believers.

I remember as a teenager, taking my friend, Henry Cranes, to visit my church. We had prayer, singing, worship, a time when people would stand and share a testimony, and great preaching with an altar call. As Henry and I drove home, he said to me, "Jack, the part of the service that really got to me was those different people standing and telling individually what God had done for them."

There is a Sunday school song that goes like this: "Be careful little feet where you go, be careful little hands what you do, be careful little minds what you think, be careful little eyes what you see, be careful little ears what you hear, and be careful little mouths what you say, for the father up above is looking down in love."

In my opinion, the reason those personal testimonies hit Henry so hard was because those same people took that Sunday school song to heart and were sincerely striving with all their might to put on the spirit of Christ.

Like I mentioned before, Steve Brimmer, my spiritual adopted brother from my teenage years, and I would always sit behind Brother and Sister Andrews in church, three times a week, month after month, year after year, and it would always be the same. We would lean forward and bow our heads with our elbows on our knees, and wind up with two puddles of tears on the black tile of the church floor. Just being near these people touched my spirit.

If we will cultivate a sweet spirit and bring that to church with us, it will help to bring out the very best in a song service, in a prayer time, and even inspire a speaker as he preaches the Scriptures.

My wife and I attended a church one time where several of the teenagers always sat in the back row. They were constantly yawning, elbowing each other, and looking at their watches. After several months of noticing this, we coined a name for this group. Are you ready for a new word? Here it comes: *Oh hummy*. This back pew was full of *oh hummys* who were constantly sighing and going "oh hum" and looking very bored. The preacher could preach his heart out and their response was always the same—oh hum, what time is it? Oh hum, how much longer before we go home?

Can you imagine trying to preach to a whole church like that? It was the same back in Paul the apostle's day; there were some that would ask, "What does this babbler have to say?" and then there were others that would cry out, "What must I do to be saved?"

So there is such a thing as preparing our hearts, loosening up the soil, and getting it ready for the good seed of faith. I really believe that we can have as much of God as we want.

It is almost free; however, there is somewhat of a price tag. You may have to invest some time, and it may even cost you some sleep in the middle of the night as you get up and pray.

In Ezekiel 3:24, it says "the spirit entered me and spoke to me." God still speaks to us today. Just how hungry are you for a greater move of the Holy Spirit in your life?

✞

Conclusion

I definitely feel led of the Holy Spirit to end with this story. A man crossing a desert ran out of water; after three days he was near death, extremely thirsty. He came upon an abandoned farm house that had burned down, with a well pump in the yard; hanging from the well pump was a canteen of water. On the cover of this canteen was a handwritten message that said, "Do not drink this water, but carefully pour it down the hole at the top of the hand pump, and while you pour, pump the handle up and down."

How many of us know that this is exactly the way you prime a hand pump, which causes fresh cold water to run out of the snout for as long as you want if you keep working the handle up and down.

The thirsty man had a choice—be satisfied with this hot, stagnant water that had been in that canteen for who knows how long, but once it was gone, it was gone. Or he could put faith in the person who wrote the note on the canteen and do exactly what was written and have an abundance of water.

This could be a picture of God's word to us. If we will dare to put faith in the divine inspired word of God and do exactly what it says, we can tap into a source that's more refreshing and has greater abundance than all the cool well water any man-made well has to offer. Jesus said it best: "I come that you might have life more abundantly."

In John 7:37, it says in the last day of the feast, Jesus stood and cried, "If any man thirst, let him come unto me and drink, he that believes on me, as the Scripture hast said, out of his inner most being, rivers of living water shall flow, but this spoke he of the Holy Spirit, which they that believe, on him should receive."

This is God's own promise to us. But remember, most of God's promises are conditional, so read His Holy Book and follow its instructions and I guarantee you, you too will hear the voice of God.

I specifically feel led to leave you with this thought from the Gospel of John 16:12-13:

> *I have yet many things to say unto you, but yea cannot bear them now. How be it when he, the Spirit of truth, is come, he will guide you into all truth: for he shall not speak of himself; but whatsoever he shall hear, that shall he speak: and he will show you things to come.*

Amen

ORDER FORM

Book title: *Obeying the Voice of God*
Jack MacDonald's Journey
As told to Donnie MacDonald

Payable by: Cash, checks or COD/no credit cards

To: Jack MacDonald
Email address: sdgondancin@cox.net

Ship to:

Name ____

Address ______________________________________

City ____

State ____________________ Zip ______________

Phone# ______________________________________

Email address _________________________________

Book Total	$ 19.99	(24 hour turnaround)
Applicable Sales Tax	$ 1.60	
Postage & Handling	$ 4.41	
Total Amount Due	$ 26.00	

To order multiple books, please contact:
Renee Kuska
Freeport Logistics
4802 W. Polk Street
Phoenix, AZ 85043
(602) 415-6003 or (602) 278-1108 Fax: (602) 269-5042
Email address: r.kuska@freeport-logistice.com